Human – Computer Interaction
for Software Designers

Tutorial Guides in Computing and Information Systems

Series Editors

Professor David Howe, De Montfort University
Dr Martin Campbell-Kelly, University of Warwick

About the series

The Tutorial Guides in Computing and Information Systems series covers the first and second year undergraduate programme and the Higher National Diploma courses in these subjects. The essentially practical nature of the books is particularly appropriate to today's courses where examinations reflect an increasing emphasis on problem-solving skills. The books are characterised by a high proportion of worked examples, practical exercises and frequent friendly tutorial-style notes in the margins of the text. The problem-solving approach also addresses the requirements of practitioners in business and industry.

Each book stands alone in its subject area; the series as a whole provides comprehensive coverage of the first two years of the undergraduate or Higher National programme.

About the Series Editors

David Howe is Head of Department of Information Systems at De Montfort University. He specializes in the analysis and design of information systems and is the author of *Data Analysis for Database Design.*

Martin Campbell-Kelly is Senior Lecturer in Computer Science at Warwick University. He teaches a number of subjects of the undergraduate programme and is a recognized authority on the history and development of computing.

Other titles in the series

Beginning Unix™
Mike Joy

Z: A Beginner's Guide
David Rann, John Turner and Jenny Whitworth

Introduction to C++
David Dench and Brian Prior

Systems Analysis Techniques
Barbara Robinson and Mary Prior

The Relational Database
John Carter

Programming in C
John Gray and Brian Wendl

Information Systems: Strategy to Design
Chris Claire and Gordon Stuteley

Software Project Management
Mike Cotterell and Bob Hughes

Foundation Discrete Mathematics for Computing
Dexter J. Booth

Human–Computer Interaction for Software Designers

Linda Macaulay

INTERNATIONAL THOMSON COMPUTER PRESS

I(T)P An International Thomson Publishing Company

London • Bonn • Boston • Johannesburg • Madrid • Melbourne • Mexico City • New York • Paris • Singapore
Tokyo • Toronto • Albany, NY • Belmont, CA • Cincinnati, OH • Detroit, MI

Human – Computer Interaction for Software Designers
Copyright ©1995 Linda Macaulay

I(T)P   A division of International Thomson Publishing Inc.
        The ITP logo is a trademark under licence

British Library Cataloguing-in-Publication Data
A catalogue record for this book is available from the British Library

---

First printed 1995

Typeset in the UK by Hodgson Williams Associates, Tunbridge Wells and Cambridge
Printed in the UK by The Alden Press, Oxford

ISBN 1-850-32177-9

International Thomson Publishing
Berkshire House
168-173 High Holborn
London WClV 7AA
UK

∞ Printed on permanent acid-free text paper, manufactured in accordance with ANSI/NISO Z39.48-1992 and ANSI/NISO Z39.48-1984 (Permanence of Paper).

Contents

Preface and acknowledgements vii

1 HCI and the software designer 1
  1.1 Introduction 1
  1.2 The importance of the user interface 1
  1.3 HCI and the software designer 3
  1.4 Rationale for this book 8

2 Understanding user needs and requirements 11
  2.1 Introduction 11
  2.2 The software designer and user requirements 13
  2.3 Understanding user needs 15
  2.4 The CAD case study 22
  2.5 Task analysis and allocation of function 42
  2.6 Summary 48
  Exercises 49

3 Designing the user interface 50
  3.1 Introduction 50
  3.2 Classes of user interface 51
  3.3 Principles of good design 52
  3.4 Evaluating designs using the principles 54
  3.5 Factors influencing the choice of colour 58
  3.6 A task-oriented approach to user interface design 63
  3.7 A case study in task-oriented user interface design 75
  3.8 Summary 93
  Exercises 93

4 Designing graphical user interfaces 95
  4.1 Introduction 95
  4.2 Design of icons 97
  4.3 Use of metaphors 100
  4.4 GUI styleguides and toolkits 104
  4.5 Portability between GUIs 109
  4.6 XVT and portability between GUIs 115
  4.7 GUI design: an object-oriented approach 123
  4.8 Case study of an object-oriented approach to UI design... 127
  4.9 Summary 135
  Exercises 135

5   Designing user interfaces to CSCW systems **136**
    5.1 Introduction 136
    5.2 Computer-supported cooperative work (CSCW).......... 137
    5.3 Characteristics of CSCW systems 143
    5.4 Examples of CSCW systems 147
    5.5 The role and characteristics of CSCW user interfaces 156
    5.6 A method of specifying and designing user interfaces
        to CSCW systems................................. 157
    5.7 A case study in user interface design for a CSCW system . 162
    5.8 Summary 172
    Exercises 172

6   Usability.. **173**
    6.1 Introduction 173
    6.2 The user's, customer's and designer's viewpoint 174
    6.3 Usability specification 178
    6.4 Stage 1: user and task analysis 180
    6.5 Stage 2: setting usability objectives and success criteria ... 182
    6.6 Stage 3: writing usability statements and identifying
        measures 184
    6.7 Stage 4: choosing techniques for measuring usability..... 185
    6.8 Stage 5: planning a usability evaluation 194
    6.9 Summary 196
    Exercises 197

7   HCI standards **199**
    7.1 Introduction 199
    7.2 HCI standards 199
    7.3 European Computer Manufacturer's Association (ECMA) . 200
    7.4 International Organization for Standardization (ISO) 201
    7.5 European Directive: Work with Display Screen Equipment 203
    7.6 BSI Guide to the Design and Preparation of
        Documentation for Users of Application Software 205
    7.7 Summary and conclusions 205

    Appendix A
    Answers to exercises 208

    References.. 213

    Useful addresses.................................... 218

    Index 220

A section of colour plates appears between pages 58 and 59.

Preface

Human computer interaction (HCI) covers a broad subject area which is concerned with the interaction between people and computers. Understanding interaction between people and computers is now recognized as vital to the design of successful computer systems.

HCI is about interaction between people and computers.

HCI is multidisciplinary, encompassing computer science, psychology, linguistics, ergonomics and sociology. Much of the recent research and development associated within the subject will be found under the heading of human computer interaction and covers a broad range of topics which affect the interaction between the computer system and the user and their organization. Other work carries the title 'human computer interface design', and often has a much narrower perspective, dealing more specifically with screen and dialogue design. Many of the recent textbooks take a particular stance, either giving a psychological perspective or a formal computer science perspective, while others focus on details of interaction devices and guidelines.

Few of the current HCI texts consider the problem of user interface design from the point of view of the software designer. The software designer is the person who is responsible for designing and implementing a user interface which will be usable in practice and which can be developed using the tools available. In fact most of the tools available for user interface design are 'passive' tools — that is, they may provide facilities for drawing windows or creating icons but the real design task still resides with the human software designer.

Most user interface design tools are 'passive'.

The purpose of this book is to emphasize those aspects of the user interface which the software designer can and should actively design. This involves the designer in understanding users and what they do, since a system which is usable by one user may not be usable by another. The designer must also understand the limitations and potential of the tools available for implementation. Thus this book is concerned with the tools and techniques which can be used by software designers in order to promote a user-oriented approach to the design and implementation of the user interface.

User interface design is considered from the software designer's point of view.

The approach of the author has been to consider how a software designer might design his or her first user interface. Consequently, specific techniques have been chosen and a step-by-step guide to applying those techniques is given. The explanation of a technique is followed by a case study showing how each step is applied in practice.

Includes step-by-step guides.

The techniques chosen are those the author has found to work in practice in a number of commercial and research projects. Specifically, they are

Techniques chosen work in practice.

techniques for understanding user needs; for designing character-based user interfaces; for designing graphical user interfaces, and for designing user interfaces to systems which support groups of users. It is not suggested that these are the only techniques, but they do work in practice and they will provide a sound basis for the first-time designer. Once the designer has grasped the techniques presented in this book, he or she will be able to make an informed comparison with those described in other HCI texts.

This approach makes the text particularly suitable for computer science undergraduates, but may be equally applicable to anyone who has to design a user interface.

The first-time user interface designer will find the task-oriented step-by-step guide (and the associated case study in Chapter Three) particularly useful in that it shows how to proceed from an initial description of users and tasks through to the detailed design of windows, menus and forms.

The more experienced designer will find the object-oriented step-by-step guide to designing graphical user interfaces in Chapter Four particularly useful because it shows how to proceed from identification of objects through to the design of icons and pull-down menus.

The perspective of the design task is broad in that the author shows that designing user interfaces is not just about designing screens, it is also about understanding user, organizational and commercial requirements. These topics are covered particularly in Chapters Two and Six. More experienced designers may find this approach refreshing.

A major future challenge for HCI is that of developing multi-media user interfaces to groupware (or CSCW systems). In Chapter Five, the author describes the characteristics of these interfaces and suggests a step-by-step approach to unravelling the complexities associated with their design. A case study of this approach shows how to proceed from group analysis to the design of windows.

As a result of reading this text it is hoped that the software designer faced with designing user interfaces for the first time will develop confidence in HCI design, and will become curious to know more about the subject. A number of complementary HCI texts are referred to in the marginal notes.

Suitable for anyone faced with designing a user interface for the first time.

Broad perspective of the design task including user, organizational and commercial requirements.

Provides a foundation for designers to learn more about HCI.

Acknowledgements

Acknowledgements and thanks to Lindsay W. Macdonald (UK Advisory Group on Computer Graphics) for permission to use the colour slides presented in plates 1 to 8 in Chapter Three; to students who have participated in my HCI design course at UMIST and who have undertaken various projects which have contributed to material within this text. In particular: John Harris for contributing to the case study in Chapter Three, Simon Mak for Plates 9 to 14 in Chapter Three, Matthew Ibbis, Yang Yong Tang and Margaret Sung Li for contributions to the XVT-Design examples in Chapter Four. Acknowledgements and thanks to M. Creppy for the quotations from an operator of an order entry system in Chapter One. To R. B. Coates and I. Vlaeminke for ideas for the case study in Chapter Three. To collaborators Andrew Hutt and Chris Fowler who contributed to the case study in Chapter Two. To members of the CRC project team who contributed to the case study in Chapter Six, and in particular, Greg O'Hare, Steve Viller, Paul Dongha, Andrew Hutt, Mary Edwards, the late Elwyn Edwards (RIP), Eric Trodd and Tom Singleton. To those who commented on versions of the text, in particular, Frank Poole and Reza Hazemi.

Thanks to all who contributed.

Special thanks to Irene Beech for the many drawings.

Any errors and omissions are all mine.

Trademarks

GroupSystems is a trademark of the University of Arizona
Macintosh is the trademark of Apple Computer Inc.
Motif is a trademark of the Open Software Foundation Inc.
OSI is a trademark of the International Standards Organisation
OPENLOOK is a trademark of USL
TeamWorkstation and Clearboard are trademarks of NTT Human Interface Labs
UNIX is a trademark of AT&T Bell Laboratories
X Window System is a trademark of Massachussets Institute of Technology
XVT is a trademark of XVT Software Inc.
MSDOS is a trademark of Microsoft Corporation
NewWave is a trademark of Hewlett Packard
NeXT is a trademark of NeXT Inc.
Amiga is a trademark of Amiga Corporation
Presentation Manager is a trademark of IBM
All other trademarks are acknowledged.

Dedication

To Patrick and our children Jon-Sebastian, Theresa and Christine, and to those less fortunate than ourselves: the author's royalties from this book will be donated to the education sponsorship section of Save the Children Fund.

Chapter 1

HCI and the software designer

The objectives of this chapter are:

- ☐ to discuss the importance of the user interface;
- ☐ to describe the scope of human computer interaction (HCI);
- ☐ to discuss the role of the software designer in the HCI design lifecycle;
- ☐ to introduce the rationale for this tutorial text.

1.1 Introduction

The purpose of this tutorial text is to emphasize those aspects of the user interface which the software designer can and should actively design. This involves the designer in understanding users and what they do and in understanding the limitations and potential of the tools available for implementation. It is concerned with the tools and techniques which can be used by software designers in order to promote a user-oriented approach to the design and implementation of the user interface.

1.2 The importance of the user interface

The user interface is the main point of contact between the user and the computer system; it is the part of the system that the user sees, hears, touches and communicates with. The user interacts with the computer system in order to carry out some specific and important task and one which is often a fundamental or critical part of the user's job. Depending on the user's experience with the interface, the system may succeed or fail in helping the user to carry out the task.

The types of problem caused by poor user interface design include reduced user productivity, unacceptable learning times and unacceptable error levels, all these factors leading to frustration and potential rejection of the system by the user. For example, one report from the operator of an order entry system reveals a lack of flexibility in the system:

Users can get frustrated by the lack of flexibility

Why can't I view the customer's past ordering history when I am entering a new order?

(Here the user cannot access all the information needed.)

Users expect the system to behave in certain ways.

Sometimes I don't know the code of a new product off the top of my head. Is there a key I can hit to see the codes on the screen rather than having to refer to my codes printout? I tried Shift-C for Codes but it didn't work!

(The user expects the system to behave in certain ways.)

You know the screen where I can page back and forth through deliveries; well, sometimes the deliveries I want to see are split across two pages. Is there a way where I can move one up at a time, rather than page forward, so that I eventually have all the ones I need on the one screen?

(The user cannot access information in small enough chunks.)

Users do not always tell designers what they want.

A typical response by systems analysts and software designers would be 'you didn't tell us that'. These problems are not necessarily caused by poor system specification, but rather by poor user interface design. More specifically, there is a lack of understanding on the part of analysts and designers, both of the user and how the user operates.

It should be noted that developers of application software such as personnel systems, stock control or order entry systems typically dedicate around 70% of the program code to manipulation of the user interface. Thus the time and cost incurred in the development of the user interface is very significant.

Users prefer graphical user interfaces (GUIs).

Graphical user interfaces (GUIs) have brought quantifiable benefits to users and organizations. Recent studies have shown that users of graphical user interfaces make fewer mistakes, feel less frustrated, suffer less fatigue, and are more able to learn for themselves about the operation of new packages than users of non-graphical or character-based user interfaces.

Designing GUIs is more complex than designing character-based interfaces.

From a software designer's point of view, however, GUIs are more difficult to design than character-based interfaces. The user's interaction with the GUI is more complex because it is based on principles of direct manipulation and concurrent user access to multiple windows, icons, menus and input devices. A character-based interface, however, normally only allows the user sequential access: first view a menu, then make a selection, then view the next screen, then enter the data. With the character-based interfaces the designer can (within limits) design the user interface so that the user will undertake a task in a predefined sequence. With the GUI, the designer can design the user interface so that certain actions are allowed on interface objects and the user will decide which actions to take and (within limits) in what order.

Systems which support groups of users working together are capable of bringing productivity gains to organizations; for example, by enabling design teams to collaborate on the development of computer-based designs and to hold discussions or brainstorming sessions over the network. Consulting companies can pool their worldwide expertise to prepare bids rapidly for complex projects. Normally groupware systems support users sharing information about common objects, such as a report, a bid or a design, in such a way that each user sees the same version of the object on their screen at the same time. The user interfaces to groupware systems are normally graphical but with the added complexity of supporting communication between group members and the sharing of common objects. Often many different media will be used to aid communication between group members; video and voice interaction may be as important as text and graphics. From a software designer's point of view, designing user interfaces for groupware systems is more difficult than designing a GUI because the designer must also consider multi-media interaction and support for communication between people.

Designing interfaces to groupware is more complex than designing GUIs for single-user systems.

The design and implementation of a successful user interface is important, therefore, not only to the software designer but also to users, groups and organizations. The next section describes the main activities which contribute to the design of the user interface and discusses the role of the software designer in each of these activities.

1.3 HCI and the software designer

The human computer interface can be thought of as the point at which the activities of the user within an organization interact with the technical computer system developed by the designer (Fig. 1.1).

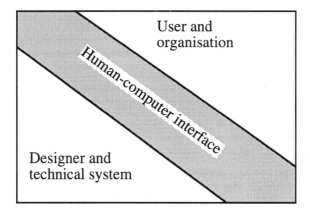

Figure 1.1 *The human computer interface.*

The human computer interface supports the organization by supporting individuals and groups.

The users inhabit their own world where they form part of an organization. The organization may be made up of a number of groups of people and each group will be helping the organization to meet management objectives. Each group may be supported by computer systems. Thus the role of the computer system is to help each individual and each group in their work.

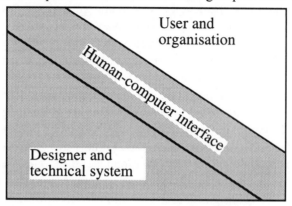

Figure 1.2   *The concern of the software designer.*

The designer inhabits a technical world where it is difficult to understand the concerns of users.

Figure 1.2 shows that the designer inhabits the technical world. The designer may or may not be part of the same organization as the user. The organization the designer belongs to may have different management objectives from that of the user, for example, where the designer belongs to a consultancy or software house. Thus one problem the designer faces is how to understand the management objectives of the commissioning organization for whom the computer system or software is to be designed.

The design process is inevitably a 'political' one because the management view of what will support the users in their work may not be the same as the user's own view. Different groups of users may require different things from the system. Indeed, the software designers will have their own interests and objectives they wish to fulfil in designing the system. Conflicts of this type are inherent in the design process and should not be ignored by the designer. It is all too easy for the designer to ignore these conflicts and simply build something that appears to them to be workable. This may bring short-term gains but in the longer term will probably prove unacceptable or create more problems within the commissioning organization.

Users inhabit a world which is constantly changing.

Figure 1.3 shows that users work within the context of an organization. Users inhabit a world which is constantly changing, due not only to external factors such as changing trade regulations, fiscal budgets or competitor action, but also to internal factors such as changes in technical strategy or in management personnel. Similarly the use of computer systems is not static; users adapt their use of them according to their changing needs. The process of ongoing change means that designers need to understand the organization so that they can design with change in mind.

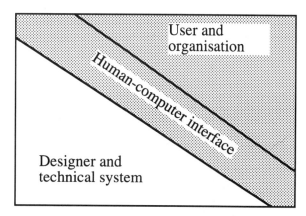

Figure 1.3   *The concern of the user*

Further, when new systems are introduced into the organization, change will inevitably occur:

1. Primary users, who use the system frequently, may have to change the way they do their job because of the computer system, or there may be fewer people needed to achieve the same task, or a greater throughput of work may be possible.

2. Secondary users, who use the system only occasionally or through an intermediary, may become more reliant on it for supporting decision making or may find that information that was once available only to them is now more widely available across the organization, thus possibly resulting in changes to the power and influence of particular individuals.

3. Tertiary users, who may never use the system but who are affected by its use, may have to change the way they work to fit in with outputs from the system. For example, storekeepers in a warehouse may have to change their order of working to fit in with the sequencing of new 'picking lists' from the computer, or a customer in a shop may be delayed by the salesperson having to enter additional data into the checkout terminal before completing a sale.

Figure 1.4 shows one view of the activities associated with the design of the human computer interface. The concerns of the software designer are shown in the bottom left hand segment, those of the human computer interface from top left to bottom right and those of the user and organization in the top right hand segment.

   This view shows the activities associated with human computer interface design as central to the design of a system which will support the user and the organization. These activities: feasibility assessment; allocation of function and requirements; user interface design; implementation and user sup-

Changes to computer systems usually mean changes to users' jobs and to the organization.

The human computer interface plays an important role as an intermediary between the concerns of the user and the concerns of the designer.

port, and evaluation, are shown as a sequence of activities. In reality there is feedback from each stage, the design process being one where decisions are being constantly reassessed in the light of new information.

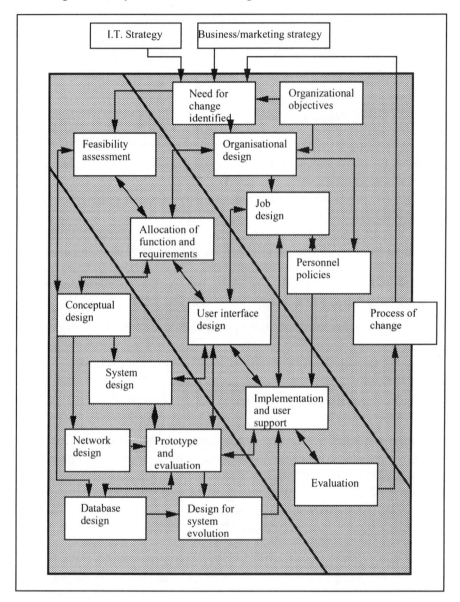

Figure 1.4   *Activities associated with the design of the human computer interface.*

Figure 1.4 illustrates the important role that the human computer interface plays as an intermediary between the concerns of the user and the concerns of the designer.

Figure 1.5 shows the main stages of HCI design lifecycle. The software designer may have different levels of involvement at each stage:

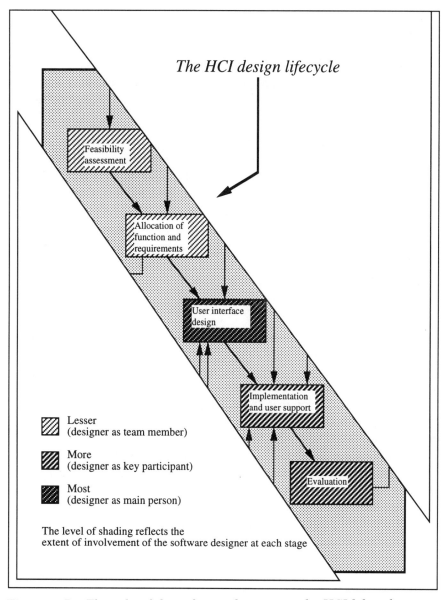

The designer has different levels of involvement in each stage of the HCI lifecycle.

Figure 1.5 *The role of the software designer in the HCI lifecycle.*

1. *The designer as team member.*
At the feasibility assessment and the allocation of function and requirements stages, the designer should form part of a team of users, managers and designers who are participating in the process of developing a shared understanding of what is needed and in understanding each other's interest in the proposed system. The designer should develop an under-

The designer as part of a requirements team.

standing of user needs which should be reflected in his or her approach to system design.

2. *The designer as the main person.*
At the user interface design stage the software designer has the major responsibility. This includes designing the user interface to meet the requirements of the team, using interface design tools to build mock ups to show the other interested parties or stakeholders, building the interface and evaluating its usefulness with groups of users prior to full implementation.

3. *The designer as key participant.*
The software designer is a key participant in the implementation within the organization and in the development of user support materials, but others, such as technical authors, professional trainers, user managers and user support staff may have major responsibility for these activities. Designers should cooperate in the process of evaluation of the system after implementation within the organization.

1.4 Rationale for this book

This book is a tutorial text, not a review of the subject. Thus the emphasis throughout is on introducing techniques and tools which may be useful to the software designer, and on illustrating the use of the techniques through examples and case studies. The reader will not find extensive discussions on possible alternative techniques and approaches; instead, one or two alternative techniques are introduced in a way that enables the software designer to learn them quickly and apply them where appropriate.

The emphasis of this book is on the main responsibilty of the software designer within the HCI design lifecycle, that of user interface design.

However, before user interface design can proceed, the designer must first gain a full understanding of user needs. Chapter Two introduces techniques which can assist in this, and which can be applied in situations where the designer is part of a requirements team.

Chapter Two discusses the role of the software designer in the requirements stage of a project. Techniques for understanding user needs are introduced, covering analyses of users and their characteristics, the tasks they carry out and the objects they interact with. The use of the techniques is illustrated by application to a computer-aided design case study. Techniques for identifying the role of the proposed system are introduced. Finally the costs and benefits of alternative allocation of function are considered from the user's point of view.

Chapter Three briefly introduces the main classes of user interface and five principles of good HCI design (naturalness, flexibility, non-redundancy, consistency and supportiveness). A task-oriented approach to user

interface design is presented, following directly from the techniques introduced in Chapter Two. This involves identifying interface tasks; techniques
for specifying dialogues and a procedure and guidelines for designing a
consistent set of screens and windows. Use of colour at the user interface is
considered, firstly through a brief discussion on the use of colour in general,
then by looking at some poorly-designed colour screens to identify some
typical mistakes that designers make. Finally, a number of guidelines on the
use of colour are presented. The chapter concludes with a case study of a
ferry reservation system showing the application of techniques from Chapters Two and Three.

A task-oriented
approach to user
interface design.

Chapter Four introduces the main elements of graphical user interfaces
(GUIs) and discusses the design of icons and the use of metaphors. An
overview of GUI style guides and toolkits is presented and issues of
portability between GUI environments are raised. The characteristics of
GUIs lead to the need for an object-oriented approach to user interface
design. The object-oriented approach includes: identifying and describing
interface objects; identifying user actions on objects; deciding on the user
interface metaphor and GUI toolkit to be used; identifying relationships
between objects (according to the metaphor) and finally deciding how to
view objects in terms of icons, menus or windows.

An object-oriented
approach to user
interface design.

The chapter concludes with a case study of this approach using the ferry
reservation system example introduced in Chapter Three. This will enable
the reader to compare and contrast a task-oriented approach to user interface
design with an object-oriented approach.

Chapter Five provides an introduction to cooperative working systems by
describing a number of systems and highlighting their general characteristics. A number of components of groupware are described, together with
systems being developed by leading edge research groups. This leads to a
discussion on the role and characteristics of user interfaces to Computer
Supported Cooperative Working (CSCW) systems and introduces a method
of specifying and designing user interfaces. The method includes: group
analysis and identification of facilitation requirements; user analysis and
role identification and conceptual design of the user interfaces. The application of the method is illustrated through a case study of a design team
engaged in brainstorming.

Approaches to
designer user
interfaces for
groupware.

Chapter Six presents the case for designing systems which are usable
from the user's, designer's and customer's point of view, briefly introducing
techniques for specifying and evaluating the usability of a system. Included
in this are techniques for identifying success criteria, writing usability
statements, identifying appropriate measures for testing for usability and
considerations associated with planning a usability evaluation. Legal requirements and directives related to software usability are described.

Techniques for
testing design results
with users.

In Chapter Seven there is an overview of the BSI standards for user
documentation and of the current ISO standards for HCI design. The book
concludes with a discussion of areas of development which may affect the
software designer.

Standards for HCI
design.

Further reading is
recommended.
Each of the main chapters has exercises for the reader to attempt. A list of references used in the preparation of the book are given at the end. Those of particular importance or those which will enable the reader to expand his or her knowledge of specific areas are referred to in the marginal notes at ·appropriate points in the text.

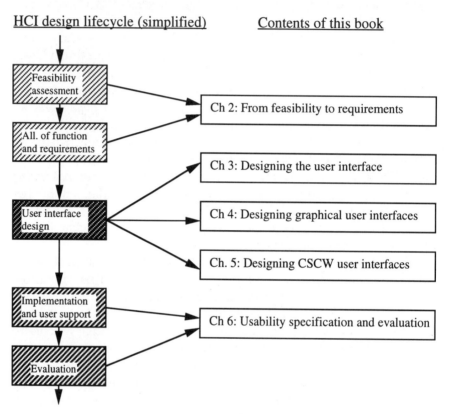

Figure 1.6   *Mapping from the HCI design lifecycle to the contents of this book.*

Chapter 2

Understanding user needs and requirements

The objectives of this chapter are:

- ☐ to discuss the role of the software designer in the requirements stage of a project;

- ☐ to describe techniques for understanding user needs through the analysis of users, objects and tasks;

- ☐ to describe techniques for identifying the role of the system through task analysis, allocation of function and cost benefit analysis of alternatives from the user's point of view;

- ☐ to illustrate the above techniques through the use of case studies.

2.1 Introduction

Developing an understanding of users, what they do now and what they will do as a result of using the proposed system is fundamental to the software designer. Without this understanding the designer will not be in a position to specify and design a usable user interface. However, the situation is complex: what should the system do in order to meet the needs of the user? Who is the user? Will the person now doing the job the system is intended to support be the one to use the system or will this job be fundamentally changed by the system? Some may argue that these are not questions the software designer should be asking and that in fact a detailed specification of requirements should have been developed before the designer becomes involved.

Who is the user?

The most traditional approach to understanding users' needs is to think of the systems analyst as responsible for 'eliciting' requirements from users. This is usually achieved through the use of interviewing techniques, where the user plays a relatively passive role. The diagram below (Fig. 2.1) illustrates how this traditional approach leads to a 'linear' human communication structure. A major problem with this approach is that it often leads to

Who is responsible for understanding user requirements?

what is referred to as the 'over the wall' syndrome, where each person will only accept responsibility for their 'part' and no one is responsible for the overall success of the system. A further consequence of this approach is that the user is often the recipient of conflicting system 'components'. For example, the job the user is asked to do by his or her manager (the job designer), once the system is installed, is not consistent with the training given (by the training staff). In addition, the training may not be consistent with what the system can do (as achieved by the designer/implementor), and quite frequently the supporting documentation (as written by the technical author) is also in conflict with what the system does.

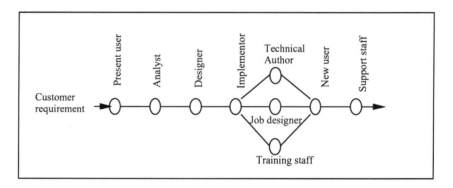

Figure 2.1 *Linear communication structure causes problems for designers and users.*

One of the major problems with the linear communication structure is that the human perception of what the system should do changes as it is passed from one person to the next (sometimes referred to as the 'Chinese whispers' effect). Thus it is argued that, for the designer to achieve 'good' user interface design, participation in the process of understanding users and evolving user requirements is essential.

Designers need to participate in order to understand requirements.

This chapter begins with a discussion about the role of the software designer in the early stages of a project, that is, in feasibility and requirements; all system development methods assume some degree of participation by the software designer, whether this is made explicit or not. A number of popular development methods are discussed. Following this, a particular method is described in some detail in order to illustrate some of the techniques associated with understanding users and assessing the feasibility of a proposed new system in the light of user needs. These techniques enable identification of what the proposed system should do. The next section then introduces techniques which help the designer to identify the role of the proposed system and the allocation of function between the user and the system. This enables identification of those tasks which will become part of the user interface.

Understanding requirements is about understanding the need for change.

2.2 The software designer and user requirements

Often 'system requirements' do not pre-exist as such. What does exist, however, is a perceived need for change and what has to be developed is a vision of that change. It can be argued that the software designer should be party to understanding the perceived need for change and should participate in evolving the system requirements and consequently the interface requirements. Different methods of requirements capture and analysis encourage differing levels of participation by designers and users. These can be broadly categorized into three groups. The first assumes little designer involvement and treats users as essentially passive, (described under the heading *Analysts 'elicit' requirements from users,* below). In the second category are those methods which encourage the active participation of users and designers (described under the heading *Users and design teams participate*). While in the third category is the more recent group of methods which recognize feasibility and requirements as a multidisciplinary activity, involving not only designers and users but also other stakeholders. These are discussed under the heading *The designer as a member of a multidisciplinary team.*

2.2.1 Analysts 'elicit' requirements from users

The most traditional approach is to think of the systems analyst as responsible for 'eliciting' requirements from users. This is usually achieved through use of interviewing, questionnaires or by observation, where the user plays a relatively passive role. In structured analysis approaches, such as SSADM (Structured Systems Analysis and Design Methodology), user views are elicited at appropriate points in the method. The requirements analysis module of SSADM has two stages. The first is an investigation of the current environment which is concerned with finding out about the business area and developing a logical picture of present activities and future needs. The second stage, business system options, derives a set of alternative courses of action for the project manager to select from. The scope of the investigation undertaken as part of the requirements analysis is relatively broad in that it tries to be concerned with the whole situation which the information system is supposed to support, not solely the system itself. However, despite the various attempts to change the approach to user involvement within SSADM the techniques recommended within the requirements analysis module are still largely process- and data-oriented. The method still relies heavily on the expertise of the analyst to model present activities, elicit requirements and develop a vision of the future to present to the project manager and other stakeholders.

SSADM is a process- and data-oriented approach. See Downs *et al.*, 1992 for an in-depth explanation of SSADM.

In contrast to the data- and process-oriented approaches, the object-oriented approach is now increasing in popularity. In particular, in object-oriented analysis (OOA) it is suggested that this approach improves analyst and problem domain expert interaction because object oriented is a natural way of thinking. OOA approaches generally still prescribe a passive role for

Object-oriented analysis is actively promoted by Coad and Yourdon, 1990.

the user, with the traditional view of users as sources of information.

The techniques employed within the above methods ensure that users are consulted, but they do not encourage them to participate actively in the decision-making process.

2.2.2 Users and design teams participate

In participative approaches all users are expected to contribute to and gain from any information system, and it is thought that participation increases the likelihood of success. Participation can take many forms. For example, in ETHICS (Effective Technical and Human Implementation of Computer Systems), the users assist in analysing their problems at work, fill in job satisfaction questionnaires and set future objectives for efficiency, effectiveness and job satisfaction. Human Factors experts at the HUSAT Research Centre at Loughborough University of Technology, UK, on the other hand, define three categories of users whose needs should be taken into account. These are: primary users, who are those likely to be frequent hands-on users of the proposed system, secondary users, who are occasional users or those who use the system through an intermediary, and tertiary users, who are unlikely to be hands-on users but will be affected by the introduction of the system or will influence its purchase.

ETHICS is a socio-technical approach developed by Mumford, 1986.

In an attempt to smooth the transition from requirements to design, the formation of a design team is recommended. There are a number of options for the construction of the design team (who also have responsibility for requirements capture) where the roles of the 'technical experts' and the 'customers' are clearly identified. The technical experts contribute their skills to the creation of a system, while the customers are concerned with the world they will have to inhabit after the change brought about by the new system. The customers also have a wide range of specific knowledge about the way the organization functions and the tasks it undertakes. The technical experts will want the system to help them advance their own design skills. Eason recommends therefore that the structure of the design team recognizes the fact that both specialists and customers have expertise to contribute and vested interests in the solutions adopted.

Design teams must be constructed to allow technical experts, users and customers to participate (Eason, 1987).

2.2.3 The designer as a member of a multidisciplinary team

More recent approaches to requirements have identified the need for including not only users and designers but also those with a stake in the system being proposed. A stakeholder is defined as anyone who stands to gain or lose from the change.

Stakeholders have a vested interest in the system being proposed. They may gain or lose depending on the scope of the system.

The stakeholders in any computer system fall into four distinct categories:

1. Those who are responsible for its design and development — for example, the project manager, software designers, communications experts, technical authors.

2. Those with a financial interest, responsible for its sale or for its purchase — for example, the business analyst, the marketing manager, the buyer.

3. Those responsible for its introduction and maintenance within an organization — for example, training and user support staff, installation and maintenance engineers and users' managers.

4. Those who have an interest in its use — for example, users' managers and all classes of users, that is, primary, secondary or tertiary .

Some of the stakeholders identified above, particularly in categories (1) and (3) have a direct responsibility for the design and development of the various system components and hence have a major interest in being involved in the requirements capture process. Those in category (2) have a financial responsibility for the success of the computer system and therefore may also need to be involved. The stakeholders in category (4) will be the recipients of the resulting computer system; they also have a major contribution to make in terms of specific task knowledge and the ability to assess the likely effects of the new system.

A cooperative approach to requirements (Macaulay, 1993 and Jirotka and Goguen, 1994).

The cooperative requirements capture (CRC) approach is described in some detail below in order to illustrate the kind of issues the software designer would need to address as a member of a requirements capture team.

2.3 Understanding user needs

Before a designer can begin system design, he or she must have an understanding of the future system that needs to be designed. How can the designer know what the future system is before design begins? The designer needs to have a 'vision' of the future system and knowledge and understanding of the target users, what they do now and what they will do in the future, and knowledge of the technological options available for building the future system.

The requirements statement embodies a vision of some future situation.

Thus the designer needs to acquire three areas of knowledge before beginning the design task:

1. Knowledge of the users present job.

2. Knowledge of the possible technological options.

3. Knowledge of the future system including the proposed new jobs.

Figure 2.2 shows a simplified view of the system design process. It illustrates the fact that knowledge of the user's present job and of the technological options acts as input to system design and that the output is the proposed new system. While broadly speaking this is true, in reality, knowledge of the future system is needed before it can be designed. This is one reason why establishing requirements for the design is complex. Knowledge of the

The future situation includes the software, the technology and the new jobs.

future system can only be acquired through projection or through developing 'visions' of the future.

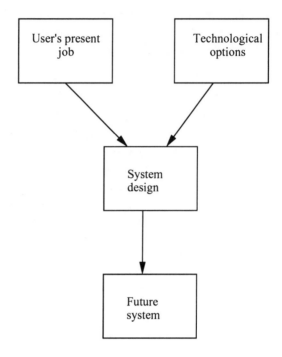

Figure 2.2   *Areas of knowledge.*

CRC encourages participation and cooperation between stakeholders.

Knowledge of the future system needs to be developed not only by the designer but also by the other stakeholders. In the cooperative requirements capture (CRC) approach, the user and the user environment provide the focus of attention for the stakeholders, and help them to develop a shared vision of the future system. They 'explore' the user environment together and they are encouraged to describe what users do now and to develop a vision of how things might change in the future. They develop a shared understanding of the potential for change and a shared terminology for discussing the problem domain. Figure 2.3 gives an overview of the CRC method.

CRC workshops are an important part of the method.

The rectangular boxes represent face-to-face meetings or workshops. Normally the meeting is supported by a trained facilitator, who guides the team through the main steps of the method and encourages all the stakeholders to participate. The oval boxes represent activities which must take place either before or after a workshop. These activities usually involve some subset of the stakeholders consulting with others outside the immediate team.

Communication and consultation is important in order to elaborate and validate the requirements before the detailed design begins.

Each part of the approach is described briefly below:

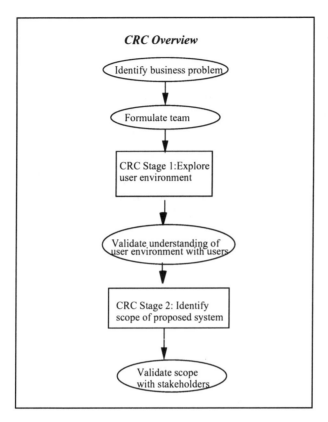

Figure 2.3 *Overview of the cooperative requirements capture (CRC) approach.*

2.3.1 Identify business problem

It is assumed that there will be some motivation for proposing that a future system be developed. That motivation may come from some specific business need, for example, the need to improve the speed of customer service at the check-in desk at an airport, or the need to provide bank customers with easy access to cash withdrawals. In some cases it may be that the commissioning organization is planning ahead and that the business problem may refer to some future need; for example, electricity distribution companies may be asking: 'What kind of computer support will control room engineers need in the year 2000?'. In other cases, it may be that only a small incremental improvement is needed, for example; an estate agent may already have a computer-based system but may be wanting to improve the quality of the information stored.

The team must understand why the system is being proposed.

If the commissioning organization is a software house or computer company it may be that they are in possession of some innovative technology and need to identify whether target users do have a need for that technology, and be able to describe what that need is.

In all these cases, a business need is identified, whether it be an improvement in customer service, a future need, a small incremental improvement to the existing system or the ability to use certain technology. There are many different motivations for proposing that a future system be developed. What is important to the application of the CRC approach is that the business need is articulated and described in such a way that it can be shared with the other team members.

User needs are investigated within the context of the business problem.

2.3.2 Formulate team

This will normally involve the project manager or initiator, and the facilitator in identifying the stakeholders and the requirements capture team. Ideally, between six and nine stakeholder representatives will participate in the CRC process. The team would be drawn from each of the four categories of stakeholders identified earlier in the chapter.

Identifying representative stakeholders to become team members is an important part of the method.

2.3.3 CRC stage 1: explore user environment

Exploring the user's environment means that the requirements capture team must collectively investigate the organizational setting the target users are in and identify and describe what the target users do. The term 'explore' is used because the team is encouraged to 'find out' afresh, to share knowledge about users and to set aside preconceptions about what users need. They also assess the likely costs and benefits of change from the user's point of view and produce a document recording the shared view of the user's environment. The structure of the 'user document' is shown in Table 2.1 below:

Table 2.1 *List of contents of the user document*

1. Management summary
   (including the business case and a brief description of the proposed system)

2. Organization/workgroups
   2.1 Workgroup control sheets
   2.2 Organization chart
   2.3 Workgroup table
   2.4 Workgroup description checklists

3. Generic users
   3.1 Generic users control sheets
   3.2 Generic users description checklists

4. Tasks
   4.1 Task control sheets
   4.2 Task hierarchy
   4.3 Task description checklists

The user document describes the user environment now and how it might change in the future.

5. Objects
    5.1 Object control sheets
    5.2 Object structures
    5.3 Object description checklists

6. Interactions
    6.1 User/task/object interactions
    6.2 Initial list of requirements and attributes

7. Consolidation
    7.1 Statement of credibility
    7.2 Further investigations needed

8. Worth proceeding?
    8.1 User/stakeholder perspective
    8.2 Business perspective
    8.3 Plan of action

9. Conclusion

The user document is produced by the cooperative requirements capture team as a result of a two day face-to-face meeting.

The initial user document is used as a basis for validating the understanding of users.

2.3.4 Validate understanding of user environment with users

Representative users do participate in the workshop but other users will need to be consulted or interviewed to ensure that the team has reliable information about all those users who may be affected by the system. After stage 1 of CRC, but before stage 2, the information recorded in the 'User Document' should be validated and then expanded or updated where necessary.

The techniques used for validation will depend on the specific problem. For a generic product, further market research may be needed; for a bespoke system, specific user interviews may be necessary. In any case, the extent of the information gathering task will depend on the extent of the knowledge and expertise of the stakeholders who took part in the workshop. A team who is highly conversant with their users may need to do very little validation. It is important to note that at this point in the development process highly detailed knowledge of all the users' tasks may not be necessary. The team needs to have enough reliable information to be able to decide which users, which tasks and which objects need to be computer supported and to decide what the extent of that support should be. That is, they need enough information to decide the scope of the proposed system.

The team needs 'enough' reliable information about users to decide the scope of the system.

2.3.5 CRC stage 2: identify the scope of the proposed system

This also involves a two day face-to-face meeting of the requirements capture team and the use of proformas and checklists. The scope of the proposed system must now be determined at a number of levels. Firstly, the stakeholders decide which jobs are to be affected and what the role of the system should be in supporting each of those jobs. In particular, task sharing, degree control and monitoring of tasks (discussed in section 2.5, *Task analysis and allocation of function*) should be considered in relation to the system. The likely acceptability of this proposed change should then be considered. In addition, for each work role identified, an initial task model is produced which helps to clarify and consolidate the understanding of the team with respect to specific roles. Secondly the team is asked to consider which objects from the user environment — that is, those contained in the user document — are likely to be of interest to the system; in other words, which objects will the system need to hold information about, which will it need to interact with and which will remain entirely in the user domain.

The scope of the proposed system is determined by the extent of support for the work roles and by the list of objects the system will need to support. In addition, both the scope of the system and the list of requirements are reviewed by each of the major stakeholders to make sure their needs are met.

Once the scope of the system is decided and the list of requirements reviewed, the team is asked to identify and agree on usability targets for the proposed system. The process involves the matching of the current situation with the proposed situation and specifying those areas where usability issues may be a problem. For example, the 'gap' between possessed and required knowledge to undertake a role or a specific task within a role may highlight a potential usability problem.

The usability is specified in five parts. The user (who), the specified activity (doing what), location (where), the targeted performance (ideal, worst case and best case), and measuring instrument (e.g. a benchmark) are all recorded in a usability specification table. Notes should be made about when in the development cycle the usability evaluation should take place (e.g. early at the prototyping stage or late at the installation stage). It is important that usabilty does not only address the end-users but also considers the facilitating users (e.g. installers and maintenance engineers).

The outcome from this stage is an 'initial requirements document' containing an agreed set of requirements for the proposed system. In addition, the software designer will have gained a thorough understanding of the users.

The initial requirements document is the major output from stage 2 of CRC. Each part is aimed at a specific set of stakeholders and covers a distinct set of issues. Table 2.2 below shows a list of contents.

Deciding the scope of the system means deciding what the system will and will not do.

The scope of the system should be such that it satisfies the needs of the stakeholders and users.

Specifying what is needed to make the system usable is part of the requirements.

Table 2.2 *List of contents of the initial requirements document*

1. Management summary
    (including the business case and a brief description of
    the proposed system)

2. The human requirements
    2.1 Description of the objectives of the commissioning organization
    2.2 List of the stakeholders together with their objectives
    2.3 List of key workgroups and users and their objectives

The initial requirements document forms the basis for the next stage of the design.

3. The high level functional requirements
    3.1 List of work roles to be supported and why
    3.2 Description of each work role in terms of users,
        objects and tasks

4. The detailed functional requirements
    4.1 Consolidated list of objects to be supported
    4.2 Descriptions of each object together with details
        of user tasks associated with each object.

5. The quality attributes
    Quality attributes may include usability, reliability,
    portability, performance, security, maintainability,
    acceptability depending on the proposed system.

6. Organization and user assistance requirements
    6.1 Documentation requirements
    6.2 Training requirements
    6.3 User support
    6.4 Human computer interface requirements.

7. The technological requirements and constraints
    7.1 Known hardware requirements (user or supplier)
    7.2 Known software constraints (user or
        supplier).

The stakeholders need to review the requirements to check whether the proposed system will meet their needs.

This initial requirements document is produced in draft form as part of CRC stage 2. The document represents a statement of the scope of the proposed system, which will then need to be validated by reviewing its contents with the stakeholders.

2.3.6 Validate scope with stakeholders

The scope of the proposed system should be validated. A range of techniques could be used at this point depending on the type of system under consideration. Appropriate techniques might include use of questionnaires, interviewing users, building mock-ups, throw-away prototypes or holding focus groups. Many techniques for measuring usability can also be used to validate the scope of the system with users and other stakeholders.

Team members need to develop a shared understanding.

Once the scope of the system has been agreed and documented, resources, timescales, tasks, milestones and deliverables can be evolved and the software designer can then proceed with the detailed design.

The next section gives a more detailed view of CRC stage 1, explaining the main steps and illustrating each step with reference to a case study.

2.4 The CAD case study

The purpose of this section is to give some insights into the kind of user-related issues covered within stage 1 of CRC and to provide illustrations of the checklists and proformas used.

The aim of stage 1 of CRC is to enable stakeholders to develop a shared understanding of users and what they do now, and to foresee what users will be doing when the proposed system is introduced. Stage 1 also encourages team members to assess the feasibility of the proposed system and of the proposed change to the user's situation, from the user's point of view.

Figure 2.4 below gives an outline of stage 1 of the CRC method showing the main steps.

What is the business opportunity?

Step 1 is where the proposer of the new system presents the case for that system in terms of business opportunity and potential business benefits. The proposer gives an initial description of the proposed system and this is discussed with the other team members.

In steps 2, 3, 4 and 5, the team members produce a list by using brainstorming techniques, classify the contents of the list according to certain criteria, select one or two important items from the list and describe those items using checklists of issues. The descriptions involve the team in thinking about the user's present job, the technological options and the proposed system.

What do users do now?

Step 6 enables the team to look for interactions between the items and issues discussed in steps 2, 3, 4 and 5. Here, a number of shortlists of user needs are generated.

Step 7 enables the team to reflect on the previous steps and to consolidate their findings into control sheets. These sheets are used by the team members to help them assess the credibility of the information they currently have about users and to identify what further work they need to do in order to get a good understanding of users.

What are the technological options?

Step 8 is part of the consolidation process, in that, as a result of steps 2,

3, 4 and 5 the team will have discussed the proposed system and the proposed changes to the users' jobs and environment. Step 8 enables the team to identify the costs of the proposed system and any benefits to the users. In some cases it may be that little or no benefit can be identified and that it is not worth proceeding. The team may need to rethink the proposed project or cancel it altogether.

What is the proposed system?

How credible is the team's understanding?

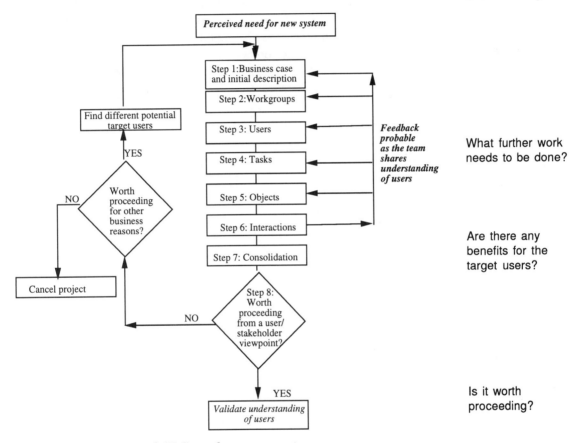

What further work needs to be done?

Are there any benefits for the target users?

Is it worth proceeding?

Figure 2.4 *Stage 1 of CRC, explore user environment.*

If it is worth proceeding, the team should undertake the further work identified at step 7; that is, they should validate their understanding of the users (after the meeting) and complete the user document.

The following discussion illustrates this process with reference to a computer-aided design (CAD) system, which assists in the planning of new construction projects such as bridges or roundabouts.

2.4.1 CRC stage 1, step 1: business case and initial description
The business case consists of a statement, made by one of the stakeholders, of the rationale for the system being proposed. This should include a description of the proposed system, a view on who the target users are and

What is the situation
now?

What is the time-
scale for the pro-
posed change?

on the perceived benefits of the proposed change to the customers and users. The business case should also identify the time perspective within which the proposed change will occur, for example, two years, five years or n years from now.

Thus in the remainder of the discussion 'now' means 'at the time of the analysis' and 'proposed' means n years from 'now'. The analysis of change centres around the end use analysis form in which the requirements team write down the current situation in the 'now' column and the projected future situation in the 'proposed' column. (CAD Figs 3, 5 and 6 give examples of end use analysis forms).

An example of a simplified business case is given below:

CAD Simplified business case

CAD case study

Business case
Overview

The proposed system is intended to support the needs of the county survey-ors' offices which are maintained by all the major civic authorities in England and Wales. The objective is to provide a computer-aided design system to assist in the planning of new construction projects. Ideally the system should be in operation in two years time.

The users of the system

The users of the proposed system are mainly found in the county surveyor's office.

Within this office, there are departments which maintain centres of exper-tise in drainage, sewage, street lighting, highways, traffic, town planning and many others. Furthermore, these departments often have to consult the legal department, the utilities (e.g. gas, water and electricity) and with the construction companies who carry out the engineering projects.

Each of the departments in the county surveyor's office consists typically of a departmental head and number of team leaders, each of whom is responsible for several projects. Each project is staffed by a small team which consists of an engineer, a tracer and a technician. The engineer is skilled in a particular area of expertise such as traffic management, and is responsible for the design decisions made on the project. The technician works for the engineer by going out on site, making observations, taking measurements and ensuring that the information is entered into the maps which form the basis of the work. The tracer is responsible for updating the maps using information collected by the technician and the designs provided by the engineer (CAD Fig. 1).

A department operates more or less autonomously, where the team leader manages the projects under his/her control by discussing progress with the engineer, who develops projects by holding informal meetings with the designated technician and tracers.

Schemes and projects

Within the county surveyor's office, a scheme can be initiated by any of the departments and, depending on their scope and impact on the environment, can involve a large number of other departments. The involvement of a department in a scheme is dependent on whether the scheme requires the skills of the staff in that department or affects the area of responsibility of that department. For example, a scheme to realign a road would be led by the highways department but, due to the movement of their pipework, may involve the public utilities.

Once a scheme is started it is separated into a number of projects, one for each of the departments involved. The lead department draws up a map for the scheme and circulates it to all the other departments.

On receiving a map, an engineer — in conjunction with the technician and tracer — sets about assessing the impact of the scheme on his/her area of responsibility. If there is an impact, they build an overlay to the map which highlights the engineer's area of interest and concern. These overlays serve to emphasize the interests of the particular engineer and de-emphasize the other parts of the map.

By this stage, a scheme is represented by a map which consists of a large number of overlays and an overall plan supporting a series of interlocking project plans. There follows a series of formal and informal meetings to clarify the design and resolve conflicts of interest. These meetings are essentially design meetings and reviews aimed at producing an agreed map which, via its overlays, reflects all the interests which need to be taken into account in order to complete the scheme.

The design phase of the scheme is completed when the plan and the map are formally signed-off whereupon the project passes into an execution phase. During the execution phase the engineers may need to consult the map and its overlays in order to resolve problems or issues.

The proposed product (initial description)

The purpose of the proposed system is to provide a graphics-based workstation which will ensure that the maps and overlays used by an individual project are up-to-date and can be worked on by several departments together.

It is intended that the system be used by the engineer, the technician and the tracer. However, due to the fact that these maps are a shared resource the system provides an opportunity for centralizing the maintenance and archiving facilities.

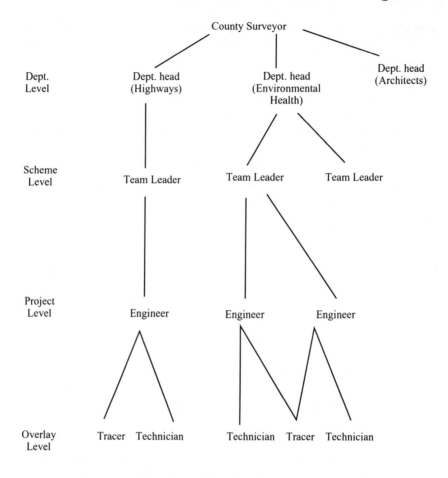

CAD Figure 1   *Simplified organizational structure.*

2.4.2 CRC stage 1: step 2: workgroups

Which workgroups
will be affected by
the proposed
system?

Each of the discussions concerning workgroups, users, tasks and objects includes a brainstorming session; an evaluation session; a prioritization session and an analysis of change session. For example at the workgroup level the team members: (i) identify on, say, a whiteboard those in the organization who might be affected by the proposed system using brainstorming suggestions for these workgroups and evaluating the list produced until the team agrees that it represents the collective view; (ii) classify the workgroups according to whether they are likely to be primary, secondary or tertiary users of the proposed system (CAD Fig. 2), then (iii) select one primary workgroup and describe it as it is 'now' in terms of social and organizational issues (CAD Fig. 3) and job issues and attempt to describe how the workgroup will change in the 'proposed' situation.

Workgroup title	Project group	Team group	Departmental group
Relationship	1	2	3
Generic users ☐	ENGINEER [1]	ENGINEER [1]	TEAM LEADER [2]
	TRACER [1]	TEAM LEADER [2]	DEPARTMENTAL HEAD [3]
	TECHNICIAN [1]	☐	☐
	☐	☐	☐
	☐	☐	☐
	☐	☐	☐

☐   Indicates the likely relationship of user or workgroup to the proposed system.

[1]   Primary relationship: likely to be frequent, hands-on users.

[2]   Secondary relationship: likely to be occasional users or those who use the system through an intermediary.

[3]   Tertiary relationship: probably will not use the system, but may be affected by its use, or may influence its purchase.

CAD Figure 2   *A workgroup table.*

Social issues are considered in order to help the designers understand social aspects of the workgroup which may affect the acceptability of the proposed system to that group. They are considered in terms of workgroup structure (size of group, location, communication structure), workgroup dynamics (leadership styles and relationships within the group), and the workgroup's status and prestige, as perceived relative to other workgroups.

Will the proposed change be acceptable to the workgroups?

Organizational issues are considered in order to understand the workgroup in its organizational context, and to help anticipate any impact upon the organization which may result from changes in working practice. Organizational issues are considered in terms of the workgroup's mission and objectives, its importance relative to other workgroups, the extent of its autonomy, its cohesion as a group, and the extent of its dependency on other workgroups.

What impact will the proposed change have on the organization?

In the CAD case study it soon becomes clear that much of the work of the tracer will be automated and that the size of the project team is likely to reduce from three or four to one or two people. Obviously the lesson for the designer is that understanding the job of the tracer is key to the design even though the tracer is unlikely to be the eventual user of the system.

Consideration of **job issues** takes the form of a diary or chart showing the time spent on particular activities within a suitable time period. It describes

What does each workgroup do in a typical day or week and how will this change? typical activities of the workgroup undertaken in a typical day, week or month as appropriate. In the CAD case study a suitable time period to consider would be a typical project. The job issues would then include a list of typical activities which occur in the lifetime of a construction design project.

Proposed System   CSCAD

Workgroup   PROJECT GROUP

Organizational and social issues

Now	Proposed (e.g. 2 years on)
Mission/objectives To complete the overlay for particular projects	same
Autonomy Low, have to work within scheme	same
Cohesion High, must work as team to complete project	must remain the same; breaking up 'the team' could have adverse effect on project completion
Dependency on other workgroups Dependent on other project groups and on scheme workgroup	same
Structure and dynamics One location	same, but small in size
Size 3/4 One Engineer, Tracers, Technicians	work of tracer less important
Prestige Viewed as equals by other workgroups	May increase with increased communications potential

CAD Figure 3   *Workgroup: organizational and social issues.*

2.4.3 CRC stage 1, step 3: users

Who are the target users? At the user level a similar procedure as for workgroups is followed. A list of generic users is agreed upon, these are classified according to their relationship with the proposed system (CAD Fig. 4).

Generic users	Relationship	Description sheets		
		Job	Person	Organization
ENGINEER	1	YES	YES	YES
TRACER	1	YES	YES	NO
TECHNICIAN	1	YES	YES	NO
TEAM LEADER	2	YES	NO	NO
DEPARTMENTAL HEAD	3	NO	NO	NO

1: Primary user
2: Secondary user
3: Tertiary user

YES: Means that a description sheet
has been completed for that user
NO: Means it hasn't

CAD Figure 4 *List of generic users.*

Selected users are described according to three sets of issues. The first set of issues is concerned with how the organization views the generic user, now and proposed. Consideration of **organizational issues** will determine the potential reactions of the organization, and the possible impact upon the organization that may result from introducing information technology into a particular user's job or occupation. Organizational issues are considered in terms of the mission and objectives of the user, the importance of the user to other users within the organization, the investment the organization has made in the user and the replaceability of the user by the organization. This checklist is not shown here. The second set of issues is concerned with the personal attributes of the generic user now and proposed and the third checklist is a typical 'day in the life of' the generic user now and proposed. Explanations of personal and job issues are given below:

How are they viewed by the organization?

Person issues are examined to identify user characteristics that may affect the design and presentation of the proposed system, to understand the potential impact of the proposed system on the user's job or work, and to anticipate any adverse user reactions to the introduction of the proposed system into the workplace. Person issues are considered in terms of the user's attitude and motivation towards work, information technology etc., the user's aspirations and ambitions, kinds and levels of skill and expertise

How will the user react to the proposed change?

possessed, and characteristics of the user's job such as whether it is lonely or sociable, dirty or clean, undertaken in hot or cold conditions and so on.

Proposed System _____ CSCAD _____

Generic User _____ ENGINEER _____

Person Issues _____

Now	Proposed (e.g. 2 years on)
Attitude Professional (traditional and cautious, positive as long as benefits can be seen)	unchanged
Motivation • easier life • to be more effective • to increase quality	• make use of maps easier • speed up information flow • increase quality
Aspiration/ambition • to be a team leader • to be seen as the 'top' engineer	to realize aspirations
Expertise High expertise (very specialized knowledge base)	• exploit expertise more fully by reducing time-consuming and/or boring tasks
Skill Most technical skills undertaken by technician or tracer, likely to be rather 'rusty'	• new set of IT skills needs to be learnt
Job Very sociable, varied with high status	unchanged

What new skills will be needed and what existing skills will no longer be needed?

CAD Figure 5   *Person issues, generic user checklist.*

Job issues are considered in the same way as for the workgroup, in terms of a diary or a chart of time spent on various activities.

In the case study the engineer is identified as a primary user and as a professional and an expert. The designer will need to identify the needs of the engineer as a key user. The 'day in the life of' begins to identify where benefits should accrue from the use of the proposed CAD system, for example, less time spent in meetings, faster corrections and changes to designs, less manual administration and record keeping. The designer can thus begin to see which tasks are crucial to the success of the system in the eyes of the user.

What does the user do in a typical day or week and how will this change?

Proposed System   CSCAD

Generic User   ENGINEER

Job Issues

Now	Proposed (e.g. 2 years on)
30min. Opens mail, has coffee. If weather good, goes on site inspection	Electronic mail facility
30min. Briefs subordinates (tracer and technician)	Content of briefing will change according to product specification
60min. Meets other prof. eng. to discuss project progress etc.	Should need fewer meetings, particularly if networked
45min. Remedial actions e.g. correct overlay or map	Can be carried out more quickly and more easily
15min. Reads technical magazines (to keep up to date)	Could increase (IT magazines)
60min. Lunch, often a liquid one!	Fewer reasons for 'working' lunches with other engineers
30min. Administration and record keeping	Should diminish
30min. Review subordinates work	Increase but more co-operative
60min. Problem-solving activities	Less 'creative' but more solutions
60min. Site visits	Unchanged but higher quality should lead to fewer problems
60min. Crises responses, answers queries, planned maintenance	More potential crises likely to be pre-empted, generally quicker and easier

CAD Figure 6   *Job issues: a typical day in the life of the generic user.*

Task Id.	Relationship	Description sheets		
		Organization	Timing	Human
INTERPRET BRIEF (e.g. build new roundabout)	3			
GATHER and ASSIMILATE (e.g. on site visits)	3			
DESIGN SOLUTION	3			
TEST SOLUTION	3			
REPRESENT SOLUTION ON OVERLAY	1			
DISTRIBUTE SOLUTION TO OTHER DEPTS.	2 or 1			
REPRESENT SOLUTION ON AGGREGATE MAP	2	YES	YES	YES
RECEIVE COMMENTS AND DATA	3			
MATCH SOLUTION TO BRIEF	3			
SIGN OFF	2	YES	YES	YES

Which tasks will be supported by the proposed system?

1: Automated task :
Likely to be totally automated, and the user will not take any action
2: Shared task:
Likely to be shared between the user and the system
3: External task:
Likely to be totally carried out by the user without system support

YES: Means that a description sheet has been completed for that task
NO: Means it hasn't

CAD Figure 7   *A list of tasks and the likely role of the system in supporting each task.*

2.4.4 CRC stage 1, step 4: tasks

A task is defined as an action carried out by a generic user on an object in order to achieve a work goal. A list of tasks associated with a workgroup is first identified, (CAD Fig. 7) and the allocation of function between human and computer is considered for each of the tasks (section 2.5). Selected tasks are fully described using checklists of organizational issues, timing issues and human issues, now and proposed, in order to understand the detail of the task and the likely effect of change.

A task is described in terms of **organizational issues**; its importance from a political viewpoint within the organization, its significance for security, the motivation for the user to carry out the task, the type of training required and the other tasks supported by or supportive of the task.

Proposed System   CSCAD

Task   REPRESENT SOLUTION

Organization Issues

What skills are associated with the tasks?

Now	Proposed (e.g. 2 years on)
Importance High	same i.e. high
affects all other departments solutions	
Security Low - initially High - final is 'frozen'	same but more problems with passwords
Motivation Important (visible) High	same i.e. high
Skill level Skill high	reduce skill level required high - low
Dependencies All other departments' solutions	same i.e. dependent on other depts.
database and knowledge base accession	same but more powerful

Why are the tasks carried out?

CAD Figure 8   *Task description sheet, organizational issues.*

The task is also described in terms of **timing issues**; that is, its frequency (i.e. how often the task is carried out by the user), the amount of time spent on it, the amount of preparation required to do it, and the degree of fragmentation of the task.

Proposed System   CSCAD

Task   REPRESENT SOLUTION

Timing Issues

Now	Proposed (e.g. 2 years on)
Time spent on task/frequency	
once per project (final only)	same but may be:
iterations (design process)	• more projects • less time for iteration
Preparation	
yes - initially	initially - same or easier
difficult later since other departments are involved	later - should be easier and more available
Fragmentation	
• initially continuous • later dependent upon responses from other departments	initially - same later - more seamless

How often are the tasks carried out?

CAD Figure 9   *Task description sheet, timing issues.*

In terms of **human issues**, CRC considers the level of discretion the user has in deciding whether or not to carry out the task, the amount of stress involved in the task and the performance criteria used to measure successful completion of the task.

Proposed System _____ CSCAD _____

Task _____ REPRESENT SOLUTION _____

Human Issues _____

Now	Proposed (e.g. 2 years on)
Task discretion no discretion dependent on project phase	same i.e. none
Task stress • intellectual pleasure • creative stress • high profile BRIEF DRIVEN	proportional to frequency, would want to reduce stress
Performance criteria • queries from departments • cost per solution • timeliness	same/more so

Can users decide whether or how to carry out the tasks?

What performance criteria are associated with the tasks?

CAD Figure 10 *Task description sheet, human issues.*

At the task level, the designer gains a greater understanding of the users and the tasks they carry out and can begin to identify which tasks will be of importance to the proposed system. In addition, the designer begins to consider the role of the proposed system in supporting the tasks, and to identify what the learning needs of the user are with respect to learning the new system-supported tasks.

2.4.5 CRC stage 1, step 5: objects

At the object level the team is asked to identify a list of objects associated with the user's environment. These objects will normally be associated in some way with users and workgroups, and they could be real-world objects, knowledge about real-world objects, procedures remembered by users or other more abstract objects. Once a list has been produced, it is then reconsidered and revised by the team, which entails clarifying the meaning of object names, looking for similar objects with different names or two different objects with similar names. In addition it may be possible to aggregate some objects with others; for example, some 'objects' may be attributes of other objects. Once an agreed list is produced, the objects are then classified according to whether they are likely to be of interest to the proposed system (CAD Fig. 11).

Which objects will be supported by the proposed system?

Object Id.	Relationship	Description sheet
AGGREGATE MAP	2	YES
OVERLAY	1	YES
SCHEME PLAN	2	YES
PROJECT PLAN	2	YES
LETTERS/NOTES/DRAWINGS	2	NO
FEATURES	2	NO
ROADS/BRIDGES etc	3	NO

1: Hidden Object:
Likely to be totally automated and not visible at the user interface.
2: Visible Object :
Likely to be supported by the system but will be visible to the user at the user interface.
3: External Object:
Not likely to be supported by the system , likely to remain external to the system, but could still be of interest to the user.

CAD Figure 11   *A list of objects and the likely role of the system in supporting each object.*

Selected objects are then described in further detail in terms of their 'now' characteristics and 'proposed' characteristics (CAD Fig. 12).

Proposed System _____ CSCAD _____

Object _____ AGGREGATE MAP

Object Description _____

Now	Proposed (e.g. 2 years on)
Description Consists of a set of overlays to a normal map	Computer support for the map and its overlays
Access to the object It is accessed by all the engineers, technicians and tracers working on a scheme	The same people will access the map but they will use a computer system
Management Controlled by the department which is leading the scheme Signed off by everybody	No change to the responsibility but a change of method, which presents a problem
Representation It is all on paper of various sorts (e.g. the overlays are on transparent paper)	Presented on a workstation and on paper
Quality This varies during the design process but each version has a status (e.g. draft)	No change to the approach but the computer system will enforce tighter control

How is each object to be described now, and how will it change?

CAD Figure 12 *Object description sheet.*

At the object level, the designer begins to identify which objects in the user environment are likely to become objects which need to be supported by the system. The designer can identify potential interface objects and their characteristics.

2.4.6 CRC stage 1, step 6: interactions
Step 6 enables the team to look for interactions between the items and issues discussed steps 2, 3, 4 and 5. Here a number of shortlists of user needs are generated. In particular, combinations of user, object and task are examined

User ID	ENGINEER
Object ID	AGGREGATE MAP
Task ID	SIGN-OFF
Interaction characteristics: a need for:
version control
'signature' facility
access from various locations
restricted 'write' access
'sign-off' security

CAD Figure 13   *User, object, task interactions.*

What user needs can be identified?

User ID	ENGINEER
Object ID	OVERLAY
Task ID	REPRESENT SOLUTION ON OVERLAY
Interaction characteristics: a need for:
version control
quick response to queries from other departments
ability to cope with interruptions
ease of amendment
intermediate quality for 'working' overlay
high quality for final overlay
support for mapping conventions
annotation of overlay
drawing capability

CAD Figure 14   *User, object, task interactions.*

in order to assess needs or requirements associated with the proposed system. The team is encouraged to make statements of the form 'There is a need for........' ; for example, 'There is a need for version control' as opposed to 'The *xyz* system of version control will be implemented'. The purpose of this is that the team should be trying to identify user and customer needs rather than deciding on the solution. (CAD Figs 13 and 14)

Figure 13 shows the interaction characteristics identified as a result of considering the engineer carrying out the task of signing off the aggregate map.

CAD Figure 14 shows the interaction characteristics identified as a result of considering the engineer carrying out the task represent solution on the overlay map.

2.4.7 CRC stage 1, step 7: consolidation

Step 7 enables the team to reflect on the previous steps and to consolidate their findings into control charts. These charts are used by the team to help them assess the credibility of the information they currently have about users and to identify what further work they need to do in order to get a good understanding of users. In particular, the consolidation session includes a review of each of workgroups, users, objects and tasks in which the team is asked to make an honest assessment of the accuracy of their collective knowledge of the users. (control sheets, CAD Figs 15, 16 and 17).

Proposed System   CSCAD

Control Sheet: GENERIC USER

Generic User ID	Relationship	Description sheets?	Target credibility	Actual credibility
ENGINEER	1	YES	1	2
TRACER	1	NO	1	3
TECHNICIAN	1	NO	1	3
TEAM LEADER	2	NO	2	3
DEPARTMENTAL HEAD	3	NO	2	3

What credibility rating would the team attach to their understanding of users?

1: Primary user	YES: Description sheet	Credibility rating:
2: Secondary user	completed for that user	1: Verified
3: Tertiary user	NO: Not completed	2: Authorative
		3: Not authorative

CAD Figure 15   *Control sheet for generic users.*

What follow-up
investigations are
needed?
The team are then encouraged in step 7 to identify follow-up investigations which are needed to ensure that the future stages of requirements capture and analysis, and the system design, are based on a sound understanding of the users. The user document is initially a collection of the proformas completed at the workshop, but should be expanded after the workshop.

2.4.8 CRC stage 1, step 8: worth proceeding?

Step 8 is part of the consolidation process in that, as a result of steps 2, 3, 4 and 5, the team will have discussed the proposed system and the proposed changes to the users' jobs and environment. The purpose of step 8 is to enable the team to identify the costs and benefits of the proposed system to the proposed users. In some cases it may be that little or no benefit can be identified and that it is not worth proceeding. The team may need to rethink the proposed project or cancel it altogether — or, as is sometimes the case, proceed with the project but seek to identify different target users.

If it is worth proceeding, then the user document provides the requirements team with an agreed set of descriptions of the target users and an

Is it worth proceed-
ing?

Proposed System   CSCAD

Control Sheet: OBJECTS

Can any benefits for
users be identified?

Object ID	Relation-ship	Descrpt. sheets?	Target cred.	Actual cred.
AGGREGATE MAP	2	YES	1	1
OVERLAY	1	NO	1	1
SCHEME PLAN	2	NO	1	2
PROJECT PLAN	2	NO	1	3
LETTERS/NOTES/DRAWINGS	2	NO	2	3
FEATURES	2	NO	3	3
ROADS/BRIDGES etc	3	NO	3	3

1: Hidden object 2: Visible object 3: External object	YES: Description sheet completed for that object NO: Not completed	Credibility Rating: 1: Verified 2: Authorative 3: Not authorative

CAD Figure 16   *Control sheet for objects.*

initial description of the requirements associated with the proposed system. The next stage in the process is to ensure that the descriptions of users are valid and to modify the user document accordingly.

The starting point for the next workshop is a validated user document. The team can then proceed to identify the scope of the proposed system by following the steps in stage 2 of CRC.

A full description of stage 2 is not given here. Instead, the following section describes one of the themes central to stage 2, that of task analysis and allocation of function. Also central to stage 2 is usability specification, covered in Chapter Six.

Proposed System   CSCAD

Control Sheet: TASKS

Task ID	Relation-ship	Descrpt. sheets?	Target cred.	Actual cred.
INTERPRET BRIEF (e.g. build new roundabout	3	NO	1	3
GATHER and ASSIMILATE INFORMATON (e.g. on site visits)	3	NO	3	3
DESIGN SOLUTION	3	NO	2	3
TEST SOLUTION	3	NO	3	3
REPRESENT SOLUTION ON OVERLAY	1	NO	1	1
DISTRIBUTE SOLUTION TO OTHER DEPTS.	2 or 1	NO	1	3
REPRESENT SOLUTION ON AGGREGATE MAP	2	YES	1	2
RECEIVE COMMENTS AND DATA	3	NO	2	3
MATCH SOLUTION TO BRIEF	3	NO	2	3
SIGN-OFF	2	NO	1	3

1: Automated task	YES: Description sheet	Credibility rating:
2: Shared task	completed for that task	1: Verified
3: External task	NO: Not completed	2: Authorative
		3: Not authorative

CAD Figure 17   *Control sheet for tasks.*

2.5 Task analysis and allocation of function

Task analysis is the process of analysing the way people perform their jobs and is important to the software designer because a major part of the design will focus on supporting the jobs people do. A number of techniques for task analysis exist, each of which tends to place emphasis on one aspect. For example, task decomposition looks at the way a task is split into subtasks, and at the order in which tasks are performed. Knowledge-based techniques look at what users need to know about the objects and actions involved in a task, and how that knowledge is organized. Hierarchical task analysis is used to decompose tasks into subtasks without any specific reference to the order in which tasks are performed, the simplest form of task analysis. In addition to task analysis, the designer should also be concerned with analysis of the objects people use when carrying out their tasks.

Task analysis is the process of analysing the way people do their jobs.

  The user carries out a task on an object. This can be thought of as the user/object/task triangle (Fig 2.5). The user, the task and the object each have particular characteristics. The user carries out a task using particular knowledge, skills, and experience and has motivation and attitudes. The task is an action carried out on an object by a user, and it will have a structure, an order of execution, dependencies on other tasks, frequency of execution and a measure of completion. An object is the thing being acted upon and will have a representation, a frequency of access and actions that can be carried out upon it.

A range of task analysis techniques are covered in Dix et al., 1993.

A task is an action carried out on an object by a user.

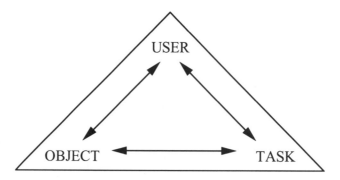

Figure 2.5 *User/object/task triangle.*

2.5.1 Hierarchical task analysis
Hierarchical task analysis is used in CRC stage 2. The first step is to identify the **invariant tasks** which users carry out. Invariant tasks are those which will not change even though the means of achieving them may change. They are fundamental to the mission of the organization. For example, the mission of a university library might be to 'lend books to students which will assist

them in their studies'. In order to do this the library must stock books, issue books to lenders and keep a record of books in stock; these are some examples of invariant tasks. The library must carry out these tasks in order to achieve its mission. However, the manner in which the task is carried out may change. For example, a library must keep a record of all the books in stock; this is fundamental to the running of the library but the manner in which stock is recorded may change. The librarian will issue books to borrowers; this is fundamental to keeping a record of where books are, although book issue could be achieved through the use of bar codes and scanners or hand-written issue slips.

> Invariant tasks are those tasks which are fundamental to the mission of the organization.

Identifying invariant tasks enables the software designer to see which aspects of the user's job are fundamental (to the user's company or organization) and which aspects can be the subject of change — that is, to which aspects can the designer apply his or her creative design skills. By taking this approach to task analysis we are more likely to achieve an innovative design for the new system as opposed to simply automating the current way of working.

> Designers can create new ways of carrying out invariant tasks.

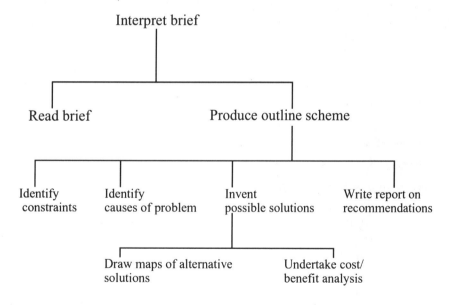

> Invariant tasks are broken down into their component parts.

Figure 2.6 *Task hierarchy for 'interpret brief'.*

This process is best described through illustration.

In the CAD case study, a new **brief** is presented to the **team group.** Their first task is to interpret that brief and to consider alternative solutions. Thus an example of an invariant task will be 'interpret brief to find the best possible solution', and another example of an invariant task would be 'to model the solution through a detailed design'. The need for these tasks will not change since they are fundamental to the 'organizational mission' of the team group. It is usual for this type of system to identify invariant tasks at the workgroup level rather than for individual users.

The next stage is to break down the invariant task into its component tasks. For example 'interpret brief in order to find the best possible solution':

In order to **interpret brief** the engineer must first **read the brief** and then **produce an outline scheme.** A problem could be identified by the county surveyor e.g. too many road traffic accidents.

His/her brief could be:

The main objective is to reduce road traffic accidents by at least 50% and preferably more. If possible, improve traffic flow and reduce noise in the town centre. Don't spend more than half a million pounds and make sure the scheme can be completed within two years.

Thus the engineer has to interpret this brief of reducing road traffic accidents into an **outline scheme**. The outline scheme typically contains critical success factors and critical constraints. The subtasks of **produce outline scheme** are:

1. **Identify constraints**
   Constraints are typically measured in terms of costs, timescales, environment, disruption etc.

2. **Identify causes of problem**
   Causes of problem are typically perceived in terms of road usage, danger spots, residents, key buildings etc.

3. **Invent possible solutions**
   (i) Possible solutions: alternatives could be bypass, tunnel, flyover, traffic lights, traffic ban, speed limiters or pedestrian barriers.
   (ii) Draw maps of alternative solutions: essentially 'sketches' highlighting the major features.
   (iii) Assess cost/benefit: this will result in the consideration of a number of possible alternative solutions.

4. **Write report on recommendations**

   (i) Making recommendations: essentially a creative process requiring much value judgement and juggling of objectives and constraints.

Interpreting the brief involves the engineer in design and in decision making. The engineer also uses a great deal of knowledge throughout this process, for example, knowledge of types and causes of accident, terrain, lighting, needs of populace and drivers, construction problems and costs.

What role should our CAD system play in order to assist the engineer and his/her team in achieving the task 'interpret brief to find the best possible solution'? Should the CAD system provide any support at all? What are the alternatives? How will the team and its various members react? Would they use the system? Would they like it and find it helpful? These issues can be addressed by considering the allocation of function between the team members and the CAD system.

Deciding on the role of the system in supporting the users involves considering alternatives.

2.5.2 Allocation of function

Allocation of function between human and computer can be thought of as a spectrum of possible allocation types from the human carrying out a task with little or no support from the computer system to the computer system carrying out a task with little or no reference to the human (Fig 2.7).

How are the functions allocated?

The system could share the task with the user.

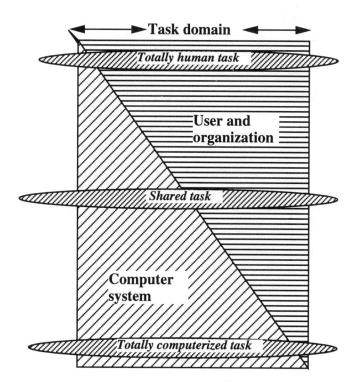

Figure 2.7 *Allocation of function.*

Sharing of tasks is only one issue associated with function allocation. Who or what **controls** the task is also important, as is the type of support the system provides i.e. **passive or active.**

The system could actively help the user with the task, or provide only general 'passive' support.

Making explicit decisions about the type of function allocation is important at this stage in the analysis, since it can be used to assess likely

reactions of the various stakeholders to the system. This prevents potential hostile reactions from users, managers or other workgroups when the system is first introduced. Function allocation is also important to help assess the alternative **cost and benefits** of the system to the users and stakeholders.

This analysis follows a tradition in ergonomics, which encourages the development team to look just as carefully at the functions expected from the human beings as from the technical system. Some examples of allocation types are given below:

The system could take control from the user, or leave the user in control of the task.

1. The system replaces the user.
    For example, an automatic cash dispenser replaces the bank teller.

2. The system carries out the task, the user provides input only.
    For example, a data entry clerk provides input concerning customer transactions, the system updates the accounts.

3. The system provides expert advice, the user inputs parameters and receives the results.
    For example, a user inputs symptoms to an expert medical system. The system carries out a diagnosis and provides advice.

4. The user carries out the task, the system controls the rate at which the task is carried out.
    For example, a user packs goods on a packing line and the system controls the rate at which the goods flow.

5. The system provides passive assistance.
    For example, a database provides structure to assist the storage and retrieval of data. A compiler provides syntax checking and compilation but does not help to design or write the program.

6. The system provides active assistance.
    For example, a fourth generation language will actively help with screen design and generation of code from a 'higher-level' specification as well as providing syntax checking and compilation.

7. The system provides general task support.
    For example, a wordprocessor or a spreadsheet.

In our CAD case study, we developed a task hierarchy for the task 'interpret brief'. It is clear that there are a number of possible alternative ways in which the computer could provide support for this task. We consider the allocation of function by drawing up a table of possible alternatives:

Alternative	User function	System function	
1. Complete automation	Specify problem Provide knowledge	Acquire implicit and explicit knowledge Develop alternative solns Check solns (cost/benefit) Produce optimum soln	Costs and benefits of alternatives must be considered from a user point of view.
2. Automatic development (design)	Specify problem Identify constraints Assess alternative solns Choose optimum soln	Develop alternative solns	
3. Automatic checking (decision making)	Specify problem Identify constraints Develop alternative solns Choose optimum solution	Acquire implicit and explicit knowledge Analyse alternatives	The expertise of the whole requirements team is needed to focus on issues and identify possible problems and acceptable solutions.
4. Partial development	Specify problem Identify constraints Consider alternatives Part design solutions	Part design solutions	
5. Partial checking	Specify problem Identify constraints Design alternative solns Partial analysis and choice of optimum soln	Partial analysis and choice of optimum soln	
6. Partial development and partial checking	Specify problem Identify constraints Part design solns and part analyse and choose optimum solution	Acquire implicit and explicit knowledge Part design solns and part analyse and choose optimum solution	
7. Administrative support	Specify problem Design alternatives Choose optimum soln Write report	Provide passive assistance Drawing facility Word processing Communications network Printing, filing	

The above table shows the major alternatives by specifying the possible allocations of function between the engineer and the CAD system. The alternatives are listed broadly in an order which has the system as the major contributor at the top and the engineer as the major contributor at the bottom.

Each option will result in a different reaction to the system by the engineer and his or her team; for example, alternative 2, automatic development, may produce adverse reactions because skill at the design function is seen as one of the major roles of the engineer and his or her project team, and they may view the system as a threat rather than an aid. Alternative 3, automatic checking, may be unpopular because identifying optimum solutions is an area of expertise developed by the engineer over a number of years and he or she may be wary of losing the power and status that this expertise gives.

User reaction to each alternative should be considered.

Each alternative must also be considered in terms of it being technically feasible; for example, alternative 1, is technically difficult, whereas alternative 7 would be technically easy to provide.

A cost/benefit analysis of each alternative should be undertaken by discussion with all the stakeholders associated with the CAD system, i.e. cost benefit associated with the social and organizational issues as well as the technical and financial issues.

Technical and financial issues should also be considered.

The user carries out a task using particular knowledge, skills, and experience, and has motivation and attitudes; the analysis carried out on the human issues at the task level of CRC stage 1 will provide this information. The task will have a structure, an order of execution, dependencies on other tasks, frequency of execution and a measure of completion, all part of the timing and organizational issues.

2.6 Summary

The role of the system in supporting the user's tasks should be explicitly decided through the designer considering a range of possible alternative allocations of function. Once the role of the system and the role of the user have been decided, the next stage in the HCI design lifecycle is to identify those subtasks which will appear at the user interface and to specify the user interface requirements. This theme is continued in the next chapter.

Members of the requirements team share their knowledge and experience to arrive at an acceptable solution.

In this chapter the author has presented some techniques for understanding user needs and requirements and has described the role of the software designer in this. Central to this is the belief that the designer should be part of a team, because the expertise of the whole team is needed to focus on issues and to identify possible problems and acceptable solutions.

Exercises for Chapter 2

2.1 Describe four different types of function allocation between user and system. Include in your answer, issues related to task sharing, task control and active or passive system support.

2.2 Give three reasons why a workgroup might find a new computer system unacceptable.

2.3 What is an invariant task and why is it important?

2.4 What three areas of knowledge does the designer need to acquire before design can begin, and why?

2.5 What are the arguments for and against a designer being part of a requirements capture team?

Chapter 3

Designing the user interface

The objectives of this chapter are:

☐ to describe briefly the main classes of user interface;

☐ to present principles of good HCI design;

☐ to encourage an understanding of the use of colour;

☐ to describe a task-oriented approach to UI design;

☐ to introduce guidelines for designing screens and windows;

☐ to illustrate the above through examples;

☐ to present a case study of a task-oriented approach to UI design.

3.1 Introduction

A well-designed user interface will provide a good match between the user's task needs, skill level and learning ability.

Well-designed interfaces provide a good match between the user's task needs, skill level and learning ability and will lead to satisfied and productive users. A good user interface will be easy to learn and easy to use and will encourage the user to experiment and try out new features within the system without getting frustrated. Well-designed interfaces will also help considerably towards 'selling' or encouraging the adoption of the computer system, either to user managers or to users themselves.

This chapter briefly introduces the main classes of user interface currently in use and suggests five principles of good design. These principles can be used to guide the design of the user interface or can be used to evaluate existing interfaces. The bulk of this chapter is devoted to an explanation of an approach to user interface design based on an understanding of user tasks and sequence of task execution. This is called a task-oriented approach and is to be compared with an object-oriented approach described in Chapter Four.

In a task-oriented design approach, the likely sequence of user system dialogue must be identified.

The task-oriented approach involves the designer in identifying those tasks which will be shared between user and system and which will appear at the user interface. The sequence in which the user will carry out the interface tasks thus needs to be specified. Once the sequence of the user system dialogue is understood, the next stage is to plan the design of the sequence of screens or windows which will support the dialogue. A procedure for planning the design is presented here, together with some of the more popular design guidelines. At the end of the chapter there is a case study of a task-oriented approach to user interface design.

This chapter also discusses the use of colour at the user interface, including general guidance on how to plan the use of colour and criticism of specific screens where colour is not used to good effect.

In order to understand what is meant by a 'good' or 'well-designed' user interface, we need to have some understanding of the classes of user interface commonly available and of their appropriateness for given situations.

Different classes of interactive dialogue will be used in different situations.

3.2 Classes of user interface

Interaction between the end-user and the system is achieved through interactive dialogues. There are a number of different classes of interactive dialogue and each of these has advantages and disadvantages depending on the situation in which they are used. The five major classes are discussed below:

1. *Command language*
    Command language dialogues are those in which the user types instructions to the computer in a formally-defined command language. For example, 'mv file1 file2', is a UNIX command for copying file1 into file2. The advantages of this approach is that it is very flexible, allowing users to create their own commands; it supports user initiative and it appeals to 'power' users, typically to software and system developers. Command language usually requires a significant level of training and a high degree of memorization.

    Command language supports user initiative and frequent users.

2. *Natural language*
    Natural language interfaces are those in which the user's command language is a significant, well-defined subset of some natural language such as English. For example 'Which women work in New York City' is a typical user input to the Intellect system from AI Corp., Cambridge, MA. Natural language interfaces are typically easy to learn, although they often require considerable typing skills on the part of the user. They can also be slow to use if the system is unclear as to the exact meaning of the user request and has to seek clarification. However, natural language systems are increasing in sophistication and a great deal of research and development work is currently being undertaken.

    A natural language statement can be syntactically correct but semantically meaningless. For example, 'square triangles taste nice'.

3. *Menu systems*
    Menu systems allow the user to issue commands by selecting choices

Menus allow the user to select from a predefined set of options.

from a menu of displayed alternatives. Menu systems are popular since they reduce learning time, reduce the number of keystrokes necessary and structure decision making. Most of the currently available fourth generation environments provide screen design tools which support the development of menu-based interfaces.

4. *Form filling dialogues*

The use of forms provides the user with a simple means of entering data.

Form filling dialogues are those in which the user enters data by filling in fields in one or more forms displayed on the screen. The use of forms on the screen considerably simplifies data entry and requires very little training to use. Forms management tools, similar to those available for menus, can be found within fourth generation environments.

5. *Direct manipulation interfaces*

Direct manipulation interfaces are those in which the user manipulates, through button pushes and movements of a pointing device such as a mouse, a graphic or iconic representation of the underlying data. An icon is a graphical symbol or pictogram used instead of words. Most direct manipulation interfaces use window systems or environments, in which the user's screen is divided into a number of possibly overlapping rectangular areas, each of which handles a specific function.

For the user, direct manipulation interfaces are WYSIWYG, 'What You See Is What You Get'.

Direct manipulation interfaces represent task concepts visually, are easy to learn and use, encourage exploration or experimentation with the system features and generally result in a high level of user satisfaction. Such interfaces are traditionally difficult to design and to program. However, most of the user interface design standards currently being put forward are based on direct manipulation interfaces.

Choosing the most appropriate class of user interface to match the needs and expectations of the users is an important aspect of good user interface design. For any given class of user interface a number of design decisions must be made by the interface designer, particularly in terms of what information should appear on the screen, how much information, in what order, what type of error messages, where should error messages be displayed on the screen and so on. To assist in making the 'right' design decisions and achieving a good user interface, a number of design guidelines are available. Some are introduced in the next section.

3.3 Principles of good design

Much guidance is currently available in the literature in the form of lists of interface design guidelines or principles. The major guidelines common to many of the texts can be summarized into five categories: naturalness, consistency, non-redundancy, supportiveness and flexibility.

1. *Naturalness*

A natural dialogue is one which does not cause the user to alter significantly his or her approach to the task in order to interact with the system. In this case the ordering of the dialogue is important. The ordering of user input, for example, should be geared towards the normal order of working of the user rather than whatever is easier for the programmer. This requires careful study of the tasks the user undertakes before, during and after each interactive session.

'Natural' to the user may not be 'natural' to the designer.

The use of language which is natural to the user is also important. Jargon may be desirable, provided that it is the jargon used every day in the user's department and not that used in the computer department. A designer might consider a task to be 'updating a file' but if the users call it 'posting P45s', then that is how the dialogue should refer to it. Phrasing should be self-explanatory; for example, words such as, 'print', 'end' and 'copy' have obvious meanings, whereas 'pip' (the CP/M keyword for copy) and 'mv' (the UNIX keyword for rename) do not. Use of non-standard abbreviations should be avoided since they slow down word recognition and introduce unnecessary stress.

Use the jargon of the user, not the jargon of the designer.

2. *Consistency*

A consistent dialogue ensures that expectations which the user builds up through using one part of the system are not frustrated by idiosyncratic changes in the conventions used in another part. For example in one system 'list' usually meant display on the screen, but occasionally meant output to a printer. Consistent layout for screens which fulfil a similar function ensures that the user knows where to look for instructions and error messages. The dialogue should also be consistent with established norms; for example, from PCs to cash dispensers, people have become accustomed to confirming a command by pressing Return or Enter. Diversion from norms will cause confusion.

The user builds up expectations of the dialogue.

The designer must be consistent.

3. *Non-redundancy*

A non-redundant dialogue requires the user to input only the minimum information for the system's operation. For example, a user should never have to supply leading zeros, for example, '00010' instead of '10'. A user should not be asked to give information which can be automatically derived by the system or which has been entered previously. Default values can be used to minimize the amount of input. Similarly, redundant information should not be output. Too much information on one screen is detrimental to the clarity of the screen and will delay the user unnecessarily when he or she tries to 'spot' a particular field or item.

User input should be minimal; no leading zeros.

4. *Supportiveness*

The supportiveness of a dialogue refers to the amount of assistance the dialogue provides to the user in running the system. It has three major aspects: the quantity and quality of instructions provided; the nature of the error messages produced and the confirmation of what the system is doing. Instructions to the user are provided both by the system's prompts and by any additional help facilities. Error messages should be helpful and not obscure, for example, 'syntax error' is not at all helpful. At the very least the system should tell the user what is the cause of the syntax error, for example, 'missing apostrophe on line 30'. Inputs should be confirmed: if their acceptance will result in an irreversible action, for example, delete file; if a code has been entered and the user has to check the associated description or when confirmation of completion of particular actions is desirable.

Displaying 'fatal error in program' is not being supportive of the user.

5. *Flexibility*
The flexibility of a dialogue refers to how well it can cater for or tolerate different levels of user familiarity and performance. This depends largely on the skill and expertise of the user in relation to a given task. Different types of dialogue may be used in different situations; for example, a hierarchical menu structure for use by a first-time user may be navigated using commands and parameters once the user becomes more experienced.

Different levels of user familiarity should be catered for.

3.4 Evaluate designs using the principles

These five principles of good design can also be used to evaluate existing user interfaces.

For example, Fig. 3.1 shows a form which is completed by a travel agent when a customer wishes to book a ferry.

Fig 3.2 shows a screen design which could be used when automating the ferry booking procedure.

This screen design is obviously unsatisfactory, but why? The five principles can be used as a basis for identifying the problems.

Five principles of good design: naturalness, consistency, non-redundancy, supportiveness and flexibility.

3.4.1 Results of evaluation of screen design
The screen design is examined against each of the five principles in turn in order to identify why the screen design in Fig. 3.2 is unsatisfactory.

Principle one: non-redundancy
Redundancy has been caused by changing from a manual system to an on-line system.

•   The screen contains superfluous information. For example, first choice and second choice do not need to be displayed at the same time. The user will be able to make a choice of outward voyage and inward voyage and if that choice is not available, the user will simply make another choice. The concept of first and second choice is only appropriate for the manual system where the form will be sent away to make the booking.

OUTWARD VOYAGE	INWARD VOYAGE	RESERVED ACCOMMODATION			
First choice From	From	Type of cabin preferred		OUTWARD Night/Day	INWARD Night/Day
To	To				
Date			Male	Female	Male	Female
Sailing time		If whole cabin is not required, No. of berths/couchettes*				
Second Choice From	From				
To	To	*delete as applicable			
Date		No. of reclining seats			
Sailing time		No. of Club Class seats			

NAME AND ADDRESS (Block capitals please)	VEHICLE DETAILS
Name	Reg. No.
Address (or Agent's stamp)	Overall length (inc. roof-top luggage) m Height under 1.83m*/over 1.83m* (inc. roof-top luggage) *delete as applicable
	CARAVAN*/TRAILER* DETAILS *delete as applicable
	Overall length (inc. tow-bar) m Height under 1.83m*/over 1.83m* *delete as applicable
Post Code	Motorcycle Reg. No. Solo/combination* *delete as applicable
Telephone No.	PASSENGERS No. of children (over 4 and under 14) No. of adults (inc. driver)

CHALET/CARAVAN/CAMPING SITE please tick appropriate box ❏ Tent rental ❏ Chalet ❏ Caravan/camping site	INSURANCE Holiday insurance ❏ Vehicle cover extension ❏ Caravan/trailer cover extension ❏
	Car make Car model
	Date of return if not stated above Age of vehicle if personalized number plate
	Please tick box if cover required for winter sports activities ❏

Figure 3.1 *Fast Ferries reservation form.*

Principle two: naturalness:

- Information is not in logical groupings. Although the information on the screen has been copied from the form, the groupings implied by the lines on the form are no longer obvious when transferred to the screen.
- The use of uppercase throughout makes for poor readability.
- The use of arbitrary abbreviations; for example, RECLIN is used to mean 'number of reclining seats'. The meaning of this abbreviation may not be obvious to the user.

Natural logical groupings have been lost when the designer has tried to get the whole form onto the screen.

The design in Fig. 3.2 is simply a copy of the form in Fig. 3.1. Why is this not a 'good' design?'

```
FAST FERRIES


                 OUTWARD VOYAGE  INWARD VOYAGE  RESERVED ACCOMMODATION
1ST CHOICE FROM STN TO SAM   FROM DIP TO WEY   CABIN  OUT DAY  IN  NIGHT
        1105  891031              2230 891222         BTHS/CHTS            1M 2F

2ND CHOICE FROM STN TO SAM  FROM SAM TO STN  RECLIN          0         0
CONFIRMED 1105 891031            2330 891222     CLUB CLASS SEATS 0        0
NAME AND ADDRESS                VEHICLE DETAILS
NAME MRS. E. CURRY              REGNO E999GGY
ADDRESS 14 CHESTER AVE          OVERALL LENGTH 3.4M HEIGHT  Y
        CHELTENHAM              CARAVAN/TRAILER CARAVAN
        GLOS.                     OVERALL LENGTH  3.3M HEIGHT  N
POSTCODE CH1 1AX                MOTORCYCLE REGNO:
TELEPHONE NO: 025437571         PASSENGERS: NO. ADULTS 3 NO. CHILDREN 0

CHALET/CARAVAN/CAMPING SITE  INSURANCE
TENT RENTAL N                   HOLIDAY  VEHICLE COVER  C/T EXTENSION
CHALET N                               Y            Y              Y
CARAVAN/CAMPING SITE  Y         CAR MAKE  FORD MODEL SIERRA COSWORTH
                                DATE OF RETURN             AGE
                                WINTER SPORTS


CONFIRM?
```

Figure 3.2 *Screen design copying form layout in Fig. 3.1*

- The screen is too full, and it is difficult to distinguish one area of the form from another.

Principle three: consistency:

Captions are used in an inconsistent way.

- Inconsistent use of captions — some are alongside the data fields, some are above.
- Some data fields have no captions, for example, sailing times and dates.
- some captions are too verbose, for example,

CHALET/CARAVAN/CAMPING SITE

Principle four: supportiveness

- Some captions do not convey the meaning of the data field; for example, HEIGHT YES is meaningless.
- It is difficult to distinguish group items from individual items.

No navigational information is given.

- It is impossible to distinguish between the captions and the data
- fields they are supposed to identify.
- No navigational information is given; for example, next screen, escape, main menu.

Principle five: flexibility

The user has no flexibility regarding the ordering or 'chunking' of data entry.

- All the information requested has to be input before confirmation.

Thus by using the five principles of good design as a basis for examining an existing user interface it is possible to identify the reasons why a particular design is poor and to see what needs to be improved.

3.4.2 How to produce a better design

The evaluation of the screen design given in Fig. 3.2 illustrates the fact that it is not sufficient just to transfer the manual way of doing things onto the user interface. Later in this chapter, two alternative approaches to designing the user interface are introduced.

The first takes a task-oriented approach, focussing on the sequence in which the user carries out the task. In the case of the ferry booking form, in Fig. 3.1, we are interested in the sequence in which the travel agent will interact with the customer and with the system. For example, the travel agent will ask the customer for a destination and preferred date of travel, and will then enter this information into the system. The system then displays a choice of crossing available and presents these to the customer. The customer makes a choice and the travel agent then asks for details about passengers and so on. The task-oriented approach is concerned with user tasks and likely sequencing of interactions.

To produce a better design, a systematic approach should be adopted, using either a task-oriented or an object-oriented approach.

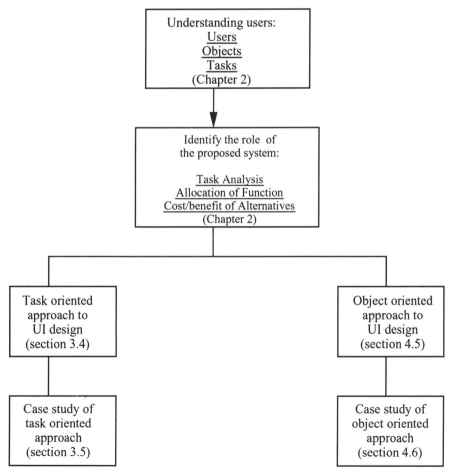

Figure 3.3   *Diagram showing the relationship between Chapters Two, Three and Four*

The second takes an object-oriented approach, focussing on the objects being dealt with by the user. In the case of Fast Ferries, the travel agent deals with enquiries, reservations, bookings, customers, tickets, receipts, payments and so on. The object-oriented approach is concerned only with objects and how they are manipulated and no sequencing is implied.

Whichever approach is adopted, it is vital to begin with a thorough understanding of the users and an agreement as to the role of the proposed system. Figure 3.3 illustrates the relationship between the techniques discussed in Chapter Two and those which follow.

No matter which design approach is followed, it is likely that the designer will consider the use of colour. The next section deals with factors which affect the choice and use of colour at the user interface.

3.5 Factors influencing the choice of colour

3.5.1 Understanding colour
The correct use of colour in screen design often causes difficulty for software designers since they often lack the training and visual perception of the graphic designer or artist.

There are no hard and fast rules associated with the use of colour.

In this section, some issues are considered in relation to the everyday use of colour. There are no hard and fast rules and perhaps the software designer can only expect to develop some empathy with the subject. Following a general discussion on colour a number of colour screen designs are evaluated. The section concludes with a number of guidelines which may assist the software designer.

3.5.2 Discussion on colour
The discussion is centred around the contents of the colour plates 1—8. These have been reproduced from a set of colour slides by Lindsay W. MacDonald, March 1993 called *Colour in Computer Graphics* under the auspices of the UK Advisory Group on Computer Graphics.

Plate 1: colours look darker and smaller against white
The appearance of a colour depends on the lightness and colour of the surrounding region, an effect known as simultaneous contrast. The result is that colours tend to look darker and smaller against white, and lighter and larger against black.

Colour depends on the lightness and colour of the surrounding region.

Plate 2: the appearance of colour changes according to the surrounding colours
Coloured surrounds can cause a coloured region to appear to be tinged with the complementary hue of the surround. Here the grey lines of the cross look yellowish against the blue background and bluish against the yellow background, even though it is exactly the same grey throughout.

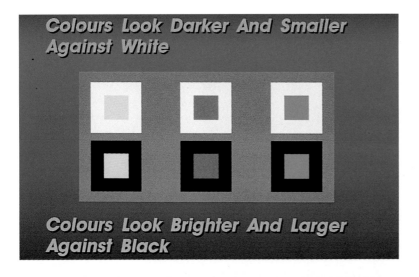

Plate 1

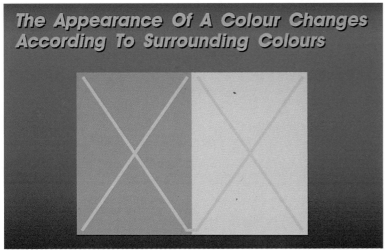

Plate 2

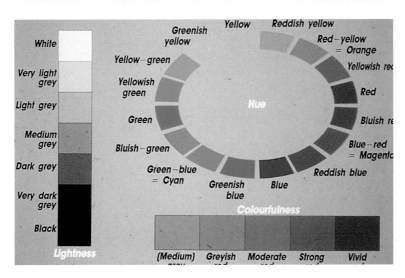

Plate 3

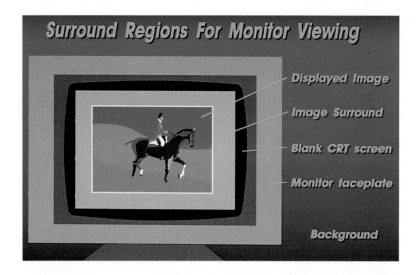

Plate 4

With THE POST he once again tried to transfer local newspaper technogy to national newspaper publication, and again he discovered it did not work. This time the process using personal computers and standard, well-proven software, was let down simply by the length of time it was taking him to produce the paper. Copy deadlines were too early, so Mr Shah's newspaper could not compete on news. One mistake which Mr Shah repeated from his first venture was not to provide what the reader wanted. That is an exclusive comodity, of course.

Mr Shah's first attempt at national newspaper publishing proved to be the catalyst Fleet Street needed to pull itself out of the dark ages. The result of the shock that was TODAY can be witnessed in Fleet Street's empty buildings and in the tabloid's colour So far the Daily Mirror is the only paper which has got the colour quite right all the way through. It has done it because it has paid for the technology necessary to do it. The Daily Mail has taken a diferent route and decided to move into flexography. There is a small capital saving with flexography,

Plate 5

Plate 6

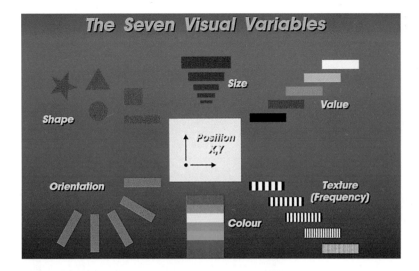

Plate 7

Plate 8

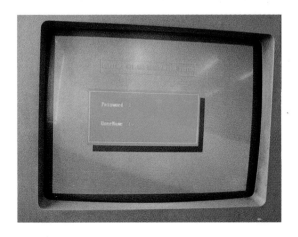

Plate 9

Plate 10

Plate 11

Plate 12

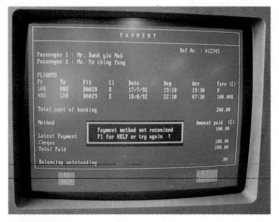

Plate 13

Plate 14

Plate 3: a simple colour naming system
Different systems will support different colour naming systems. For example, some may provide the user with the means of specifying a colour for a graphic object on the screen display in terms of hue, saturation and brightness.

Colour depends on the palette provided by the implementation platform.

Plate 4: surround regions for monitor viewing
The appearance of a colour always depends on the conditions under which it is viewed. One of the most important factors is the surrounding field. A typical computer screen consists of several concentric zones. The most important is the image background, over which the application has full control, but which is often neglected. A light surround will make the image look darker, through the simultaneous contrast effect, (Plate 1), and vice versa.

The lightness and colour of the blank CRT screen, monitor faceplate and office surround, being successively further away, affect the image appearance to a lesser degree but cannot be ignored. Ideally they should be unobtrusive, neutral in colour and graded in lightness from the image background.

Colour depends on the condition under which it is viewed.

Plate 5: text manipulation applications
There are four categories of colour-related task, which make different demands on the user: text manipulation, chart and graph design, monitoring and modelling. Legibility is the most important criterion for text processing systems, and monochrome monitors are frequently preferred because of their inherently greater sharpness. On a colour monitor, however, satisfactory legibility can be achieved through attention to presentation and font design. Here colour is used to good effect for both association, highlighting in yellow the results of the word-search for all occurrences of 'Mr. Shah', and for differentiation by highlighting in red all spelling errors.

Legibility of text is often better on monochrome monitors.

Plate 6: modelling applications
In modelling applications the display is intended to represent the appearance of an object or scene. The purpose of the image should be clearly understood. Is it to portray a real product as realistically as possible, or to impress the observer into believing something about the product represented by the image? The art of the graphic designer is to achieve a memorable result with an economy of means. Here the potency of the car has been conveyed through the vibrancy of the red, whilst the illusion of depth is enhanced by using reddish colours for the foreground and bluish colours for the background.

The appearance of an object can change through appropriate use of colour.

Plate 7: the seven visual variables
Colour should generally be used not just for aesthetic purposes, but as a means of increasing the information content of a display or of improving the

display by making it easier to interpret. The principles of good graphic design are just as important to computer displays as they are to the more traditional media. In particular, colour should be used in conjunction with other visual attributes of position, shape, size, brightness, orientation and texture. A good principle is to ensure that the layout is meaningful in monochrome ('get it right in black and white') and to then add colour sparingly.

Colour can be used to increase information content.

Plate 8: icons and colour conventions

Colour has the ability to evoke emotional responses or to trigger memories. Warm hues (red, orange, yellow) generally imply action or warning, whereas cool hues (green, blue, grey) can imply passivity or safety.

These associations of colour are used to advantage in many of the familiar objects in the everyday world, such as the highly systematic colour codes and icons in road signs. Traffic lights, for example, can be employed as metaphors in graphic displays, conveying to the user a message consistent with real-world experience. A particularly effective symbol is the red STOP sign, which grabs visual attention and conveys an unambiguous command.

'Get it right in black and white' and then add colour sparingly.

3.5.3 Discussion on colour screens

The screens showed in Plates 9—14 were produced as part of a student project for a system which deals with flight enquiries, reservations and bookings and illustrate a typical approach to the use of colour. Although some planning of the 'colour scheme' has occurred, there are too many colours and in some cases poor combinations of colours. Following is a brief discussion of the good and bad points associated with the screen designs and the use of colour.

The principles of good design (naturalness, consistency, non-redundancy, supportiveness and flexibility) introduced in section 3.3 are used as a basis for the discussion, together with issues related to the use of colour raised earlier in this section.

Use everyday colour conventions and icons.

Colour designs should also follow the five principles of good design.

Plate 9: the login screen

The first screen is the Login screen, in which the name of the application AIRLINE RESERVATION SYSTEM is barely visible because there is insufficient contrast between the turquoise lettering and the grey background. (Plate 2). Also the black 'shadow' effect on the window in the middle of the screen gives the window the appearance of 'floating'. This is because of the effect of the surround regions, that is, the black CRT screen and the grey monitor (Plate 4). The screen in Plate 14 is much better in this respect because the whole screen is a single colour and simple lines are used as borders for windows.

The window appears of 'float' in Plate 9.

Plate 10: main menu

Here the user selection from the main menu is highlighted by changing the colour of the selected item. The black lettering on the turquoise background is difficult to read. This screen when viewed with Plates 11—14 illustrates the inconsistent use of colour and position for the navigation commands. In Plate 10 the 'help' 'button' appears in the middle of the screen, in Plates 11—13 it is on the mid left and in Plate 14 it is on the bottom left. 'Help' should appear in a consistent and predictable position on every screen.

Black on turquoise is difficult to read in Plate 10.

In addition, the line at the bottom of Plate 10 tells the user to use 'arrows' to select a menu item and to press Return to confirm the choice. On all other screens the user is asked to use function keys and these appear as small 'windows'.

Plate 11: error window
Here the choice of colours is much improved: white on a blue background is normally very readable. Also the red on black small screen in the middle is used to warn the user of a problem or error situation. The use of red for warnings is consistent with issues raised in Plate 8.

White lettering on a blue background is easy to read in Plate 11.

Plate 12: navigation commands
The grey lettering on a bright green background is difficult to read. The navigation 'buttons' have moved from those in Plate 11. The navigation commands are also combined with other user options which are logically different. F2 PAYMENT, F4 NEXT PASSENGER, F5 PREVIOUS PAS-SENGERS, F6 SEAT RESERVATION deal with making a reservation, while F1, F3 and ESC deal with navigation. Also there are too many choices in the list of this type ('small windows'); they are not grouped logically and the use of capital letters makes reading slow.

Grey lettering on bright green is almost impossible to read on Plate 12.

Plate 13: unavailable selections
Here the warning for 'invalid input' is shown in yellow, whereas in Plate 11, warnings were shown in red. This is inconsistent. Some of the 'small windows' at the bottom of screen are shown in as 'faded' notifying that these selections are not available from this screen. This contravenes the principle of non-redundancy — why display information of the screen which is of no use?

Inconsistent use of colours between Plate 11 and Plate 13.

Plate 14: highlighted captions
The single blue background with white lettering for captions and yellow lettering for data items is now consistent and easy to read. However, there are still some problems with this screen; for example, why is one caption red? Why is the data items' 'total' in white when all others are in yellow? The warning window should be red as in Plate 11, rather than yellow.

Arbitrary use of colour in Plate 14.

3.5.4 Some guidelines on the use of colour
The above discussion illustrates the danger of using colour without due consideration as to how or when to use it. In this section some points of

guidance on the use of colour are offered. First there are some major points on how to approach the inclusion of colour into a design, then some specific guidance is given concerning the amount of colour, background colours, user needs and choice of colour.

The major points are:

Develop a plan of when, where and why colour should be used.

1. 'Get it right in black and white' and then add colour sparingly.

2. Develop a plan of when, where and why colour should be used. The plan should cover the 'suite' of screens or windows that are to be designed. Be consistent.

3. Test colour designs using the palettes available on the target computer systems — colour designs on paper may not transfer well to the system. Colours which work well together on one platform may not work as well on another.

Amount of colour

Not more than three or four colours per screen.

- Use the minimum number of colours and not more than three or four per screen.
- Do not overuse colour. The benefits of colour as an attention getter, information grouper and value assigner are lost if too many colours are used.

Background colours

- Use background colours in large blocks.
- Group related elements by using a common background colour.

Use darker and weaker colours as background.

- Use bright colours for emphasis and weaker colours for background areas.
- Not all colours are equally readable. Extreme care should be exercised with text colour relative to background colours. As a general rule, the darker colours such as blue, magenta and brown make good backgrounds

User needs

Be consistent with user expectations.

- Use colour coding consistent with user expectations.
- Similar colours should denote similar meaning.
- To avoid frequent refocussing and visual fatigue, extreme colour pairs such as red and blue or yellow and purple should be avoided.
- Older users may need higher brightness levels to distinguish colours.
- Colour blind users may not be able to distinguish some colour combinations, for example, red and green should be avoided.
  (between 7 and 10% of the population are colour blind).

Avoid extreme colour pairs such as red and blue, or yellow and purple.

Choice of colours

- Brightness and saturation draw attention.
- Link the degree of colour change to event magnitude.
- Colours change appearance as ambient light level changes.

- Opponent colours go well together. Yellow and blue are good combinations.
- The user could be allowed to choose their own preferred colour combinations, which may be helpful in cases of visual handicap.

These are suggestions only; there are too many variables in colour display, colour copying and human interpretation to make hard and fast rules. Plan the use of colours, experiment on the target system and test the designs with users.

Consider the lightness of the colour of the surrounding region.

Jackson *et al.*, 1994, provides a detailed, practical guide on the use of colour.

3.6 A task-oriented approach to user interface design

In Chapter Two, techniques for understanding user requirements were introduced. These involved considering the users from three perspectives: the users themselves, what they do, and their skills, attitudes and motivations; the tasks undertaken and the characteristics of the tasks; and the objects manipulated by the users. The CAD case study provided an example of how to do this in practice. The task hierarchies associated with the proposed system were identified next and the allocation of function decided.

The next stages in the HCI design process are to:

1. Identify which tasks will be shared between user and system.

2. Specify the flow of interaction between the user and the system in carrying out those tasks.

3. Plan the design in order to design a consistent set of screens and windows to support that interaction.

A task-oriented approach involves understanding users and tasks, and the sequencing of user actions.

Figure 3.4 shows the main stages that a designer might follow when taking a task-oriented approach to user interface design.

Stages 1 and 2 were explained in Chapter Two. The remainder of this section is concerned with the stages 3 to 7, while section 3.7 presents a case study of the first six stages. This case study is based on the ferry booking form for Fast Ferries, the example discussed earlier in this chapter.

3.6.1 Stage 3: identify shared tasks

This stage is illustrated with reference to the CAD case study presented in Chapter Two. Given the task hierarchy for 'interpret brief' (Chapter Two, Fig. 2.6) and the discussion which followed on allocation of function (Chapter Two, Table 2.3), it is likely that alternative 4 or 5 may be chosen. Both alternatives would allow the professional engineer to continue as 'expert' and the system should simply provide support for the design. Alternative 5 would also assist in assessing the costs and benefits of alternative designs.

If alternative 5 is chosen then it becomes possible to identify those tasks which will have a user system interface.

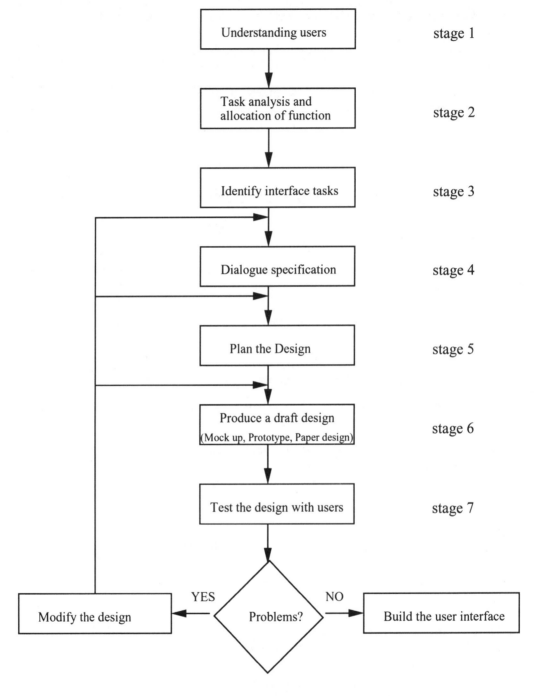

Figure 3.4   *The main stages in task oriented user interface design.*

These tasks can be marked on the task hierarchy (Fig. 3.5). The shared tasks for alternative 5, 'partial development and partial checking' are indicated thus: **. Note that the subtask 'write report on recommendations' has been excluded by the choice of alternative 5, and is not now considered to be part of the CAD system. However, the designer may need to be aware of the fact that the engineer will still need to carry out this task and therefore that the CAD system may need to be capable of providing input to some document preparation system.

Those tasks which are shared between user and system will have a user system interface.

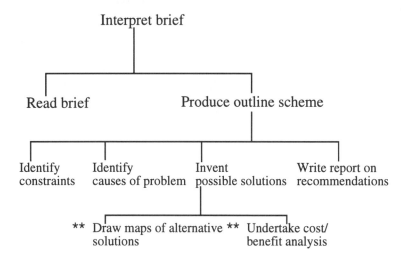

Figure 3.5 *Task hierarchy for interpret brief showing interface** tasks.*

3.6.2 Stage 4: specify user system dialogues

Having identified the share task, the next stage is to analyse them in more detail in order to specify the dialogue between user and system. Several techniques are available to achieve this, as follows.

Two techniques for specifying the dialogue between user and system are introduced.

The first technique, dialogue network diagrams, is based on the use of state transition networks and enables the designer to specify the sequence of a dialogue between the user and the system. This technique is useful for systems where the user dialogue is primarily driven by a reasonably predictable sequence of actions. It can help the designer to consider the user interaction with the system from the user's point of view.

The second technique, logical dialogue controls (LDC) and logical dialogue outlines (LDO), is useful for specifying dialogues such as those for data entry systems, where the primary task of the user is to populate the database. This technique links user inputs directly to data items.

Both of these techniques are described below:

Dialogue network diagrams

Dialogue network diagrams are a specialization of state transition diagrams in which the progress of a dialogue between user and computer can be viewed as a series of transitions from one state to another.

The dialogue may be in a particular state awaiting input from the user, and it will progress to one of several possible states depending on the nature of the input received. This can be represented as a transition network (Fig. 3.6). Each state is represented by a node, denoted here by a circle. A node is defined as any point at which the dialogue outputs a message to the user or requests an input from the user. Transitions between nodes are indicated by directed arcs connecting two nodes; a label on the arc indicates the condition under which it is traversed. Note that there may be several arcs connecting two nodes, indicating that more than one condition can cause the transition to occur.

Dialogue network diagrams help the designer to consider user interaction with the system from a user point of view.

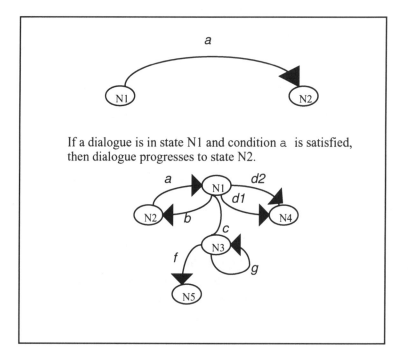

Figure 3.6 *Nodes and arcs in a dialogue network.*

Network diagrams can be nested hierarchically to deal with complex sequences. A square is used to represent a call to a sub-dialogue sequence. Sub-dialogue sequences are labelled on the top-level diagram.

For example consider the case of the library mentioned earlier (section 2.5). Here we identified 'keep a record of books in stock' as an invariant task. The task hierarchy for this is given in Fig 3.7, and after a discussion of possible allocation of function it was decided that those tasks marked with ** will be shared between user and computer and hence will appear at the user interface. The other tasks in the hierarchy will be carried out by the user without the assistance of the computer.

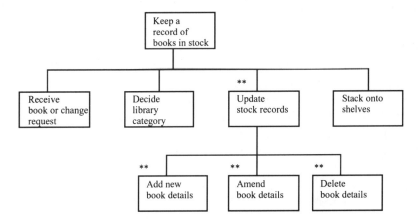

Figure 3.7 *Task hierarchy showing interface** tasks.*

A more detailed analysis of how the user carries out these tasks may now be needed for the designer to establish the details of the sequence of the dialogue between user and system.

For the task of 'update stock records' a possible dialogue network diagram is shown in Fig. 3.8, where each of the squares is itself a dialogue network diagram for a sub-dialogue.

The designer needs to envision the actions the user will take.

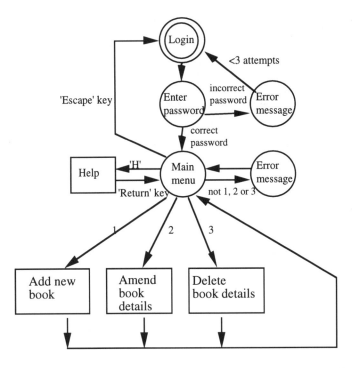

Figure 3.8 *Example of a dialogue network diagram for update stock records.*

Logical dialogue
outlines also repre-
sent dialogue se-
quences, but are
closer to the pro-
grammer's view of
the world, showing
data items and
updating files (Downs
et al., 1992).

Logical dialogue outlines

Specifying the interaction between user and system is referred to as dialogue design within SSADM (Structured Systems Analysis and Design Method) Dialogue design takes place in the system design phase of SSADM, i.e. as part of Stage 5: process design. Dialogue design is used in SSADM to model the on-line screen handling and human-computer interaction of the required system. A flowchart, called a logical dialogue outline or LDO, is used to represent the progression of screens for a particular event.

The SSADM dialogue design procedure is as follows;

1. Identify on-line events.

2. Identify I/O data items.

3. Create an LDO, one per event.

4. Review LDOs against data flow diagrams.

5. Create logical dialogue controls (LDCs).

6. Validate the diagrams with appropriate users.

The objectives of the dialogue design step are to represent dialogue sequences, to communicate screen handling and interface concepts to the users and to provide a basis for the physical program design. Each LDO uses symbols similar to those used in flowcharts: a rectangle represents a single screen, a triangle represents a user decision point (one which requires a value judgment by the user) and start/stop and flow symbols are directly analogous to their flowchart equivalents.

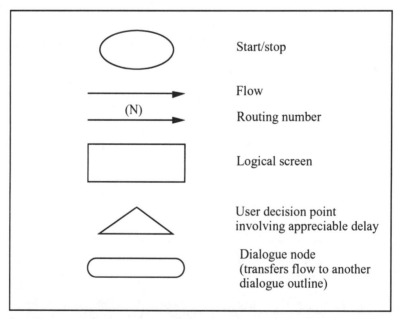

Figure 3.9   *SSADM dialogue design symbols*

Figure 3.10 shows a dialogue (LDO) which allows a user to update a book entry in a library system.

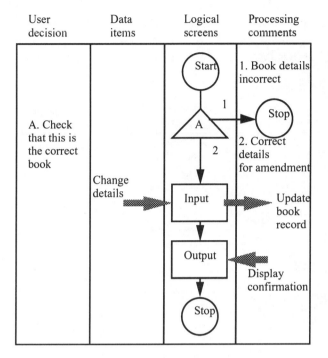

Figure 3.10 *Example of a logical dialogue outline (LDO) for a library cataloguing system.*

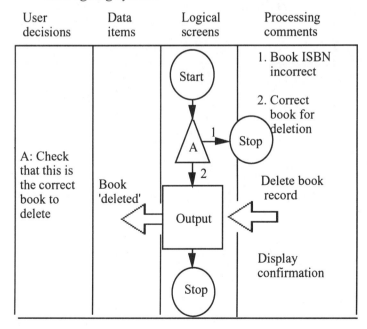

Figure 3.11 *LDO for delete book details.*

Figure 3.11 shows a dialogue (LDO) which allows the user to delete book details.

LDOs are then linked together into charts to represent a higher level grouping of screens which are called logical design controls (LDCs). Related LDCs are usually linked together to form the lowest level of menu hierarchy.

Figure 3.12 shows the LDC which links the LDOs given in Figs 3.10 and 3.11.

Specifying user system dialogues enables the designer to identify the sequence of screens or windows that need to be designed.

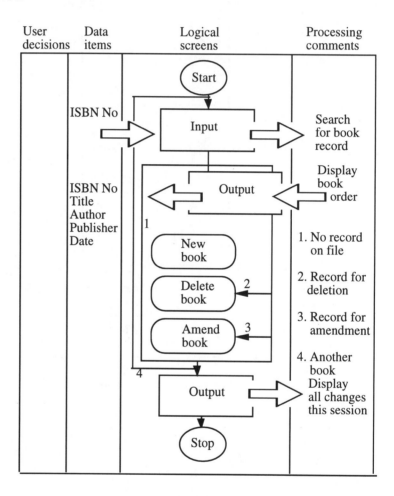

Figure 3.12 *Example of SSADM logical dialogue control (LDC) for a library cataloguing system.*

Having specified the logical screens, sequencing of interactions and logical groupings of information, the next step is to design a consistent set of screens and windows associated with a particular application.

3.6.3 Stage 5: Plan the design of the user interface

Planning the design can be divided into four main steps:

1. Deciding what information should be displayed in each window.

2. Deciding how the information should be displayed.

3. Deciding where each field will appear.

4. Deciding what highlighting is required.

The designer should plan the design of the sequence of screens and windows specified in stage 4.

Stage 5, step one: what information should be displayed?
Don't display information just because it is available. **Only the information which is relevant** to the user at that point in the dialogue should be displayed.

On the other hand **all the information relevant** to the user at that point should be displayed. This may involve some repetition from screen to screen, for example, the customer's name and address. Users should not be expected to remember information from one screen to another.

Information should be displayed in logical groupings i.e. a set of information which must be viewed as a composite entry in order to achieve a task. Logical groupings should not be split across screen or window boundaries. One window may contain one or more logical grouping(s).

Careful planning will ensure consistency within the design.

Some guidelines for menu design
- menu lists should be in logical order and in logical groupings;
- hierarchical menus should be in logical groupings;
- each menu should permit only one selection by the user;
- each new option should be on a new line;
- selection should be by pointing device where possible;
- wording of menu options should be commands not questions;
- selection should be by initial letter, not by arbitrary code.

Decide what information is needed by the user at each point in the dialogue.

Actions for the designer in step one   Study the tasks which the user will perform during an interactive session with the system and identify logical grouping of information. These may be groupings which are related together in time, for example, a series of questions concerning an enquiry or those related by topic, such as all the information relating to a customer. For each logical group produce a list of the required data items. Give each logical group a name, such as customer details, enquiry details. The window in Fig. 3.13 shows an example of a logical group of information.

Information should be displayed in logical groupings.

Stage 5, step two: how should the information be displayed?
Information should be presented in an immediately usable form. The user should not be required to manipulate the information, for example, look up codes, decipher dates and so on.

Decide how to display information so that it is immediately useful to the user.

```
┌────────────────────────────────────────────────────────┐
│                  Passenger Information                  │
├────────────────────────────────────────────────────────┤
│                                                        │
│   Surname...............................................│
│   Forenames.............................................│
│   Title.................................................│
│   Address...............................................│
│                                                        │
│   .....................................................│
│                                                        │
└────────────────────────────────────────────────────────┘
```

Figure 3.13 *A logical grouping of information.*

'Logical groupings' refers to information which is related together in time, or linked by topic.

Some guidelines on information presentation
- use upper and lower case (as in road signs);
- use normal conventions; for example, accountants easily recognize negative values which are displayed in red or in brackets;
- caption names should be as brief as possible but with meaningful abbreviations;
- captions should be positioned in a natural and consistent physical relationship to the corresponding data fields.

Follow well-established guidelines for information presentation.

Some guidelines on data entry
- explicit entry: users should be asked to check data before entry;
- explicit movement between fields: users should use Tab or Return or some other key to move explicitly from field to field;
- explicit delete: users should always be required to confirm any request for deletion;
- provide undo: wherever possible allow users to backtrack to a 'previous state', i.e. to undo their last action.

Actions for the designer in step two
- for each data item choose an appropriate caption;
- for each data item decide on the size and format, such as car registration — eight alphanumeric or null, return date — dd/mm/yy, caravan length — 99.9 or null;
- decide on the position of the data item relative to the caption.

The window in Fig. 3.14 shows the captions appearing consistently on the top of the columns.

Stage 5, step three: where should the information be displayed?

Some guidelines on positioning of text
- leave approximately half of the total screen (window) blank;
- every screen (and window) should be self contained;

Leave half the screen blank.

Voyage: Dover to Calais							
Mon	Tues	Wed	Thurs	Fri	Sat	Sun	
06.30	06.30	06.30	06.30	06.30	07.00	07.00	
07.00	07.00	07.00	07.00	07.00	09.00	09.00	
08.00	08.00	08.00	08.00	08.00	11.00	11.00	
10.00	10.00	10.00	10.00	10.00	13.00	13.00	
11.30	11.30	11.30	11.30	11.30	15.00	15.00	
12.30	12.30	12.30	12.30	12.30	17.00	17.00	
13.30	13.30	13.30	13.30	13.30	19.00	19.00	

Planning the design will ensure consistency in the presentation of information.

Figure 3.14 *Captions appear in a consistent position.*

- there should be an obvious starting point — usually top left — then proceed left to right and top to bottom;
- the same information should be displayed in a consistent and predictable relative position on the screen throughout the application, e.g. error messages should appear in a consistent position throughout the whole interactive session.

Some guidelines for presentation of text
- upper and lower case together can be read 13% more quickly than upper case only;
- UPPER CASE CAN BE USED TO ATTRACT ATTENTION;
- right-justified text with variable spacing is more difficult to read than evenly spaced text with a ragged margin;
- optimal spacing between lines is equal to or slightly greater than the height of the characters themselves.

Design of windows   The advantages of multiple windows include:
- allowing users access to multiple sources of information;
- allowing information to be viewed from different perspectives, for example in program debugging;
- the user may examine the same information at different levels of detail, for example, overviews in one window with related windows containing further detail;
- allowing the system to attract the user's attention, for example, by displaying a new window in the middle of the screen;
- allowing the user to control multiple concurrent tasks in an environment where multitasking is provided.

The disadvantages of multiple windows include:

- the danger of 'overcrowding' on the screen;
- distraction from the task in hand by causing the user to manipulate the interface in order to obtain the information required;
- the 'desk-top' metaphor becoming the 'untidy desk top' metaphor.

Information should
be displayed in a
predictable and
consistent position.

Some guidelines for the design of windows:

- the contents of a window should form a logically-related group;
- the borders of each window should be clearly delimited;
- avoid filling the screen with a multiplicity of small windows;
- windows should appear initially in a consistent position and have a consistent size;
- the default position and size should be adjusted to reflect user preference;
- the contents of each window and of each screen should reflect a logical ordering and consistent format and use minimum highlighting;
- the spatial positioning of windows on the screen should reflect a logical ordering.
- use of colours across the whole screen should be minimal and consistent;
- allow 'popping-up' of windows to attract user attention.

Actions for the designer in step three   Use a template for screen layouts or hand draw draft designs. Plan the design of a sequence of screens (Fig. 3.15)

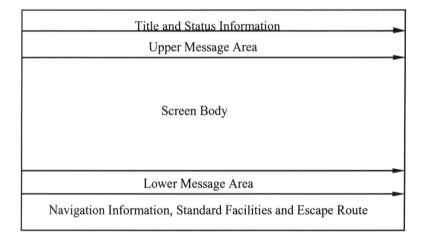

Figure 3.15   *Example of a screen template.*

Stage 5, step four: when to use highlighting?
- Use only to make particular areas of the screen stand out from the rest;
- use blinking highlights only in extreme circumstances (rapid blinking could trigger an epileptic fit);
- use guidelines for use of colour but always experiment on actual system with target users;
- use beeps etc. to attract attention but take care in certain environments;
- use reverse video to highlight error situations.

Actions for the designer in step four   Only use highlighting and colour when some positive advantage can be identified. Try out any colour design on the actual screen. See section 3.5 for further discussion on the use of colour.

3.6.4 Stage 6: Produce a draft design
Use screen layout sheets, screen design aids, paper mock-ups or prototyping tools to produce a first draft.

3.6.5 Stage 7: Test the designs with users
Evaluate the layout in terms of the five design principles, then evaluate the effectiveness of the design through experimentation with target users.

The case study which follows illustrates the seven stages of task-oriented user interface design.

3.7 A case study in task-oriented user interface design

This is a case study of a task-oriented approach to user interface design. The full analysis is not shown but representative; selected parts of the analysis and design are given to illustrate the process and concepts associated with the approach.

The case study used is that of the Fast Ferries reservation system referred to earlier in this chapter. Below is an overview of the sections which follow:

Stage 1: Understanding users
1.1 Business case
1.2 Workgroup table
1.3 Workgroup: sales staff: job issues
1.4 Generic user: travel agent: person issues
1.5 Task: enquiry: organization issues
1.6 Task: booking: organization issues
1.7 User, object, task: travel agent, voyage details, enquiry
1.8 User, object, task: travel agent, booking details, booking.

Stage 2: Task analysis and allocation of function
2.1 Task analysis
2.2 Allocation of function.

Stage 3: Identification of shared tasks

Stage 4: User system dialogues
4.1 Dialogue network diagrams.

Stage 5: Plan the design
5.1 Full-screen window template
5.2 Error popup window template.

Stage 6: Design of screens and windows
   6.1 Main menu
   6.2 Some enquiry windows
   6.3 Some booking windows.

3.7.1 Stage 1: understanding users
The following subsections are an extract from the CRC stage 1 forms.

   (1.1) Business case
   (1.2) Workgroup table
   (1.3) Workgroup: sales staff: job issues
   (1.4) Generic user: travel agent: person issues
   (1.5) Task: enquiry: organization issues
   (1.6) Task: booking: organization issues
   (1.7) User, object, task: travel agent, voyage details, enquiry
   (1.8) User, object, task: travel agent, booking details, booking.

(1.1) Business case
The proposed system is intended to support the sales staff in travel agents, the aim being to provide a fast and more efficient enquiry and booking service. Ideally the system should come into general use over a period of one year, starting in one year's time. The buyers of the proposed system are the travel agent management, whose objectives are to improve the quality of customer service by reducing the number of errors in bookings and improving the speed of dealing with customers.

   The users of the proposed system are mainly the sales staff in Fast Ferries accredited travel agents. Their customers are the general public, who make enquiries and bookings for ferry services. Some customers visit the travel agency, others telephone them. Fast Ferries itself has a sales department.

   Enquiries by potential travellers concern routes, sailing and journey times, facilities and services. Bookings are for a specific outward and, optionally, a specific inward journey. Fast Ferries needs to know the total number of people travelling and the characteristics of any vehicle.

   Fast Ferries also sells additional services: holiday and travel insurance, reserved accommodation, and a booking service for holiday sites.

   The purpose of the proposed system is to provide an on-line system for enquiries and bookings at each sales position. It is intended that the system should support detailed enquiries and validate bookings as they are entered. The system should require minimum staff training time.

(1.2) Workgroup table
The workgroup table in Fig. 3.16 shows the three main workgroups within the travel agents. The management group and the financial group are likely to use the proposed system less frequently than the sales staff. These two

groups may still be important from the point of view of the user interface design and hence some further CRC type analysis may be required. However, in this case study, only the sales staff are described in more detail.

Work Group Title	Sales staff group	Management group	Financial group
Relationship	1	2	2
Generic users ☐	TRAVEL AGENT ☐1	SENIOR ☐1 TRAVEL AGENT	MANAGER ☐2
	ASSISTANT ☐1	MANAGER ☐2	ACCOUNTANT ☐2
	SENIOR ☐1 TRAVEL AGENT	SECRETARY ☐3	☐
	☐	☐	☐
	☐	☐	☐
	☐	☐	☐

☐   Indicates relationship of user to the proposed system

Figure 3.16 *Fast Ferries workgroup table.*

(1.3) Workgroup: sales staff: job issues
The sales staff are a primary workgroup, whose job issues are described in Fig. 3.17. The 'now' column indicates what the sales staff do in a typical week, with the percentages indicating the proportion of time spent on each task. The proposed column indicates what the proposed or desired situation will be once the system has been introduced. In this case there is quite a lot of potential for change and improvements which would help to meet the management objectives.

This form also helps the designer to identify key tasks which the system needs to support. For example, it is proposed that the time spent on enquiries is reduced from 25% to 15%, the time spent on bookings is reduced from 15% to 10% and that filing and paperwork is reduced from 10% to 4%. The design of the user interface will affect the workgroup's ability to achieve these reductions in time taken.

The other workgroup issues related to the social and organization aspects of the sales staff would also be considered, but they are not included here.

Proposed system   FAST FERRIES

Work-group   SALES STAFF

Job issues   (A typical week)

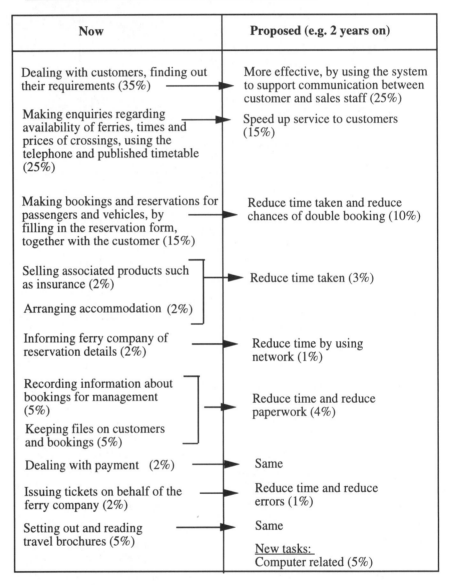

Now	Proposed (e.g. 2 years on)
Dealing with customers, finding out their requirements (35%)	More effective, by using the system to support communication between customer and sales staff (25%)
Making enquiries regarding availability of ferries, times and prices of crossings, using the telephone and published timetable (25%)	Speed up service to customers (15%)
Making bookings and reservations for passengers and vehicles, by filling in the reservation form, together with the customer (15%)	Reduce time taken and reduce chances of double booking (10%)
Selling associated products such as insurance (2%) Arranging accommodation (2%)	Reduce time taken (3%)
Informing ferry company of reservation details (2%)	Reduce time by using network (1%)
Recording information about bookings for management (5%) Keeping files on customers and bookings (5%)	Reduce time and reduce paperwork (4%)
Dealing with payment (2%)	Same
Issuing tickets on behalf of the ferry company (2%)	Reduce time and reduce errors (1%)
Setting out and reading travel brochures (5%)	Same New tasks: Computer related (5%)

Note:
% indicates the proportion of the working week spent on that particular task by the workgroup.

Figure 3.17 *Fast Ferries sales staff job issues.*

Next the primary users within the sales staff group are described. The next section shows the travel agent person issues, now and proposed.

(1.4) Generic user: travel agent: person issues

The travel agent enjoys dealing with customers and wants to be helpful towards them. The proposed system should support this communication rather than obstruct it. The job is very visible to customers and the travel agent wants to be seen to be acting for a prestigious ferry line. The travel agent has knowledge of routes and booking routines and enjoys acquiring and using this knowledge.

Thus the designer needs to take account of the travel agent's view of the job and to design the system so that the positive aspects of the job are unchanged.

Now	**Proposed**
Attitude	
Sociable	Unchanged
Likes helping people	
Motivation	
To be more helpful	More up-to-date information
Commission on voyage and service sales	Less hassle
Aspiration/ambition	
To act for a prestige ferry line	Unchanged
More commission on sales	
Expertise	
Knows ferry routes and timetable in outline	Unchanged
Knows booking routine	
Skill	
Many are touch typists, but are out of practice	Typing skills preferred, but high speed not essential
Job	
Very visible to customers	Unchanged
Seated, at a desk or counter	Unchanged
Office-like environment, with public access	
Similar to building society branches	
Much paper clutter	Less clutter

Other primary users may be described. For example, the assistant may be responsible for much of the filing and paperwork and as such would be affected by the proposed change. Also it is important for the designer to understanding how filing and other paperwork is done now.

Next, some of the tasks of the travel agent are described.

(1.5) Task: enquiry: organization issues

Now	**Proposed**
Importance	
High	Same
Many sales depend on it	
Helps avoid under — or over — booking	Same but more accurate
Security	
No security issues	Same
associated with the timetable	
Availability of sailings is inaccessible and security risk is low	High: commercially and financially sesnsitive if collated over all sailings and whole year
Motivation	
High	Same
Used to help customers	
Skill level	
Medium	Low: less reliance on memory
Dependencies	
Accuracy of timetable and availability	Same, but more up-to-date information

(1.6) Task: booking: organization issues

Now	**Proposed**
Importance	
High	Same
Is selling the core product	
Is selling additional profit-making services	

Now	Proposed
Security	
High	Same
Information must not be lost	
Includes personal data	May imply additional legal requirements
Other agent's bookings	Commercially and financially sensitive
Motivation	
High	Same
Skill level	
Booking: medium	Low: less reliance on memory
Data entry: low	Medium: Touch typists have advantage
Dependencies	
Accuracy of timetable	Same, but more up to date
Availability information	Is now accessible immediately

(1.7) User, object, task: travel agent, voyage details, enquiry

Interaction characteristics   There is a need for:
- route and timetable information;
- vehicle and accommodation availability information;
- up-to-date information;
- enquiry to be fast enough for telephone enquiries;
- enquiry/lookup to be available during booking;
- enquiry details to be transferred to booking details without re-typing.

(1.8) User, object, task: travel agent, booking details, booking

Interaction characteristics   There is a need for:
- details to be checked for inclusion of vital data;
- details to be checked for consistency;
- details to be checked against up-to-date timetable and availability information;

- booking to be fast enough for telephone bookings;
- enquiry/lookup to be available during booking;
- enquiry details to be transferred to booking details without re-typing;
- reminder of additional services available.

3.7.2 Stage 2: Task analysis and allocation of function

Task analysis

A key invariant task which can be identified is that of 'serve customer'. Subtasks of 'serve customer' are 'answer customer enquiry' and 'make customer booking'. The task hierarchy is shown below in Fig. 3.18.

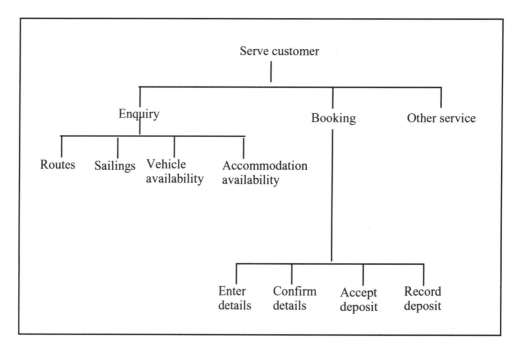

Figure 3.18 *Task hierarchy for 'serve customer'*

Allocation of function

This section discusses the allocation of function between the computer system and travel agent staff.

Sharing between user and computer

1. *Fully automated: rejected.* Automatic ticket machines. The customer would find it difficult to enter all the details correctly without assistance, and is unlikely to buy extra services such as insurance. The travel agent would feel the machine clashes with the office environment, as well as taking up too much space.

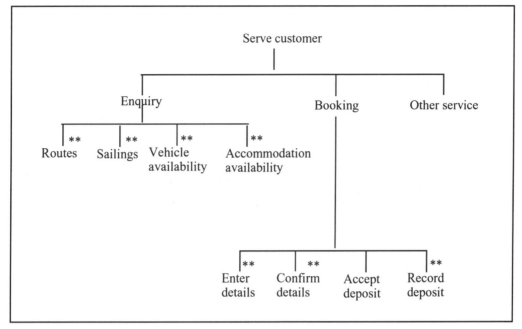

Note: ** denotes shared tasks.

Figure 3.19 *Task hierarchy for 'serve customer' showing tasks which are to be shared between user and computer.*

2. *System supplies general task support: rejected.* (Just word processing and printing.) The user would feel that the system is not an improvement over the existing pen and paper methods. Possibly it would be viewed as worse.

3. *System and user share the tasks: accepted.* The system provides task-related assistance and knowledge.

Who or what controls the task?

1. *The system totally controls the user: rejected.* This implies that the customer is also constrained in every way. This is liable to upset the customers who might not choose to be customers of Fast Ferries.

2. *The user totally controls the system: rejected.* Fast Ferries requires certain rules to be obeyed, such as knowing what type of vehicles are to be carried.

3. *The system enforces rules, leaving the user free in other respects: accepted.* The travel agent staff can work at the customer's pace, and in the customer's way if untypical.

Type of support provided by the system

1. *Active: rejected.* It is not clear what active support could be provided.

2. *Passive: accepted.* The system essentially records what the user and customer wants. The system does this in a helpful way, of course.

3.7.3 Stage 3: Identification of shared tasks

The task hierarchy in Fig. 3.19, has ** against the tasks which will be shared between user and system with respect to 'serve customer'.

3.7.4 Stage 4: user system dialogues

Dialogue network diagrams are drawn for the shared tasks in order to specify user system dialogue. The designer should draw the diagrams bearing in mind the interaction between the travel agent, the customer and the system. The designer should ask such questions as: in what order will the conversation take place? What information is needed at a given point? How can the system help the travel agent deal with any errors that may arise? What are the likely and unlikely actions of the travel agent at a given point? How will the system respond?

Below are the dialogue network diagrams for some of the shared tasks.

Conventions used

The diagrams use double circles for both entry and exit points. Where there is any doubt, entry and exit points are labelled with the name of the previous or next diagram or state. Return indicates that the next state is the one occupied just prior to entering the diagram.

Figure 3.20 shows the main menu for 'serve customer', where the user selects E for dealing with the enquiry and B for making a booking. This can be described as a level 1 diagram because it is the first level of shared task in the task hierarchy.

Figure 3.21 shows the network diagram for 'enquiry'. This can be thought of as a level 2 diagram because it shows the second level of shared task. The enquiry menu asks the user to select which they wish to see: ferry routes, sailing times, vehicle availability or accomodation availability. The choice will depend on the outcome of the travel agent's discussion with the customer; the order of selection cannot be predicted.

Figure 3.22 shows a level 3 diagram for the routes window, which would be selected by choosing R in the level 2 diagram in Fig. 3.21.

The routes window needs to display all the routes and a scrolling window is specified.

Figure 3.23 shows a level 3 diagram for the sailings window, which would be selected by choosing S from the enquiry menu in Fig. 3.21.

Figure 3.24 shows a level 2 diagram for making a booking, This would be selected by choosing B from the level 1 diagram in Fig. 3.20. Note that the logical groupings of information associated with making a booking each forms a subdialogue; for example, 'enter voyage details' or 'enter customer details' are subdialogues. Note also that the user does not need to enter all the data at once but may select whichever logical grouping is of concern and

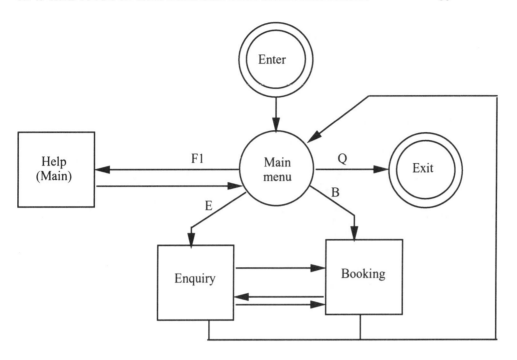

Figure 3.20 *Level 1 diagram, main menu for 'serve customer'.*

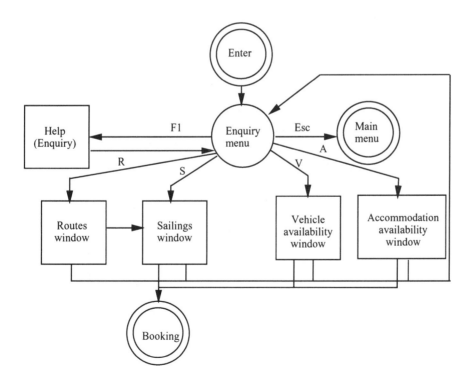

Figure 3.21 *Level 2 diagram, menu for dealing with an enquiry.*

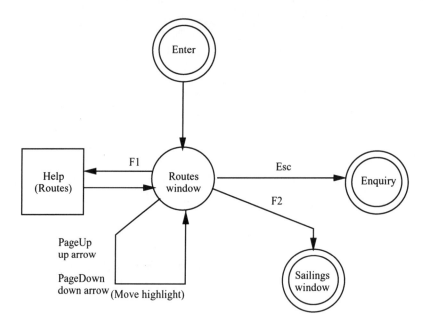

Figure 3.22 *Level 3 diagram, dialogue for routes of ferries.*

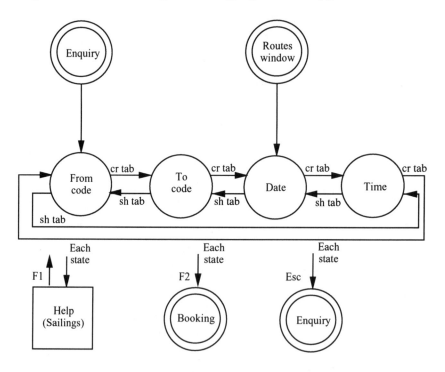

Figure 3.23 *Level 3 diagram, dialogue for times of sailings.*

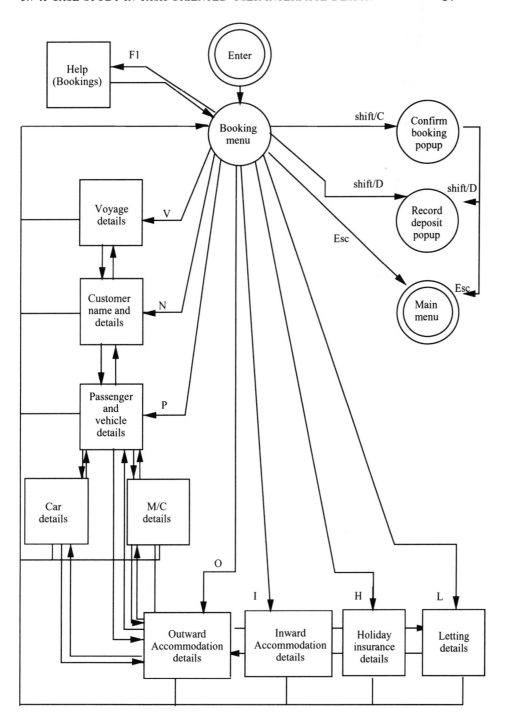

Figure 3.24 *Level 2 diagram, making a booking.*

may enter the subdialogues in any order. However, the option is also provided for the user to move sequentially from one logical grouping to the next, if preferred.

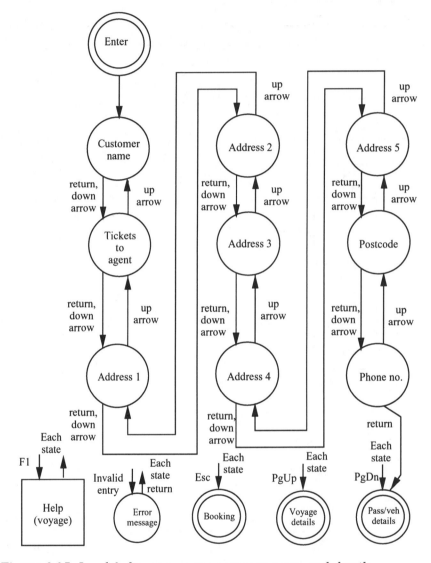

Figure 3.25 *Level 3 diagram, enter customer name and details.*

Figure 3.25 shows a level 3 diagram for entering customer details. This would be selected by choosing N from the level 2, 'make a booking' diagram, (Fig. 3.24). At this level of detail, the network diagram is showing one item of information at a time, normally the lowest level of detail represented in a dialogue network diagram.

The above dialogue network diagrams represent only part of the full design.

3.7.5 Stage 5: plan the design

Full-screen template
Figure 3.26 shows the template for the screen design for an IBM PC DOS character screen.

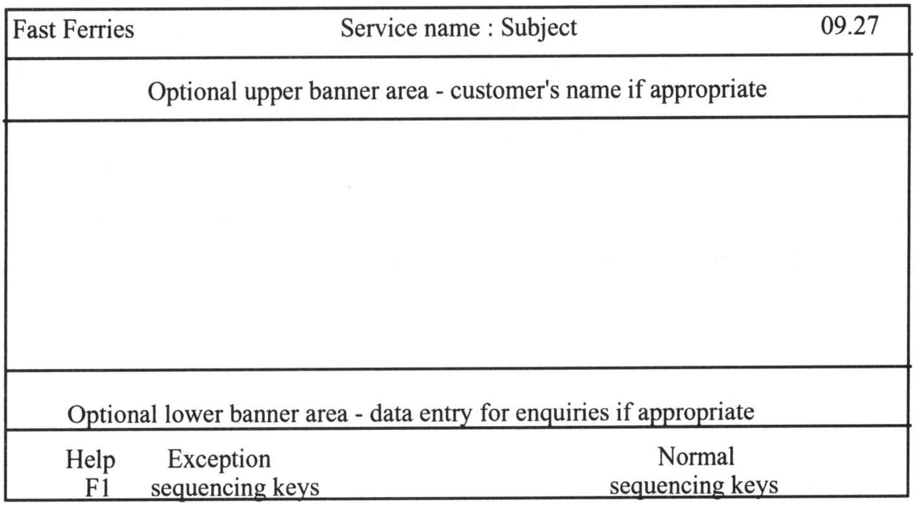

Fast Ferries	Service name : Subject	09.27
	Optional upper banner area - customer's name if appropriate	
	Optional lower banner area - data entry for enquiries if appropriate	
Help F1	Exception sequencing keys	Normal sequencing keys

Figure 3.26 *General screen template for Fast Ferries screens.*

Template for a pop-up window
Figure 3.27 shows the general design for a pop-up window.

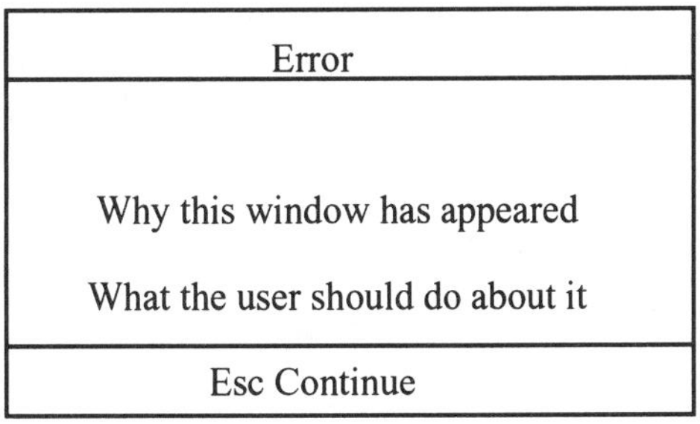

Error
Why this window has appeared
What the user should do about it
Esc Continue

Figure 3.27 *General template for pop-up error messages.*

3.7.6 Stage 6: design of screens and windows

Main menu
Figure 3.28 shows the screen design for the network diagram seen in Fig. 3.20. It shows the main menu for 'serve customer'

```
┌─────────────────────────────────────────────────────────────────────┐
│ Fast Ferries                   Main menu                      09.27   │
├─────────────────────────────────────────────────────────────────────┤
│                                                                       │
│                 Fast Ferries enquiry and booking service             │
│                                                                       │
│          E : Enquiry service - routes,  timetables, availability      │
│                                                                       │
│          B : Booking service                                          │
│                                                                       │
│          Q : Quit - stop using the enquiry and booking system         │
│                                                                       │
│                                                                       │
├─────────────────────────────────────────────────────────────────────┤
│          Press the indicated key for the service or action you want   │
├─────────────────────────────────────────────────────────────────────┤
│ Help                                                                  │
│  F1                                                                   │
└─────────────────────────────────────────────────────────────────────┘
```

Figure 3.28 *Main menu for 'serve customer'.*

Some enquiry screens
Figure 3.29 shows the screen design for the network diagram shown in Fig. 3.21, that is, the enquiry menu.

```
┌─────────────────────────────────────────────────────────────────────┐
│ Fast Ferries                   Enquiry menu                   09.27   │
├─────────────────────────────────────────────────────────────────────┤
│                     Fast Ferries enquiry service                     │
│                                                                       │
│          R : Routes - countries, ports, port codes                    │
│                                                                       │
│          S : Sailings                                                 │
│                                                                       │
│          V : Vehicle space available                                  │
│                                                                       │
│          A : Accommodation available - cabins, berths/couchettes      │
│                                                                       │
├─────────────────────────────────────────────────────────────────────┤
│          Press the indicated key for the information you want         │
├─────────────────────────────────────────────────────────────────────┤
│ Help   Main menu                                                      │
│  F1      Esc                                                          │
└─────────────────────────────────────────────────────────────────────┘
```

Figure 3.29 *Menu for making an enquiry.*

Figure 3.30 shows the screen design associated with the network diagram in Fig. 3.22, indicating ferry routes. The highlighted line selects the 'from' and 'to' ports if F2 is pressed. The PageUp key moves the highlighted line up the table of routes, and PageDown moves it down the table.

Fast Ferries			Enquiry : routes			09.27
.... From......................			.... To.............................			Hours
Country	Port	Code	Country	Port	Code	
England	Folkestone	FOL	Belgium	Ostend	OST	10
	Dover	DVR	France	Calais	CAL	2
	Dover	DVR		Dunkirk	DUK	2.5
France	Calais	CAL	England	Dover	DVR	2
	Dunkirk	DUK		Dover	DVR	2.5
Belgium	Ostend	OST	England	Folkestone	FOL	10
Help	Enquiry menu					Sailings
F1	Esc					F2

Note:
Highlighted line selects the From and To ports if F2 is pressed.

Figure 3.30 *Routes of ferries.*

Figure 3.31 shows the screen design associated with the network diagram in Fig. 3.23, indicating the times of sailings. Note that the currently selected sailing is highlighted in the table.

Fast Ferries			Enquiry : sailings				09.27
21.02.94				Dover to Dunkirk			27.02.94
	Mon	Tues	Wed	Thur	Fri	Sat	Sun
	01.00	01.00	01.00	01.00	01.00	01.00	01.00
	05.00	05.00	05.00	05.00	05.00	05.00 *	05.00
	09.00	09.00	09.00	09.00	09.00	09.00 *	09.00
						11.30 *	
	13.00	13.00	13.00	13.00	13.00	13.00	13.00
						14.30	
	17.00	17.00	17.00	17.00	**16.30** *	17.00	17.00
					19.30 *		
	21.00	21.00	21.00	21.00	21.00 *	21.00	21.00
					21.30		
From	To	Date	Time		* : Fully Booked		
DVR	**DUK**	**25.2.94**	**16.30**		* : Check Availability		
Help	Enquiry menu						Booking
F1	Esc						F2

Figure 3.31 *Times of sailings.*

Some bookings screens

Figure 3.32 shows the screen design associated with the level 3 network diagram in Fig. 3.25, showing 'enter customer details'.

```
┌─────────────────────────────────────────────────────────────────────┐
│ Fast Ferries              Booking : Customer details           09.27 │
├─────────────────────────────────────────────────────────────────────┤
│                                                                       │
│   Customer's name          : (Miss S G Barrington-Bayley             │
│                                                          )            │
│   Tickets to agent (Y/N)    : (N)                                     │
│                                                                       │
│   Customer's address        : (Rose Cottage                          │
│       (if needed)             (Delphi Lane                 )          │
│       (for tickets)           (Alsager on the Wold         )          │
│                               (Cheshire                    )          │
│                               (via Stoke-on-Trent)         )          │
│             Post code       : (ST7 1XY   )                 )          │
│             Phone           : (04889 012 3457_)                      │
├─────────────────────────────────────────────────────────────────────┤
│ Help    Booking menu                            Next/Prev             │
│  F1        Esc                            PageDown/PageUp             │
└─────────────────────────────────────────────────────────────────────┘
```

Figure 3.32 *Enter customer name and details.*

Figure 3.33 shows a confirm booking pop-up window. This would appear as a result of making a selection of C from the booking menu in Fig. 3.24.

```
┌──────────────────────────────────┐
│         Confirm Booking          │
├──────────────────────────────────┤
│                                  │
│      Confirm all booking details │
│        and print deposit receipt │
│                                  │
│                                  │
├──────────────────────────────────┤
│  F1 Confirm          Esc Cancel  │
└──────────────────────────────────┘
```

Figure 3.33 *Confirm booking pop-up.*

3.7.7 Stage 7: test the designs with users

These designs should then be tested with some target users: for example, the designer could talk through a typical scenario of use with the user. A sequence of enquiry, reservation and booking screens could be shown. These could be paper- or computer-based designs. The designer should also check the designs against the five principles of good HCI design.

3.8 Summary

This chapter has covered both theory and practice of user interface design. The five principles: naturalness, consistency, supportiveness, flexibility and non-redundancy were introduced and these can be used both as a basis for designing user interfaces and as criteria for evaluating existing interfaces. Some guidelines have been given on the form and content of screen designs and on the use of colour.

A task-oriented user interface design method was introduced and illustrated through the use of a case study. This method is useful for those applications where the user interaction with the system occurs in a reasonably predictable sequence. The chapter which follows describes an object-oriented user interface design approach which is useful for those applications where the sequence of user interactions is not easily predicted. However, the guidelines and principles introduced in this chapter still apply.

Exercises for Chapter 3

3.1 The screen shown below appears upon selection of the 'Enquiry about performance' from the main menu of the Theatre Booking System. Give five examples of how the screen design contravenes widely-recognized screen design guidelines.

Enquiry About Performance Screen

ENTER CUSTOMER NAME AND ADDRESS

WHICH PERFORMANCE?

WHICH NIGHT?

HOW MANY TICKETS?

ENTER TIME OF SHOW

METHOD OF PAYMENT

What Next? EXIT TO MAIN MENU? (press Q)   QUIT (press E)

3.2 Compare the following two techniques for dialogue specification:

    1.   Dialogue networks diagrams.

    2.   Logical dialogue outlines as used in SSADM.

3.3 What criteria would you use in order to evaluate the design of a user interface?

3.4 There are some inconsistencies in the screen designs in the Fast Ferries case study. Can you spot what they are?

Chapter 4

Designing graphical user interfaces

The objectives of this chapter are:

- ☐ to introduce the main elements of a graphical user interface;

- ☐ to examine the design of icons;

- ☐ to discuss the use of metaphors in GUI design;

- ☐ to introduce GUI styleguides and toolkits;

- ☐ to discuss issues of portability between GUI environments;

- ☐ to describe an object-oriented approach to UI design;

- ☐ to illustrate the above through use of examples;

- ☐ to present a case study of an object-oriented approach to UI design.

4.1 Introduction

Graphical user interfaces (GUIs) bring quantifiable benefits to users and organizations. Recent studies have shown that experienced users of graphical user interfaces make fewer mistakes, feel less frustrated, suffer less fatigue, and are more able to learn for themselves about the operation of new packages than users of non-graphical interfaces.

Temple *et al.*, 1990, shows that GUIs bring quantifiable benefits to users.

The development of applications with graphical user interfaces differs from the development of traditional approaches both in the technology that is used and in the design of the interface itself. It is more difficult to acquire the skills required to design a GUI that will provide users with a natural and intuitive interface. The main tasks are the creation of appropriate metaphors, the specification both of the functions provided by the interface and of its behaviour, and the design of the graphical displays.

The purpose of this section is to introduce some of the basic concepts of GUIs and to introduce some of the tools available to aid their effective design and implementation.

One of the main goals of a GUI is to create the illusion of objects that can be manipulated; for example, moved across the screen and discarded into a 'waste bin'. GUIs use an object-action paradigm where the user indicates an object first and then gives the command. Figure 4.1 shows features typical of most GUIs.

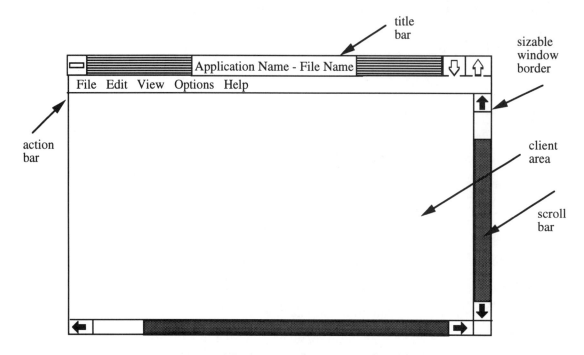

Figure 4.1 *A typical GUI screen.*

GUIs support an object-action paradigm where the user indicates an object and then decides on the action.

Most GUIs have a pointing device, usually a mouse; a bit-mapped display, with a WYSIWYG (What You See Is What You Get) screen where what you see on the screen is what you get on the printout; windows which can be resized; on-screen menus which appear or disappear under pointer control; icons, which represent files, folders and devices, and widgets such as dialog boxes, buttons and scroll bars.

From a user's point of view, a graphical user interface has three main elements which contribute to its 'look and feel' :

- The visual appearance
  This includes items such as the position and layout of menu and scroll bars, the design of icons used to represent applications and files and the shape and size of the mouse controller.
- Behaviour
  The behaviour of an interface is the way in which it responds to actions taken by the user; for example, a double click on a file icon will result in that file being activated.

- Metaphor
  The term 'metaphor' is used to describe the analogy used in the design and implementation of the GUI. The use of a metaphor can help users to foresee the consequences of their actions.

The first four sections of this chapter examine GUIs in greater detail, firstly by considering how icons should be designed and introducing some of the current standards associated with icon design. Icons are often linked with the use of metaphors and some popular metaphors are briefly discussed. Next follows an introduction to GUI styleguides and toolkits. Portability between the various styles is discussed, together with examples of how a portability toolkit is used in practice.

The 'look and feel' of a GUI includes the visual appearance, the behaviour of the interface and the metaphor for use.

The remaining two sections of this chapter are concerned with how a software designer might approach the design of a GUI. Since GUIs adopt an object-action paradigm, an object-oriented approach to user interface design is presented. Section 4.8 presents a case study of the object-oriented approach for the Fast Ferries problem.

4.2 Design of icons

An important component of the visual appearance of GUIs is the icon. There have been various attempts to classify icons; for example, the original Xerox Star classification separates icons into data icons and function icons. A data icon is defined as representing an object on which actions can be performed, for example, documents, folders and files and anything that can be done to one data icon can be done to all, for example, move, copy, delete. Function icons, in contrast, represent objects which perform actions, for example file drawers, in-trays, calculators. Most function icons will accept any data icon; for example, the in-tray receives a document and places it in a stack of documents.

Icons can represent objects upon which actions can be performed.

Other researchers distinguish between form and function. In Fig. 4.2, four forms of icon are identified:

1. *Resemblance icons*
   These depict the underlying referent through an analogous image. Figure 4.2(a) shows falling rocks.

2. *Exemplar icons*
   These depict a typical example of a general class of object. For example, Fig. 4.2(b) illustrates the availability of food.

3. *Symbolic icons*
   These convey the underlying referent at a higher level of abstraction than the image itself. Figure 4.2(c) means 'fragile'.

4. *Arbitrary icons*

These bear no resemblance to the referent. For example, Fig. 4.2(d), shows a biohazard sign.

Icons can represent
objects which
perform actions.

Icons can be sym-
bolic or exemplar.

The design of icons
is still poorly under-
stood.

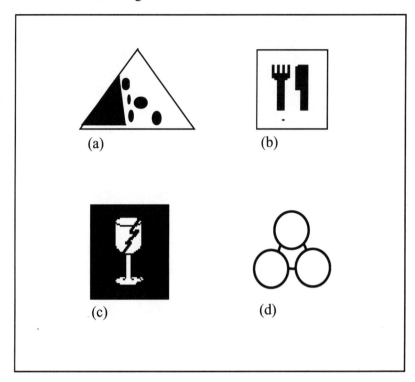

(a)   (b)

(c)   (d)

Figure 4.2   *Examples of different forms of icons, after Rogers 1989.*

In contrast, the function of an icon relates to the task demands.

The design of icons is still poorly understood, although most current methods advocate user participation in the design of the icon. Some recommend getting the user to 'doodle' in an effort to facilitate visualization of some aspect of the user environment. Tools which allow icons to be drawn rapidly and prototyped with the user are also available to assist the designer.

The Icon Book
(Horton, 1994)
provides many
examples of icons.

Icons are highly pictorial representations and can be used to represent actual objects such as documents, folders or waste bins. Specific operations can be represented through analogy; for example the in-tray represents the process of mail arriving for the user while the out-tray is used to send outgoing mail. Icons can also be abstract representations of system states, such as an hourglass icon to indicate that the system is processing data and that the user must wait.

ISO (the International Organization for Standardization) suggests as part of its ISO/IEC CD 11581-1.2 1993 Draft Standard that there are two main types of icon: interactive icons and non-interactive icons. Interactive icons represent the objects, pointers, controls and tools which mediate user interaction with the software application. Non-interactive icons are normally status indicators.

Figure 4.3 shows the ISO classification of icons and indicates that part of the standard where these icons are further described. Each part includes rules for the graphical representation of objects and actions as icons; a set of commonly-used graphical representations that follow these rules; definitions of functionality of the icons in the set, and rules and recommendations for interactive properties of interactive icons.

ISO standards exist for the design of interactive and non-interactive icons.

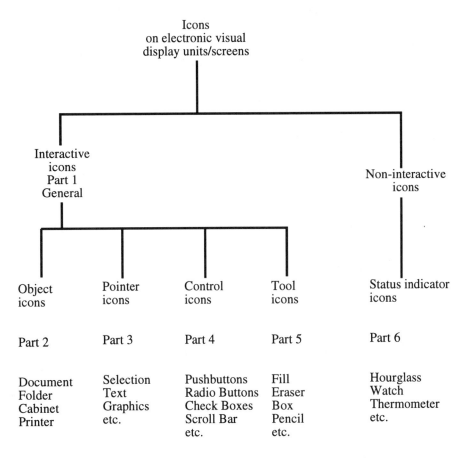

Figure 4.3 *Graphical symbols: classification used in this standard (ISO/ IEC CD 11581-1.2 1993 Draft Standard).*

For example, part 2 of the standard covers object icons and suggests a framework for specifying object icons based on Fig. 4.4 below. The object icon provides a visual link between a function and the metaphoric environment, and is itself a metaphor for an object in that environment. Figure 4.4 illustrates how the icon metaphor helps to mediate the conceptual link between the graphical symbol displayed on the screen and the function it represents.

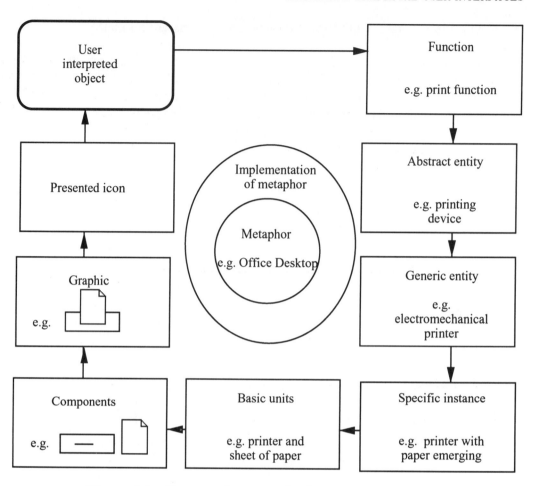

Figure 4.4 *Framework to specify object icons (ISO/IEC CD 11581-1.2 1993 Draft Standard).*

The object icons specified in the standard include: document; folder; filing cabinet; mail; mail in-tray; mail out-tray; printer; waste paper can; display; keyboard; mouse; workstation; network; fixed storage device; removable disk; diskette; telephone; facsimile machine; calculator; clock; audio device; indexed list; notebook and scheduler: all of these belong to the office metaphor. The software designer is advised to refer the most recent ISO standard before embarking on the design of an icon. A contact address is given in the bibliography at the end of this book.

A metaphor can help the user foresee the consequences of his or her actions.

4.3 Use of metaphors

Graphical user interfaces were initially targeted at office system users. In an attempt to provide an interface which was natural, consistent and supportive of such users, designers looked for analogies in the clerical performance of similar tasks. For example spreadsheets are based on the metaphor of the ledger book.

Three examples of analogies are:

1. The physical object metaphor.

2. The desktop metaphor.

3. The travel holiday metaphor.

The physical object metaphor

Here items are represented by the physical object and exhibit real-world behaviour. Thus files are sheaves of paper or folders, directories are drawers in a filing cabinet, while clerical operations involve physical actions on these objects. Thus to store a file, the human will pick up the sheaves of paper, walk across to the filing cabinet, open the drawer and place the file inside. To rename the file, the human will erase the old name and write in the new one.

The physical object metaphor seeks to eliminate the dichotomy between the syntax and semantics of the task and the syntax and semantics of the computer system by modelling the interface on the natural human performance of the task.

> Icons can represent physical objects and exhibit real-world behaviour.

The desktop metaphor

The desktop metaphor suggests that the interface should provide the user with a similar type of flexibility as the desktop: for example, there should be access to several information sources and a variety of formats such as pictures or graphs. The system should permit easy access and should facilitate swapping from one type of task to another; for example, from a spreadsheet for financial planning, to a wordprocessor. Tools such as calculators, clocks, notepads, and diaries should also be available.

An extension of the desktop metaphor was used in the early designs of the IBM Common User Access Workplace Environment (Berry, 1988) in which the system is portrayed as an extension of the real world. The Workplace Environment has three types of primary windows: the workplace window (Fig. 4.5), the list handler window (Fig. 4.6) and the object handler window (Fig. 4.7).

> The interface can represent a desktop.

In addition icons were organized into three classes with each class possessing its own properties: (i) container icons such as folders or baskets; (ii) data icons such as charts, spreadsheets or documents and (iii) device icons such as printers or a telephone.

The workplace window has a set of pull-down menus associated with it (File; Edit; View; Options; Help) representing the operations which can be carried out on the icons at this level. Various classes of icons are shown.

The list handler window was obtained by selecting from a container icon (Folder — Project X), whereupon a list of the contents of the 'container' are displayed. The list handler window allows a different set of operations to be performed on each icon (File; View; Help). The icons displayed within the list handler window are data icons.

The IBM CUA Workplace Environment uses an extension of the desktop metaphor (Berry, 1988).

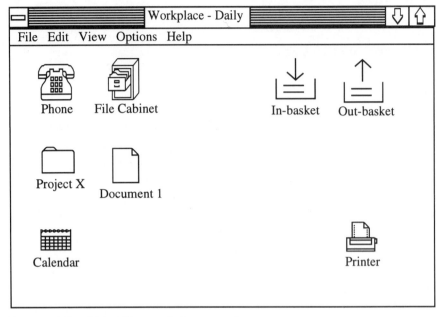

Figure 4.5   *The CUA workplace window.*

There are three classes of icons: container icons, data icons and device icons.

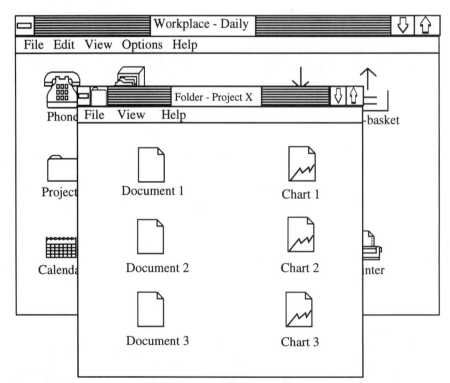

Figure 4.6   *The CUA list handler window.*

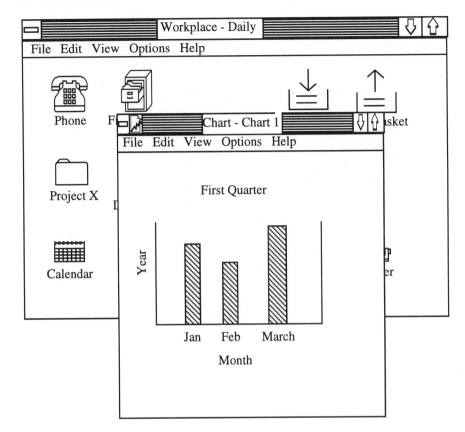

Figure 4.7   *The CUA object handler window.*

A different set of operations is performed on each class of icon.

The object window is displayed when a data icon is selected, for example, Chart 1. The operations (File; Edit; View; Options; Help) which can be performed on the contents of the window are specific to this data icon.

The desktop metaphor will not be appropriate for all application types. The software designer is attempting to provide an interface which is natural and consistent and which is also appropriate for the class of users and tasks under consideration. The designer may well need to identify different types of icons and different analogies depending on the situation.

The travel holiday metaphor

The travel metaphor has been used within learning environments and is based upon the user's understanding of tours, guides and navigation. An example of this was developed for a computer-aided learning (CAL) system for psychology students at York University, England, UK. The aim of the system was to provide the student with a large amount of information, together with various means of accessing it.

The general metaphor of the **travel holiday** was used, plus display frames representing **places to visit**, and various facilities representing the ways and means of travelling around. Within the general metaphor, a number of more

A travel holiday metaphor can be used to help navigate large amounts of information.

specific ones were subsumed. First, there were two explicit forms of navigation, reflecting the extremes of student controlled versus system controlled. These were **go-it-alone** travel and **guided tours.** Second, a **map** facility allowed the student to see where they were and where they had been. Third the **index** (notionally the index of a guide book) provided a mechanism for keyword-based access.

'Guided tours'
provide a guide
through the information as a preset
sequence.

Guided tours were the main tutorial mechanism supported by the system. A tour is initiated when the student uses the mouse to select a **coach** icon (labelled with the topic of the tour). They are then guided around a sequence of screens on a given topic until the tour ends. The student can leave the tour at any time and re-join it later. The system allows for considerable flexibility, with the possibility of branching or embedded tours (these are termed **excursions** within the metaphor).

The metaphor should be used with great care since too strict an adherence to a metaphor could lead to an unnecessarily restricting interface.

In 'go it alone' travel,
a 'map' is provided
for users to find their
own way round the
information.

This section briefly discussed how icons should be designed, and introduced some of the current standards associated with icon design. Icons are often linked with the use of metaphors and a number of popular metaphors were briefly discussed. The next section provides an introduction to GUI styleguides and toolkits.

4.4 GUI styleguides and toolkits

Graphical user interface software can be difficult to build since these interactive interfaces must handle at least two asynchronous input devices, typically mouse and keyboard. They must also provide real-time feedback to users, multiple windows, and dynamic, direct manipulation graphics. Most graphical interfaces are created using toolkits which usually contain a set of interaction techniques known as widgets or gadgets for menus, scroll bars, and buttons.

Most GUIs are
created using
toolkits.

A GUI styleguide determines the 'look and feel' of the user interface and determines how the user will interact with it.

The main GUI styles are IBM's Common User Access (CUA), Apple Macintosh, the Open Software Foundation's (OSF) Motif and AT&T's OPEN LOOK (these styles are discussed in more detail in the next section). Associated with each style is a toolkit, for example, Microsoft Windows and IBM's Presentation Manager are toolkits for developing CUA style interfaces.

A GUI styleguide
determines the 'look
and feel' of the user
interface.

The Garnet toolkit developed at Carnegie Mellon University (Myers *et al.* 1990) provides high-level design aids as well as a toolkit. Some of the gadgets in Garnet's toolkit are shown in Fig. 4.8.

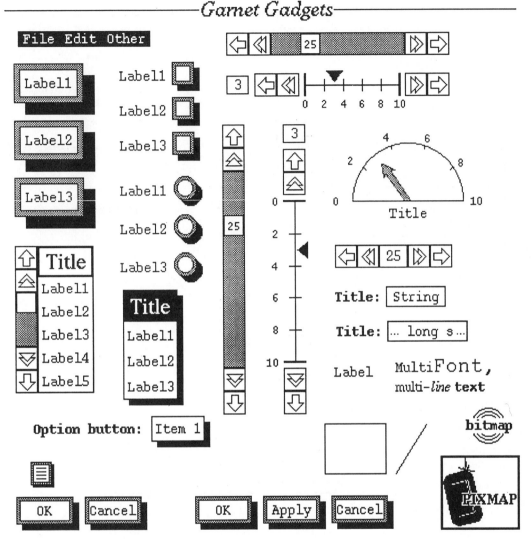

Figure 4.8 *Garnet Gadgets.*

Each GUI toolkit will have an associated window system; for example, OPEN LOOK and OSF Motif use the X Window System.

The X Window System was originally designed for use with the UNIX operating system. Figs 4.9 and 4.10 contrast the architecture of a UNIX-based system with and without a GUI.

The main concepts underlying the X Window System are outlined below.

The X Window System

The X Window System has become the the industry standard for window-based applications developed in the UNIX environment. It provides a high performance graphic system based on a set of hierarchical resizable win-

Toolkits contain widgets. A widget enables the designer to create menus, scroll bars and so on.

Each GUI toolkit has an associated window system.

dows. The X Window System does not provide a specific user interface style, but instead supports an extensive set of tools to build user interfaces.

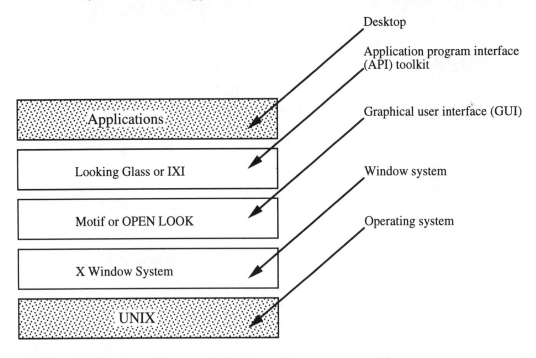

Figure 4.9 *UNIX with a GUI.*

The X Window System provides an extensive set of tools to build user interfaces.

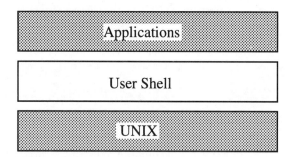

Figure 4.10 *UNIX without a GUI.*

The design goals for the X Window System include the following:

- the system should be capable of implementation on a variety of displays;
- applications must be display device independent;
- the system must be network transparent;
- the system should be extensible.

The first three of these goals distinguish X from other windowing systems; for example, the Macintosh window system does not meet these criteria.

The client server architecture of the X Window System
These design goals have led to a client server architecture for the X Window System in which there is an explicit division between the interface and the input/output device control code. The input/output devices are controlled by the display server process and the interface defined by the library code linked into the application process. This division into separate processes allows the display server and application to execute on different machines.

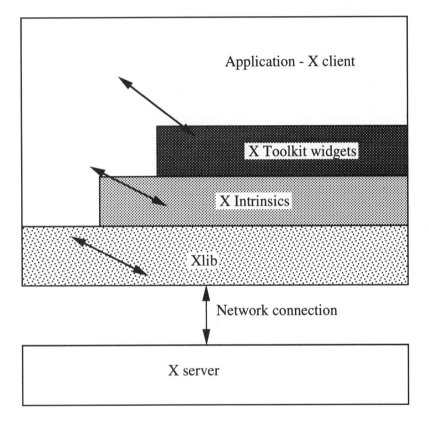

The X Window System has a client server architecture.

Figure 4.11 *The X Window System client/server architecture.*

Draper *et al.* (1990) is a video explaining the X Window System.

The network connection shown in Fig. 4.11 is known as the X protocol and describes all communication between an X client application and an X display server. If the client and server are on the same machine then local interprocess communication is used. If they are on different machines then an inter-machine connection is established, for example, via TCP over an Ethernet. Thus networking and multiprocessing applications are an inherent part of the X Window System.

Xlib, the X protocol interface
Xlib (Fig. 4.11) is the programming language interface to the raw X protocol. This level of interface provides access to all the functionality of the

display server but entails a high programming overhead and therefore is only used to generate application-specific functions.

X Intrinsics and widgets

An X widget encapsulates the appearance and behaviour of an interaction object.

X Intrinsics is a library of 'widgets'. A widget is the basic building block of an X Window user interface and encapsulates the appearance and behaviour of an interaction object. Widgets are built from a hierarchy of widget types (Fig. 4.12). The core widget defines the data and functionality shared by all widgets and a subclass of the core widget is the simple widget, which is used to build buttons, labels and so on. The X Intrinsics library provides the necessary support facilities to build combine and operate the widgets.

The X Window System acts as a foundation on which to build GUI toolkits.

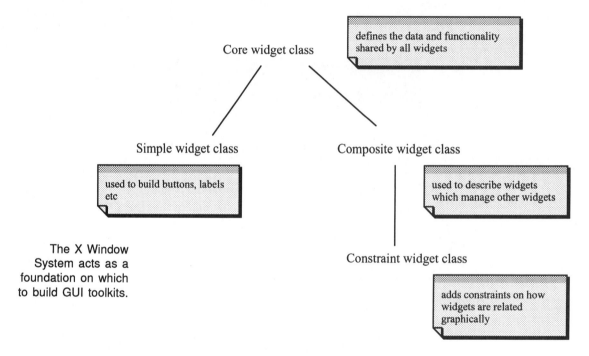

Figure 4.12 *Hierarchy of X Window widget types.*

X toolkits

The Joy of X (Mansfield, 1993) provides a comprehensive coverage of X.

The X Window System is not a GUI. It is a portable, network transparent windowing system that acts as a foundation on which to build GUI toolkits such as OSF/Motif or OPEN LOOK. The X Window System provides a standard means of communicating between dissimilar machines on a network.

This section provided an introduction to GUI styleguides and toolkits and a overview of the X Window System. In the next section portability between the various GUI styles is discussed, together with examples of how one portability toolkit is used in practice.

4.5 Portability between GUIs

Because of the variety of graphical user interfaces available today it is often difficult to compare one GUI directly with another. Peddie, 1992, has suggested an organizational model of a GUI which aids comparison. In Fig. 4.13, six main layers are identified which reside between the application and the processor:

GUIs developed in one environment cannot be readily transferred to another environment.

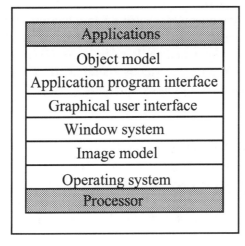

GUI toolkits can be compared using the organizational model suggested by Peddie, 1992.

Figure 4.13 *Organizational model of a GUI, after Peddie, 1992.*

1. *The object model*
    The object model represents a new trend towards object-oriented GUIs. It is the most recent addition to GUIs and, in fact, is not included in most GUIs. The object model is most noticeably manifest within Hewlett-Packard's NewWave in which an object consists of data and the application program that generates and manipulates that data. NewWave is built around an object management facility which is an object database manager with three functions: application/data building, maintaining information links between applications, and object integration.

2. *The application program interface*
    The application program interface (API) is a set of programming language calls that are used by application developers to communicate with the GUI. A programmer can specify which functions (for example, windows, menus, scroll bars and icons), are desired and when.

3. *The graphical user interface*
    The GUI is where the screen actions and elements reside, such aspop-up or pull-down menus, and scroll bars. The boundary between the GUI and the window system varies from supplier to supplier.

4. *The window system*

The X Window System resides here. Other window systems such as Microsoft Windows include both the GUI and the window system.

5. *The image model*

The NeXt Book
(Webster, 1991).

The X Window System does not have an image model, although in some GUIs such as Sun Microsystem's NeXT, the screen can be turned over to a complete graphics imaging system.

6. *The operating system*

In some cases the operating system is an integral part of the GUI, such as the Macintosh or Amiga. Here, the GUI appears automatically when the system is first switched on. In other cases the GUI sits on top of the operating system and the user is required to choose which GUI to invoke. Most of the GUIs based on the X Window System fall into this category.

GUIs based on the X Window System

OSF/Motif and OPEN LOOK are both based on UNIX and X.

Using the organizational model described above goes some way towards permitting comparison between different GUIs. For example, OSF/Motif and UNIX International's OPEN LOOK are both based on UNIX and on the X Window System. Figs 4.14 and 4.17 show their organizational structure.

Motif

OSF/Motif is the standard graphical interface to computer applications being promoted by the Open Software Foundation (OSF). OSF is a worldwide nonprofit organization dedicated to developing an open computing environment in which all hardware and software can work together more easily.

OSF/Motif has a distinctive bevelled 3-D appearance.

Desktop	**Applications**
Object model	Third-party
API/Toolkit	Digital's API toolkit
GUI	Motif
Window system	XII
Image model	PostScript
Operating system	AIX
Processor	680x0, RS6000, MIPS

Figure 4.14 *Open Software Foundation's Motif, after Peddie, 1992.*

Motif is based on the Digital Equipment Corporation's XUI (X User Interface) technology and on Digital's UIL (User Interface Language) and toolkit. Motif has the distinctive bevelled three-dimensional appearance or look and feel of Hewlett-Packard company's 3D windowing system (NewWave), as well as Microsoft/IBM's Presentation Manager behaviour. OSF combined Digital's XUI widgets with HP's widgets to produce the Motif widgets (Fig. 4.15).

See OSF/Motif User's and Style Guides.

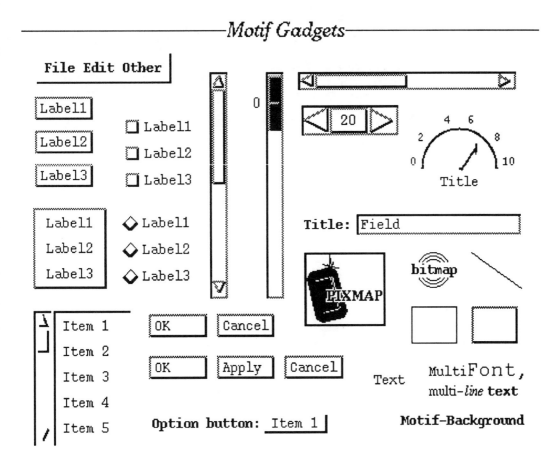

Figure 4.15 *Motif Gadgets.*

UNIX International has also endorsed Motif since it meets the five criteria for an approved GUI for UNIX system, version 4.: (i) it conforms to the X Window System; (ii) the specification is freely available; (iii) there are no legal encumbrances on its use; (iv) it is a real product; and (v) it must run on top of UNIX, version 4. Figure 4.16 shows the basic window components of Motif.

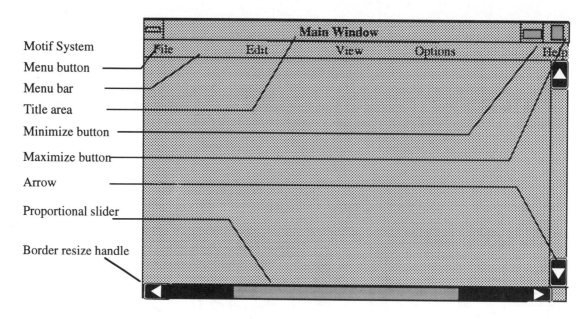

Motif System
Menu button
Menu bar
Title area
Minimize button
Maximize button
Arrow
Proportional slider

Border resize handle

Figure 4.16 *The basic window components of Motif after Marcus, 1992.*

OPEN LOOK

OPEN LOOK, (1989) provides the GUI styleguide and functional specification.
In contrast, OPEN LOOK is not a product, but a user interface architecture defined by a specification and a style guide. It is not a piece of software but a book called *OPEN LOOK Graphical User Interface Specification.* The architecture was developed by Sun and AT& T and others and describes what a user sees on the computer screen, and the way a user controls the computer in any applications program based on OPEN LOOK. The OPEN LOOK user interface is different in that it standardizes the user interface but does not specify the API. Sun's implementation of OPEN LOOK is Open Windows.

Desktop	Applications
API/Toolkit	Third-party
Object Model	GUIMS
GUI	OPEN LOOK
Window system	XII
Image model	PostScript
Operating System	Unix
Processor	680x0, MIPS, SPARC

Figure 4.17 *UNIX International's OPEN LOOK, after Peddie, 1992.*

The OPEN LOOK user interface specification is designed to give applications a 3D 'look and feel'.

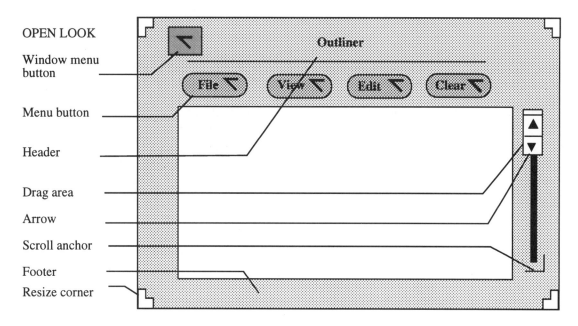

Figure 4.18 *Basic window components of OPEN LOOK after Marcus, 1992.*

OPEN LOOK and Motif are based on UNIX and X Windows, while other GUIs such as Macintosh (Fig. 4.19), and Presentation Manager have their own architecture which does not necessarily fit well into Peddie's model. However, the architectures shown below do highlight the differences between UNIX-based GUIs and others.

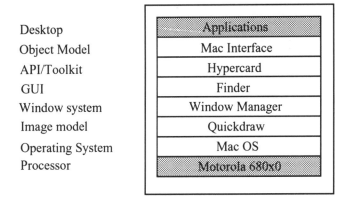

Figure 4.19 *Macintosh GUI structure, after Peddie, 1992.*

Presentation Manager is the standard graphical user interface and toolkit for the OS/2 operating system. Presentation Manager provides a GUI which is consistent with IBM's Common User Access (CUA) guidelines (Fig. 4.20).

IBM, The Official Guide (1992) describes CUA guidelines.

Desktop	Applications
Object Model	Third-party
API/Toolkit	User Interface Controls
GUI	Presentation Manager
Window system	Presentation Manager
Image model	Graphics Programming Interface
Operating System	OS/2
Processor	Intel 80x86

Figure 4.20 *IBM's Presentation Manager, after Peddie, 1992.*

Presentation Manager windows typically have a title bar, system icons, min/max icons, an action bar and sizable borders (Fig. 4.21).

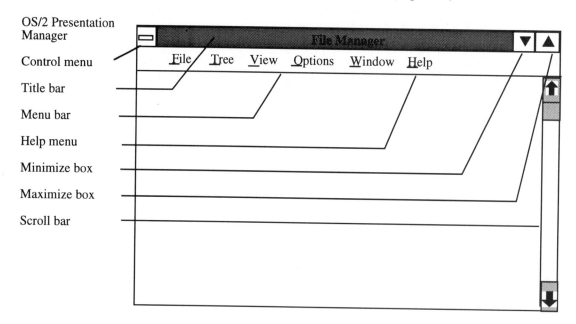

OS/2 Presentation Manager

Control menu

Title bar

Menu bar

Help menu

Minimize box

Maximize box

Scroll bar

File Manager

<u>F</u>ile   <u>T</u>ree   <u>V</u>iew   <u>O</u>ptions   <u>W</u>indow   <u>H</u>elp

Figure 4.21 *Basic window components of Presentation Manager after Marcus, 1992.*

There is hardly any portability from one GUI to another. If an application is to be mounted across different platforms, the GUI has to be rewritten for each platform. For example, if some users have only Motif and others have only Presentation Manager, then the user interface must be designed and developed twice, once for each environment.

4.6 XVT and portability between GUIs

There are a large number of GUIs available, each with an associated toolkit which allows the programmer to develop applications which comply with a particular GUI's style. GUI toolkits typically require considerable effort to learn and consequently programmers tend to commit to a single environment or system. This limits the portability of applications from one system to another.

There is hardly any portability from one GUI environment to another.

XVT Software has developed XVT (Extensible Virtual Toolkit) which provides a common API and a set of libraries for each popular environment: the X Window System (both OSF/Motif and OPEN LOOK), Macintosh, Microsoft Windows, Presentation Manager and for a number of character-based displays (Fig. 4. 22).

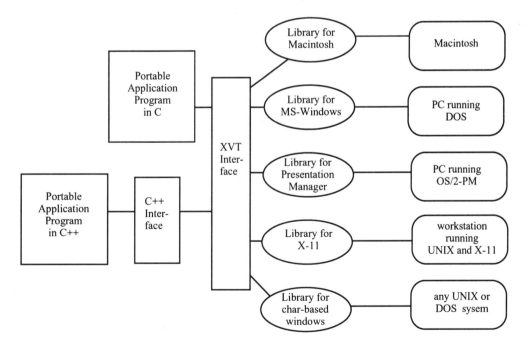

Figure 4.22 *XVT architecture* XVT Corp.

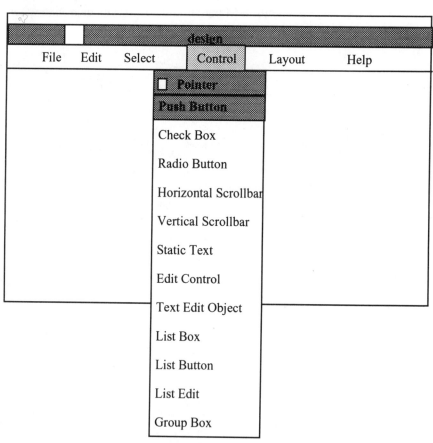

XVT allows software designers to create a GUI using XVT-Design, and provides software libraries which generate C or C++ code which can be executed in the chosen GUI environment.

With XVT, software designers can write interactive applications that use graphics, menus and dialogues and then port them to different environments. Particularly helpful in this respect is XVT-Design which enables the designer to build the user interface interactively by allowing the design of one screen at a time. C (or C++) code can be generated for each screen and then the screens linked together to form the code for a sequence of screens. This application interface code can then be presented to the appropriate XVT library and executed on the associated platform. For example, if a sequence of screens is designed using XVT-Design running on Open Windows on the SUN, the application interface code generated in C can be executed using Presentation Manager on an IBM PC.

The process of generating user interfaces is further illustrated below by showing how push buttons and menu bars are created using XVT-Design. These illustrations are based on version 1.1 of XVT-Design.

With XVT, the interface need only be designed and built once, but can run on different platforms.

Figures 4.23 to 4.28 show how XVT-Design can be used to create a push button and a menu bar. They show how the designer can create user interfaces simply through interacting with the design tool and without programming.

The designer creates the user interface by interacting with the XVT-Design tool. No programming is necessary.

Figure 4.23 *Drawing of initial screen from XVT-Design.*

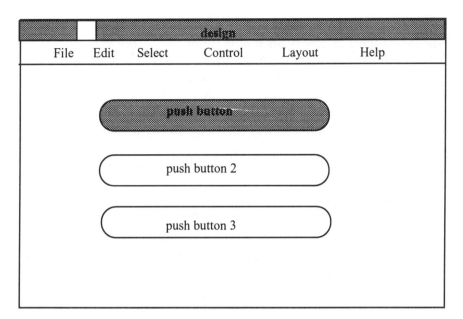

This example illustrates some of the basic features of XVT-Design.

Figure 4.24 *Three push buttons are created using XVT-Design.*

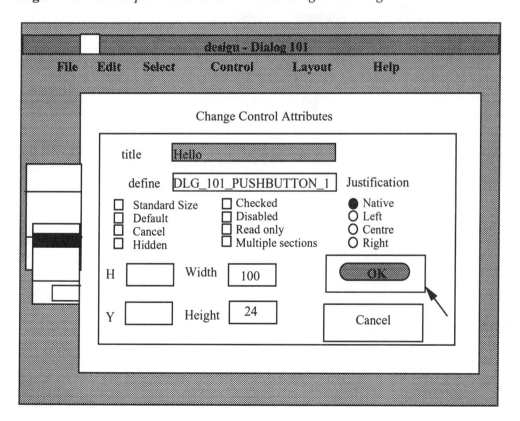

Figure 4.25 *The attributes of a push button can be selected.*

4.6.1 Creating a push button

First the designer selects 'Push Button' from the Control menu.

A dialogue box appears and the designer simply double clicks for each push button required; for example, three double clicks will create three push buttons (Fig. 4.24).

By double clicking a push button, an attributes dialogue box will appear, whereby the designer can select the attributes the push button should have (Fig. 4.25).

The push button is then created and the attributes stored.

4.6.2 Creating a menu bar

Choose 'menubars' from the Select menu (Fig. 4.26).

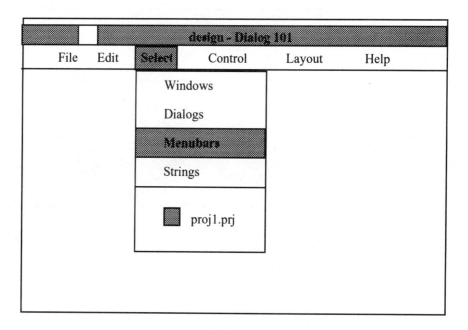

Figure 4.26 *Drawing of initial screen from XVT-Design.*

This causes the Menubar Editor to appear. Selecting 'new' causes a new menu bar to appear, which must be given a name; in this case, 'menu-bar 1'. Selecting 'edit' from the Menubar Editor will cause the menu editor to appear (Fig. 4.27).

The Menu Editor allows the designer to create the menu associated with the menu bar. Each item in the menu can be given attributes or can have a submenu (Fig. 4.28).

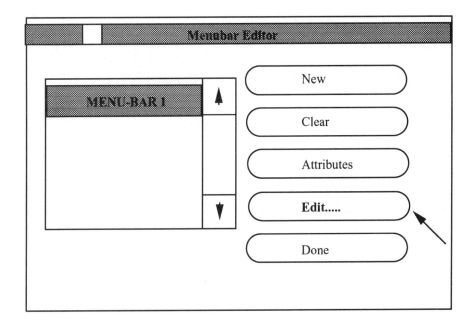

Figure 4.27 *The Menubar Editor.*

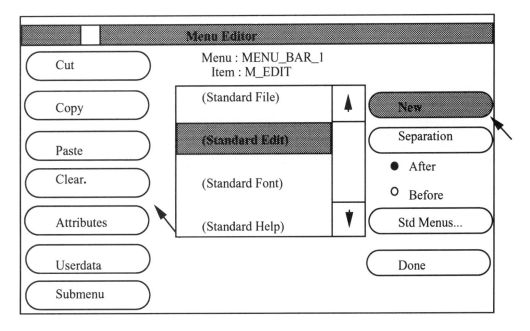

Figure 4.28 *Menu Editor.*

4.6.3 Designing screens for Fast Ferries

XVT-Design provides basic constructs for building a user interface, but the **design** of the user interface is still the responsibility of the designer.

The examples below illustrate how some of the features of XVT can be used in a specific case; here, the designs are of screens from the Fast Ferries enquiries and reservation system. Other features supported by XVT include areas for static text which are used to prompt the user. Static text is usually associated with edit control areas which are used to obtain typed information from the user. For example in Fig. 4.29, 'From' is static text and the edit control box adjacent to it would be used to enter the date of the outward journey.

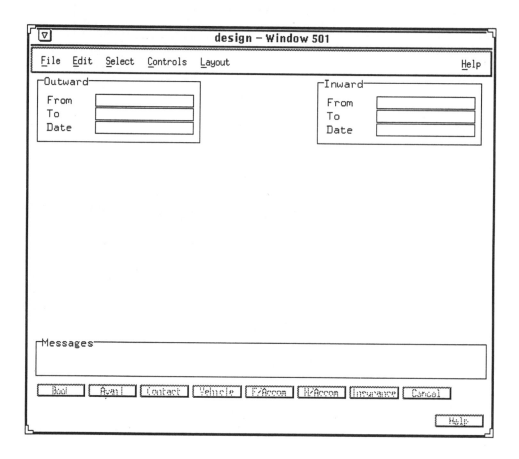

Figure 4.29 *Static text and the edit control box.*

Horizontal and vertical scrollbars can be created. List boxes, such as the availability detail window (Fig. 4.30) are used to choose between a variable list of options. The list box includes a vertical scroll bar.

```
 ┌─────────────────────────────────────────────────────────────┐
 │ [▽]              design – Window 501                         │
 ├─────────────────────────────────────────────────────────────┤
 │ File  Edit  Select  Controls  Layout                   Help │
 ├─────────────────────────────────────────────────────────────┤
 │ ┌Outward─────────────────────┐   ┌Inward──────────────────┐ │
 │ │ From   [_____]   │   │ From   [_____]  │ │
 │ │ To     [_____]   │   │ To     [_____]  │ │
 │ │ Date   [_____]   │   │ Date   [_____]  │ │
 │ └─────────────────────────────┘   └────────────────────────┘ │
 │  Origin          Destination      Date     Time    Vacant   │
 │ ┌──────────────────────────────────────────────────────┬─┐  │
 │ │                                                        │▲│  │
 │ │                                                        │ │  │
 │ │                                                        │ │  │
 │ │ Availability Detail Window                             │ │  │
 │ │                                                        │ │  │
 │ │                                                        │ │  │
 │ │                                                        │▼│  │
 │ └──────────────────────────────────────────────────────┴─┘  │
 │ ┌Messages─────────────────────────────────────────────────┐ │
 │ │                                                          │ │
 │ └──────────────────────────────────────────────────────────┘ │
 │ [ Book ]   [Contact][Vehicle][F/Accom][H/Accom][Insurance][Cancel] │
 │                                              [ Help ]       │
 └─────────────────────────────────────────────────────────────┘
```

Figure 4.30 *A list box with a vertical scroll bar.*

Group boxes are used to group together a number of edit controls within the workspace. For example, in Fig. 4.31 below, four group boxes are used, one for details of the outward journey, one for details of the inward journey, one for contact details and one for messages. The use of group boxes aids user understanding of what is required and contributes significantly to the clarity of the design.

At the bottom of each of the above windows are radio buttons which are used to select one option from a list.

The Fast Ferries example illustrates how XVT-Design can be an aid to good design by providing the basic constructs needed to build a user interface. However, it should be remembered that the software designer must first create the design by hand and by considering the needs of the

```
┌─────────────────────────────────────────────────────────────────┐
│ ▽              design – Window 501                               │
├─────────────────────────────────────────────────────────────────┤
│ File  Edit  Select  Controls  Layout                      Help   │
│ ┌Outward─────────────────────┐      ┌Inward──────────────────┐   │
│ │ From  [            ]        │      │ From  [            ]   │   │
│ │ To    [            ]        │      │ To    [            ]   │   │
│ │ Date  [            ]        │      │ Date  [            ]   │   │
│ ┌Contact Details Window──────────────────────────────────────┐   │
│ │                                                            │   │
│ │  Name    [                        ]                        │   │
│ │                                                            │   │
│ │  Address [                                              ]   │   │
│ │          [                                              ]   │   │
│ │          [                                              ]   │   │
│ │                                Post Code [            ]     │   │
│ │  Tel. Number   [            ]                               │   │
│ │                                                            │   │
│ ┌Messages────────────────────────────────────────────────────┐   │
│ │                                                            │   │
│ │                                                            │   │
│ ┌────┐ ┌─────┐      ┌───────┐┌───────┐┌───────┐┌─────────┐┌──────┐│
│ │Book│ │Avail│      │Vehicle││F/Accom││H/Accom││Insurance││Cancel││
│ └────┘ └─────┘      └───────┘└───────┘└───────┘└─────────┘└──────┘│
│                                                     ┌──────┐      │
│                                                     │ Help │      │
│                                                     └──────┘      │
└─────────────────────────────────────────────────────────────────┘
```

Figure 4.31 *Group boxes.*

users. The GUI tools only aid implementation; the designer is still responsible for creative design and for meeting the needs of users.

Once the window designs are complete, the application code (C or C++) is generated for each window. The windows must then be linked together by adding additional C code (in version 1.1 of XVT-Design but not in later versions). The order of linking will depend on the sequence in which windows can be viewed by users, specified of course, through discussion with users. The code is then compiled and linked to the application. In this way the designer can create the required user interface.

4.7 GUI design: an object-oriented approach

GUIs use an object-action paradigm where the user indicates an object first and then gives the command. Thus when considering the design of graphical user interfaces it is natural to adopt an object-oriented approach.

> GUIs use an object-action paradigm where the user indicates an object first and then decides the action.

The techniques described in Chapter Two showed how the designer might undertake an analysis of the user's needs within the context of business objectives and stakeholder needs. User needs were considered from three perspectives: firstly the users, the workgroups they belong to and their characteristics; secondly the tasks performed and their characteristics and thirdly the objects and their characteristics. It is suggested here that this early analysis can form the basis for an object-oriented approach to interface design in the same way that in Chapter Three it formed the basis for a task-oriented approach to interface design.

This section describes an object-oriented approach to user interface design and the following section presents a case study showing the application of the approach to the Fast Ferries reservation system. It is hoped that the reader will consider the contrast between a task-oriented approach and an object-oriented approach both in terms of the process and in terms of the resulting user interface.

Figure 4.32 shows an overview of the procedure which can be followed when taking an object-oriented approach to user interface design.

> An object-oriented approach to GUI design is presented.

4.7.1 Stage 1: understanding users

Stage 1, understanding users, was covered in Chapter Two. However, two important inputs to this process are the workgroup table and the job issues for each workgroup. These provide descriptions of what the users do now and a basis for identifying objects.

> Always begin by understanding users and what they do.

4.7.2 Stage 2: list objects associated with all users and workgroups

Stage 2, list objects associated with all affected users and workgroups, was covered at an inital level in Chapter Two. This is an important stage because any given system will only support one set of objects, no matter how many users or workgroups use the system. Different users will carry out different actions on the same object; for example, the manager at a theatre may create a seating plan for a show, the box office clerk will update the seating plan with customer bookings, and the marketing manager may wish to amend the seating plan in order to optimize revenue. The tasks of primary and secondary workgroups should be considered first. These tasks should be set out in a list for each workgroup and all the nouns underlined. Some of these nouns may not be of any relevance to the proposed system but at this stage everything should be included. The outcome of this stage will be a long list of potential objects.

> Make a list of all the objects associated with users and workgroups.

> Users carry out actions and objects.

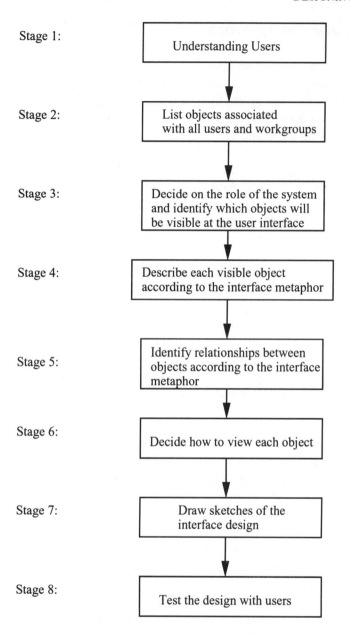

Figure 4.32 *Stages in object-oriented user interface design.*

4.7.3 Stage 3: decide on the role of the system and identify visible objects

Stage 3 is concerned with deciding upon the role of the system, which objects should be supported by the system and which objects will remain as they are now.

1. *Decide the role of the system*
There should be some general statement about the role of the system in supporting the users and workgroups, as discussed in section 2.5, *Task analysis and allocation of function.*

Decide on the role of the system. Which objects should the system support?

2. *Classify objects*
Once the role of the system has been decided, it is then possible to classify the objects. Objects classified as '1' are to be fully automated and will not be visible at the user interface; objects classified as '2' will be visible at the user interface and the user will be able to carry out actions on them; objects classified as '3' will be external to the system and will remain totally the user's responsibility. Each object in the list generated in stage 2 should be classified as 1, 2 or 3. At this point some duplication of objects will normally be identified (for example, customer and customers, are probably the same object) and so the list can be slightly reduced. The choice of classification of each object will depend on the role of the system.

Classify objects: '1' — fully automated; '2' — will be visible at the user interface; '3' — will remain external to the system.

3. *Identify aggregations, different names and reports*
Next, only those objects with a classification of 1 or 2 need be considered and a list should be drawn showing just these objects. The next step is to shorten the list by looking for aggregations, different names and reports.

Aggregations
Upon inspection, some of the objects may be seen to be attributes of other objects and hence can be aggregated into one object. For example, name, address and telephone number could be aggregated into customer.

Consider objects classified as '1' or '2' and look for aggregations, different names and reports.

Different names
In other cases, two objects may be the same object but their names are different; for example, 'bookings' and 'files on bookings' are probably the same object, so one can be removed from the list.

Reports
Some objects may simply be outputs or reports from the system which can be generated as a result of user actions on other objects; for example, a receipt for payment may have been listed as a object initially but the important object may be payment, and the user can ask the system to issue a receipt. There is no need to treat 'receipt' as an object in its own right.

4. *Revised list of objects*
The outcome of stage 3 is a revised and usually much shorter list of objects.

Produce a revised list of objects.

4.7.4 Stage 4: describe each visible object

The next stage is to describe all the visible objects, that is, those objects with a classification of '2'. Obviously the designer must be constantly reassessing whether this is the 'correct' set of objects, as there is no single answer.

Each object with a classification of '2' will appear at the user interface, i.e. is a visible object.

1. *'Now' and 'proposed' descriptions*

   Each object can be described according to its 'now' and 'proposed' characteristics as discussed in Chapter Two. Describe them in terms of: who has access to the object, who is responsible for the management of the object and its representation and quality.

2. *Descriptions according to metaphor adopted*

   In addition, each object can be described according to the interface metaphor being adopted. For example, if the CUA interface metaphor is used, there will be three classes of objects:

Each visible object should be described.

Container objects:	The container object holds other objects. Its purpose is to provide a way for a user to group related objects for easy access and retrieval, for example, folders.
Data objects:	The data object conveys information such as text or graphics.
Device objects:	The device object often represents a physical object in the real world. The primary purpose of this kind of object is to provide a means of communication between a computer and another physical or logical object. For example, a printer object represents a physical device, whereas an electronic mail out basket represents a logical device.

The CUA metaphor is described in *IBM, The Official Guide* (1992).

4.7.5 Stage 5: identify relationships between objects

The next stage is to identify relationships between objects, in terms of which object is associated with another object, which one contains another object and which one is sent to another object. The nature of the relationships will also depend on the interface metaphor adopted. In the main, however, this stage involves understanding how the user will interact with the system.

Identify relationships between objects such as association or containment.

4.7.6 Stage 6: decide how to view each object

Next the designer must decide how each object should be viewed in order to give the user the best access to the objects and the information they contain.

Views of objects such as icons, menubars, menu items, forms, etc. must be decided.

The designer should produce lists detailing the contents of each menu bar, each pull down menu, each form, table or list. In addition, icons should be described in terms of allowable user actions and their consequences. For example, dragging a reservation icon onto the printer will cause the reservation form to be printed.

4.7.7 Stage 7: draw sketches of the interface design

Hand-drawn sketches of the interface design or rapidly put-together sketches are useful. Their main purpose is to discuss the proposed design with the user. The design will probably change as a result of the discussion and so the designer should not spent too much time on drawing a draft of the design.

Draw sketches of the GUI design and discuss possible scenarios of use with the users.

4.7.8 Stage 8: test the design with users

User reaction should be sought concerning the choice of objects, the views of each object, the allowable user actions on each object and the representation of each object. The design should be modified to reflect user reaction.

The case study which follows illustrates the above process using the Fast Ferries example discussed in Chapters Two and Three. Only selected parts of the design are shown.

4.8 Case study of an object-oriented approach to UI design

The aim of this case study is to illustrate how the designer might proceed from user analysis to graphical user interface design taking an object-oriented approach.

4.8.1 Stage 1: understanding users

Another look at the workgroup table in Fig. 3.16 reminds us that there are potentially three workgroups who might be users of the proposed system.

The job issues associated with each workgroup can be used as a basis for identifying objects. Figure 3.17 shows the job issues associated with the sales staff workgroup.

The job issues are used in stage 2.

4.8.2 Stage 2: list objects associated with users and work-groups

The nouns in each of the job issues table are underlined. This is the first stage in identifying objects.

SALES STAFF WORKGROUP: (from the job issues table in Fig. 3.17)

Deals with customers, finding out their requirements.

Makes enquiries regarding availability of ferries, times and prices of crossings, using the telephone and published timetable.

Makes bookings and reservations for passengers and vehicles, by filling in the reservation form, together with the customer.

Sells associated products such as insurance.

Arranges accommodation.

Informs <u>ferry company</u> of <u>reservation details</u>.

Records <u>information about bookings</u> for <u>management</u>.

Keeps <u>files</u> on <u>customers</u> and <u>bookings</u>.

Deals with <u>payment</u>.

Issues <u>tickets</u> on behalf of the <u>ferry company</u>.

Sets out and reads <u>travel brochures</u>.

MANAGEMENT WORKGROUP: (from the job issues table — not shown).

Produces monthly and annual <u>reports for head office</u>.

Monitors <u>performance of sales staff</u>.

Markets the <u>services of the travel agent</u> by accessing <u>customer files</u>.

Makes <u>forecasts</u> and <u>plans for future business</u>.

Deals with <u>complaints from customers</u>.

Deals with <u>exceptions</u>.

Deals with <u>other agencies</u> and <u>travel companies</u>.

FINANCIAL WORKGROUP: (from the job issues table — not shown)

Produces monthly and annual <u>financial reports for head office</u>.

Produces <u>financial statements for tax returns</u>.

Produces daily and weekly <u>summaries of takings</u>.

4.8.3 Stage 3: decide the role of the system and identify visible objects

Decide on the role of the system and decide which objects will appear at the user interface

1. *The role of the system*

    From the workgroup level analysis, the main advantages can be gained by reductions in the time taken to deal with customers, reservations and bookings, and to record information about customers and sales for management. These are all tasks which must be shared between the user and the system. Very few tasks, except those at the lowest level such as calculation of totals, will be fully automated. Most will remain either totally manual or shared between user and computer.

2. *Classification of objects*
   Objects are classified as follows:

   (i) fully automated and not visible at the user interface;
   (ii) visible at the user interface and the user can carry out actions on the object;
   (iii) totally manual and the system will not be aware of this object.

List of objects (from Stage 2)	Classification
customers	2
requirements	part of customer
enquiries	2
ferries, times and prices of crossings	same as timetable
telephone	2
timetable	2
bookings	2
reservations	2
passengers	2
vehicles	2
reservation form,	2
~~customer~~	duplicate object
products	2
insurance	2
accommodation	2
ferry company	3
~~reservation details~~	duplicate object
information about bookings for management	2
files on customers	2
files on bookings	2
payment	3
(but information about payment will be needed)	2
tickets	2
~~ferry company~~	duplicate object
travel brochures	3
reports for head office	3
performance of sales staff	3
services of the travel agent	3
~~customer files~~	duplicate object
forecasts	3
plans for future business	3
complaints from customers	3
exceptions	3
other agencies	3

travel companies	3
financial reports for head office	3
financial statements for tax return	3
summaries of takings	2

The allocation of 2s and 3s above reflects the decision that the role of the system should be that of a straightforward enquiries, reservation and booking system providing very little management information. If the decision had been made to provide more support for management, then the allocation would have been different.

3. *Aggregations, different names and reports*
   Next the objects with an allocation of 1 or 2 need to be reconsidered:

customers	2
enquiries	2
telephone	2
timetable	2
bookings	2
reservations	2
passengers	2
vehicles	2
reservation form	2
products	2
insurance	2
accommodation	2
information about bookings for management	2
files on customers	2
files on bookings	2
information about payment	2
tickets	2
summaries of takings	2

Look for aggregations, different names and reports
Some of the objects can be aggregated into one object, while some may simply be the same object but given different names. Some objects may simply be outputs or reports from the system which can be generated as a result of actions on other objects.

Aggregations
Insurance and accommodation availability details could be aggregated into products, to allow for any future products which may be added. However, insurance and accommodation booking details associated with a particular customer may need to be treated as separate objects.

Different names
Customers and files on customer; bookings and files on bookings; reservations and reservation form.

Reports
Information about bookings for management; summaries of takings; information about payment (although there should probably be a payment object).

4. *Revised list of objects*

> customers
> enquiries
> telephone
> timetable
> bookings
> reservations
> products
> tickets
> payment
> insurance details
> accommodation details
> vehicle.

4.8.4 Stage 4: describe each object

1. *'Now' and 'proposed' descriptions*
Each object can be described according to its 'now' and 'proposed' characteristics as discussed in Chapter Two. That is, in terms of: what it is, who has access to the object, who is responsible for the management of the object and its representation and quality.

For example, the reservation object 'now'

What is it?
The reservation object now is a pre-printed form (Chapter Two, Fig. 2.1) and contains passenger-related information such as details of inward and outward voyage (first and second choice), passenger details, vehicle details and requirements for insurance and accommodation.

Who has access to the object?
The object is accessed and completed by the travel agent through discussion with the customer and the customer is given a copy.

Who is responsible for the management of the object?
The management of the reservation form is the responsibility of the travel agent. If it is lost or if it contains incorrect information, the travel agent is held responsible.

What is its representation and quality?
The reservation form is represented only in paper format on multipart stationery. Three copies are made in all, one for the customer, one for the travel agent and one for the bookings file. The quality (accuracy) of the information on the form is dependent on the accuracy of the questions asked by the travel agent and the responses made by the customer. The quality in terms of readability will depend on the handwriting of the travel agent.

How will the object change? The reservation object 'proposed'

What is it?
The description of the object will be similar in that it contains passenger-related details. However, there will be no need to keep information concerning first and second choice because with an on-line system the customer can make any number of choices, and each choice will be treated independently (unless it is decided to keep a history of unsatisfied customer choices). There is no mention of payment in the reservation object now; payment could be part of the reservation object so that there is no need to have a separate booking object.

Who has access to the object?
The proposed situation is similar to the situation now. The customer will still require a copy.

Who is responsible for the management of the object?
Same as now.

What is its representation and quality?
The accuracy of the information may improve because some internal consistency checks can be carried out by cross referencing details within the form. Handwriting will be eliminated, so readability should improve.

2. *Descriptions according to the interface metaphor adopted*
   In addition, each object can be described according to the interface metaphor being adopted. Here it is the CUA interface metaphor. This includes three classes of objects:

   (i) Container objects: The container object holds other objects. Its purpose is to provide a way for a user to group related objects for easy access and retrieval, for example, folders.

(ii) Data objects: The data object conveys information such as text or graphics.

(iii) Device objects: The device object often represents a physical object in the real world.

Container objects
Enquiry, reservation.

Data objects
Customer, timetable, products, passenger, payment, vehicle, accommodation, insurance.

Device objects
Telephone, tickets.

4.8.5 Stage 5: identify relationships between objects

The next stage is to identify relationships between objects. This involves understanding how the travel agent will interact with the system. For example, details concerning choice of crossing and accommodation or insurance may be gathered during the enquiry. If the customer has reached a decision and is ready to make a reservation then the travel agent would want to pass these details onto the reservation object, rather than having to retype it. This could be achieved by dragging the enquiry object onto the reservation object for a particular customer. Figure 4.33 shows the relationships between the objects which reflects this description of the interaction.

There is no single 'correct' answer. Identifying the relationship between objects is an important part of the design and should be carried out where possible in consultation with target users.

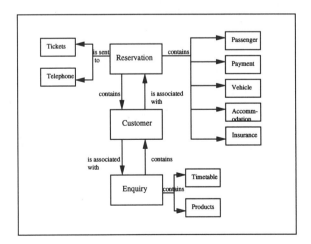

Figure 4.33 *Relationships between Fast Ferries Objects.*

4.8.6 Stage 6: decide how to view each object

Next, the designer must decide how each object should be viewed in order to give the user the best access to the objects and the information they contain.

For example, the reservation, customer and enquiry objects may be viewed as icons. On selection of the reservation object, a menu bar will appear containing passenger, payment, vehicle, accommodation and insurance, as well as help and other standard items such as file and edit.

Each of the items in the menu bar will have associated with it a pull-down menu showing the allowable actions associated with that object. For example, on selection of 'passenger', the pull-down menu might include 'new'. When this is selected, a blank form will appear for the travel agent to complete. This might include 'existing', and when this is selected, the travel agent is asked to enter the passenger name. Once confirmed, the existing passenger details will appear in a completed form.

The designer should produce lists detailing the contents of each menu bar, pull down menu, form, table or list.

4.8.7 Stage 7: draw sketches of the interface design

Figure 4.34 shows a sketch of the screen design showing the most important objects (from the travel agent's point of view) as icons. The device icons are also shown.

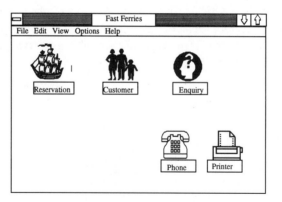

Figure 4.34   *Draft screen layout for Fast Ferries reservation system.*

4.8.8 Stage 8: test the design with users

Designers can simply show the screen designs to potential users and discuss a typical scenario of use with them. This might involve getting the user to describe some typical daily activity and to 'walk through' the screen designs to see how this activity would be done using the proposed system. Other techniques which may be useful are described in Chapter Seven.

4.9 Summary

This chapter has covered both the theory and practice of graphical user interface design at an introductory level. Various texts have been referred to which cover the material in more depth.

It's Time to clean your Windows: designing GUIs that work (Galitz, 1994) is recommended.

The object-oriented approach to user interface design enables the designer to take advantage of the direct manipulated facilitates available on present day systems. The approach adopts an object-action paradigm and is therefore useful in situations where the sequence of user actions is not readily predictable. The tools and techniques described in this chapter assume that the designer is concerned with the design of user interfaces for systems which support a single user. The next chapter deals with that class of system which supports groups of people working together.

Exercises for Chapter 4

4.1 Using the organizational model of a graphical user interface (GUI) compare the Open Software Foundation's Motif (OSF/Motif) and Sun Microsystems OPEN LOOK.

4.2 From a user's point of view, a GUI has three main elements which contribute to its 'look and feel': the visual appearance, behaviour and metaphor. Explain what is meant by each of these elements.

4.3 Each GUI toolkit has an associated window system, for example, OPEN LOOK and OSF Motif use the X Window System. With respect to the X Window System:

   1. What benefits does the client server model give the user?
   2. How is an X client structured?

4.4 What type of interface components does a typical X toolkit provide?

4.5 Describe a typical workplace environment as specified as part of the IBM Common User Access advanced user interface design standard. What are the major classes of icons used in CUA? Describe typical attributes of each class.

Chapter 5

Designing user interfaces to CSCW systems

The objectives of this chapter are:

☐ to introduce computer-supported cooperative working (CSCW) systems;

☐ to highlight the general characteristics of CSCW systems;

☐ to discuss a number of examples of CSCW systems;

☐ to discuss the role and characteristics of user interfaces to CSCW systems;

☐ to introduce a method of specifying and designing user interfaces to CSCW systems;

☐ to illustrate the application of the method through a case study.

5.1 Introduction

This chapter provides a brief introduction to computer systems which support groups of people working together. The popular name for such systems is CSCW (computer-supported cooperative working) systems. Section 5.2 provides a brief outline of a number of enabling technologies, followed, in section 5.3, by a discussion of the general characteristics of CSCW systems. In order to illustrate these characteristics, and to provide a basis for understanding user interfaces to CSCW systems, a number of exemplar systems are described in section 5.4.

CSCW is concerned with how groups of people work together using computer technology.

Section 5.5 contains a brief discussion of the differences between the role of the user interface in single-user systems and its role in CSCW systems. The typical characteristics of CSCW user interfaces are described, thus highlighting the difficulties facing the designer. Section 5.6 presents an approach to specifying and designing user interfaces to CSCW which may be helpful to the designer. This is followed in the next section with a case study which serves to illustrate the main features of this approach.

5.2 Computer-supported cooperative work

CSCW is concerned with how both large and small groups of people can collaborate using computer technology. Of necessity, it draws on a diverse set of more established disciplines including computer science, cognitive science, psychology, sociology, anthropology, ethnography and management, each contributing a different perspective and methodology for acquiring knowledge about groups and suggesting how the group's work could be supported.

5.2.1 Groupware

Intimately linked with CSCW is groupware which is software that supports and augments group work. Examples of groupware include: electronic mail, bulletin boards, asynchronous conferencing, group schedulers, group decision support systems, collaborative authoring systems, screen-sharing software, and video conferencing. A CSCW system will combine various groupware technologies depending upon the objectives of the group.

Groupware is the software that supports and augments groupwork.

5.2.2 Group

A group is a collection of people who work together on a common task. Groups can be made up of a diverse set of individuals each with their own objectives and each with different knowledge and skills to contribute to the completion of the common task. Individuals become part of a group when they have a stake in completing the common task. A group need not have a fixed or closed membership. Typically groups are formed when the task needs to be done and taken apart when it is completed.

Groups work together on a common task.

5.2.3 Computer support for group work

Group work need not always take place during a face-to-face meeting; the group may be geographically distributed and be communicating via the CSCW system. The group members may decide to login to the system at the same time, that is, work synchronously, or may allow group members to work on the common task as and when they have time, that is, they may choose to work asynchronously.

Figure 5.1 shows four possible situations in which groups may operate depending on their geographical and temporal distribution.

Face-to-face meetings occur at the same time and place. **Asynchronous login** occurs at one place at different times (there are very few examples of this). Interaction at the same time but at different places is **distributed synchronous meetings**. **Fully distributed** interaction occurs at different places and times.

CSCW systems may support one or more of the situations shown in Fig. 5.1. In what follows, approaches to providing computer support for groups are discussed from a user point of view. Included are:

Group members need not be in the same place at the same time.

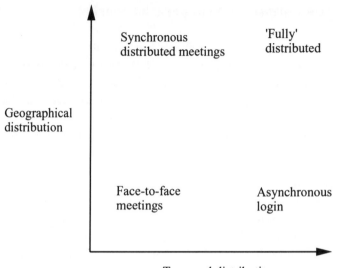

Figure 5.1 *Four situations in which groups may work together.*

1. Presentation support software.

2. Computer-supported meetings.

3. Group decision support.

4. Use of telephones.

5. Public windows.

6. Computer conferencing.

7. Group writing.

8. Group memory management and project management.

The computer system may help the group to organize their thoughts and ideas.

1. Presentation support software
Presentation support software can be used by a team working in a face-to-face situation, with individual workstations, but each member sharing the same view of the presentation. The team will also communicate verbally, as they would in a non-computer-supported meeting (Fig. 5.2).

Team members collaboratively prepare a presentation. The system helps the group to organize their thoughts collaboratively by guiding them through brainstorming, ordering and evaluation of content, style and purpose of the presentation.

2. Computer-supported meetings
In this case each team member has a private workspace and then chooses to show the other team members the results of his or her work by displaying it on a large central screen (Fig. 5.3). The team will then

discuss the contents of the screen. Meetings held in this way often employ a trained person to facilitate the discussion and help the group reach a decision.

Some information may be private, some may be for all the group to see.

Figure 5.2 *Presentation support software.*

Figure 5.3 *Computer-supported meetings.*

Team members work directly with computers, working privately during the meeting and displaying their work for others to see. For example, they may be working on a jointly-produced report.

3. Group decision support systems (GDSS)

One workstation may be shared between group members.

A more traditional style of decision making is to hold a face-to-face meeting supported by decision-support software (Fig. 5.4). Such software will typically provide a model of a particular problem situation. For example, senior management within a bank may meet to decide on the distribution of the marketing budget for the coming year. The system would provide a model to enable the managers to assess the relative merits of spending more or less on particular aspects of marketing.

Figure 5.4   *Group decision support.*

One workstation is used by each team member in turn to enter their anonymous judgement on some issue. The GDSS asks them about their own uncertainties, and to self-rate their expertise. The system then aggregates their opinions and feeds back a first set of judgements from the group. The group discusses the judgements made and expresses opinions until a decision is reached.

4. Use of telephones

This is an example of a distributed synchronous meeting, where group members are geographically distributed but all agree to login to the system at the same time and to use the telephone for verbal communication (Fig. 5.5).

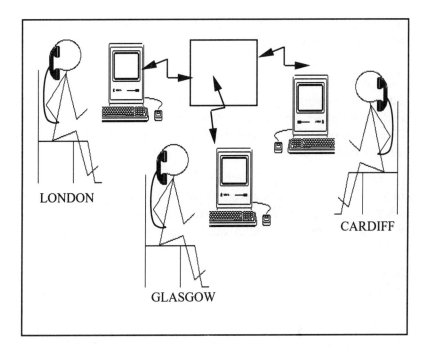

LONDON

CARDIFF

GLASGOW

Group members may speak over the telephone sharing information via the system.

Figure 5.5 *Use of telephones.*

A team meeting is booked for 2.0.pm. Each team member has a screen display that shows who is present and who is talking at a given time. Members can speak to all other group members at the same time, and can send data to each others' terminals.

Group members can share the same view of information, sometimes called WYSIWIS windows ('What You See Is What I See', Stefik, 1987).

5. Public windows

A common feature of a CSCW system is to have a public window. This window appears on everyone's workstation and is kept up to date on each person's screen. It is similar to having a white board in a meeting in that everyone in the meeting shares the same view of the window (Fig. 5.6).

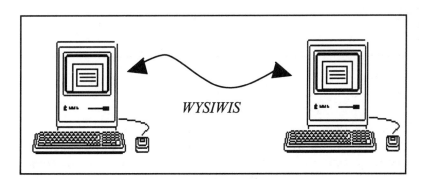

WYSIWIS

Figure 5.6 *Public windows.*

Public windows are often referred to as WYSIWIS (What You See Is What I See) windows.

6. Computer conferencing

Computer conferencing can be either synchronous or fully distributed and can be thought of as a group version of electronic mail, used for sending messages, holding discussions between team members and the filing of messages by group or by topic. Many CSCW systems include some element of conferencing.

A typical scenario might be where six team members based in three countries check the team's conference twice a day, see what has happened since they were there last, make their own comments and leave. Working documents, graphics and so on are exchanged through the conferencing system.

Groups may wish to produce a document jointly.

7. Group writing

An important aspect of group working is the co-authoring of documents. Groups may wish to work synchronously or fully distributed. Each team member will normally have some private workspace and a public (WYSIWIS) window. The public window will show the current state of the document (Fig. 5.7).

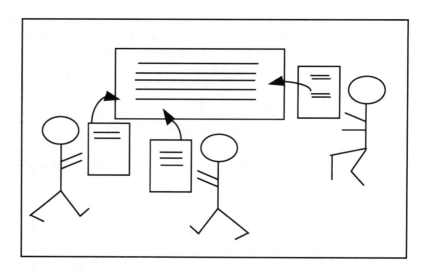

Figure 5.7   *Group writing.*

Group authoring software allows team members to make document revisions, with the system remembering who made the changes. Members suggest changes without 'wiping out' the original text and comparisons can be made between alternative drafts. The goal is to improve the speed and quality of group writing.

8. Group memory management and project management

Some CSCW systems will provide support for helping the team to remember statements made, actions taken or decisions reached by the group. A typical scenario might be, 'I remember it was an idea we had a couple of days ago. I think it was Susan and it has something to do with the notion of "optimization".'

Systems can contain notes from team meetings, with links between the words and concepts. Various paths through words, data and people can be tried in order to locate the lost idea.

Project management software can help teams in planning and coordinating the common task, to help plan what needs to be done, track progress and coordinate activities of individual members.

Groups may need help with tracing decisions made and the associated ideas and discussions.

5.3 Characteristics of CSCW systems

In this section, a number of characteristics of CSCW systems are discussed. Each characteristic is explained in terms of why it is needed, how it manifests itself within particular systems and the potential benefits and limitations associated with it.

CSCW systems as a whole can be thought of as having the following characteristics:

They provide support for

- communication between group members;
- sharing of information;
- coordination and control of shared objects;
- sharing of workspace;
- organization and common understanding of the work process;
- decision making.

Not all CSCW systems have all these characteristics; a specific system may have only one of them. Below is a brief discussion of each of them.

5.3.1 Communication between group members

Face-to-face meetings between group members can be as informal and unstructured as the group wishes. Often a great deal can be achieved in a setting in which people can see each other and be sensitive to each other's behaviour and reactions. Someone seen tapping their fingers on the table may be clearly annoyed; someone yawning may have lost interest in the discussion; another person leaning forward and pointing may be agitated or trying to make a point forcefully.

Face-to-face communication can be broken down into audio and visual channels, which in turn encompass language content, vocalizations such as

Human communication between people via computer is less 'rich' than direct human communication.

'er' or 'um', the general appearance of group members, facial expressions, body movement and psycho-physiological responses. The model shown in Fig. 5.8 illustrates the richness of face-to-face communication.

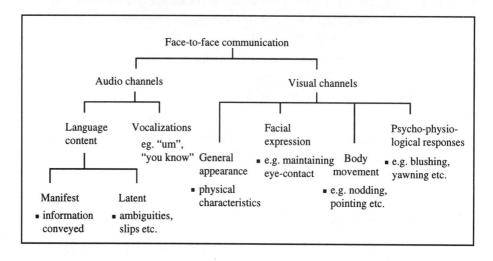

Figure 5.8   *The richness of face-to-face communication.*

Multi-media may improve the 'richness' of computer-mediated communication.

In contrast, computer-mediated communication is often limited to visual channels only, where the user can read written messages (Fig. 5.9).

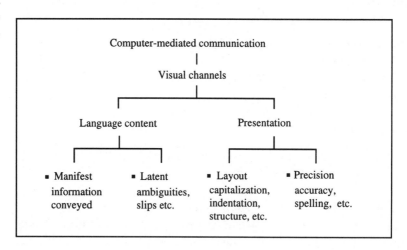

Figure 5.9   *Computer-mediated communciation.*

This can have an effect on the quality of communication between group members. However, additional context can be conveyed through specific use of layout, indentation or structuring of the text. Further, the members will often take longer to compose a message, attempt to structure their response and provide a more precise response than might be possible in a face-to-face setting.

Computer-mediated communication can also affect turn taking. In face-to-face conversations, cues are conveyed as vocalizations, through body language, and by facial expression. Removal of the cues leads to the need for an additional media of communication other than textual.

Examples of communication systems include:

- advanced electronic mail systems with voice and video; message components;
- real time 'desk top video conferencing' systems;
- large video wall screen systems.

5.3.2 Sharing of information

Sharing of information is important to groups in order to prevent unnecessary duplication of effort and to ensure that all members are using the same information. The group needs facilities to support the input, storage, navigation and retrieval of that information by all members of the group. The information may be in text, numeric, graphic, image or video format.

> Changes to shared objects should be immediately available to all group members.

Examples of shared information facilities include:

- multimedia, multi-user hypertext;
- shared optical discs or CD-ROM systems;
- multi-user databases.

5.3.3 Coordination and control of shared objects

Coordination and control of objects which are shared between group members is important for a number of reasons. For example, consider a design team attempting to develop a design diagram where the diagram is maintained on paper: time can be wasted drawing and re-drawing the diagram; there are delays in circulating amendments within the team; a number of versions of the diagram can accumulate and become difficult to manage; more that one person may be modifying the diagram at the same time and there may be a proliferation of associated notes, papers and diagrams which become difficult to maintain.

> The group needs support for version control.

The design team needs support such that changes are immediately available to all team members; versions of the diagram and cross-referenced documents are effectively maintained, and multiple amendments can be prevented or controlled.

Examples of systems which support coordination and control of shared objects include:

- Shared editors for synchronous group meetings;
- Co-authoring systems for asynchronous working, including facilities for planning the work, allocating tasks among team members, exchanging drafts and comments;
- Shared diaries.

5.3.4 Sharing of workspace

Group members need a shared workspace on which to develop their ideas.

Face-to-face meetings are often supported by the use of a white board or flip chart on which people can write their ideas for other members of the meeting to see. The results of a brainstorming exercise may be recorded or a list of important items may be developed by the members of the meeting. One person may be responsible for writing on the board but everyone can see what is written and can suggest changes or additions. Used in this way the white board or flip chart represents a shared workspace.

Examples of technologies which support the sharing of workspace include:

- The use of WYSIWIS or public windows which appear on the individual's workstation;
- Large electronic screens in face-to-face meeting rooms;
- Electronic whiteboards which provide support for drawing and organization of information and which include the ability to store and recall documents and drawings.

5.3.5 Organization and common understanding of the work process

Group members need support in the process of working together.

People who work together sometimes know what they have to do and how they are going to do it; for example, most meetings will have an agenda and a chairperson to facilitate the meeting. If this is not the case, people must first decide what they have to do and agree upon the process of achieving it. This process may include agreeing on the role of each individual, setting specific objectives and deadlines and deciding on some way of keeping informed as to how each person, and the group, are progressing.

Examples of technologies which support organization and common understanding of the work process include:

- co-authoring tools to support the joint writing of documents;
- agenda management tools;
- work flow systems which enable electronic forms to be sent on predefined routes of people and roles.

5.3.6 Decision making

Groups need support to reach decisions.

Central to a group of people working together is the ability of the group to reach a decision. The decision may be concerned with the objectives of the common task of the group, the method of working to be adopted by the group, the choice of the group members and their roles and the choice of techniques for making decisions, for example, voting.

Examples of technologies which support decision making include:

- decision-support tools to display facts and options available;
- argumentation tools to help the members of the group make their position explicit and to understand the views of other members;
- naming tools to help groups define their terminology;
- idea generation and prioritizing tools to aid group creativity.

In summary, a CSCW system can have one or more of the six characteristics discussed above. The next section provides further details of systems developed by particular companies or research laboratories.

5.4 Examples of CSCW systems

CSCW systems from the following companies and research labs are now described in order to provide some insights into recent developments within CSCW: The Microelectronics and Computer Technology Corporation (MCC) in the USA; The University of Calgary in Canada; The NTT Human Interface Labs in Japan and the University of Arizona in the USA. The projects described also provide a context for the description of a specific system called CRC, which was developed at UMIST, UK and which is used in the case study later in this chapter. The descriptions provide a summary of information available from sources in the public domain (these sources are listed at the end of the book).

5.4.1 MCC, USA

The Software Technology Program at the Microelectronics and Computer Technology Corporation (MCC) has been responsible for some significant CSCW research. They started with studying meetings and meeting improvement in Project Nick, and have proceeded to study real-time groupware, in particular, producing the GROVE group outline editor. They have also examined groupware toolkits and post-session group process feedback.

Project Nick (Cook *et al.*, 1987)

Their primary area of concern is real-time groupware. The work done by MCC is focussed on the support for design teams in large systems design projects. Project Nick examined meetings support, and GROVE is a group outline editor for use by co-located and distributed teams working synchronously.

GROVE (GRoup Outline Viewing Editor), is a prototype outline editor specifically designed for use by a group of people interacting synchronously during a work session. The group may work face-to-face in a room equipped with several workstations in a distributed manner, using office workstations and speaker phones for an audio-link. Mixed-mode sessions, where some participants are face-to-face and others are distributed, are also possible. GROVE has been used by several groups of computer scientists within an organization for a variety of design tasks, from planning joint papers and presentations to brainstorming.

GROVE editor (Ellis *et al.*, 1991)

GROVE focusses attention on those features that are required by real-time groupware tools and that are not concerns in building single-user tools. Consequently, although GROVE is a simple editor with a limited repertoire of outline editing operations, it emphasizes the provision of a fine-grained concurrent editing capability. It supports a team of people working very closely together in a number of modes. For example, people can share a view of the outline such that if one person scrolls, all the windows showing the view are immediately scrolled. Or several people can type into the same sentence at the same time, and immediately see the effects of each other's edits. Grove embodies the three main concepts characteristic of real-time groupware, those of **session**, **group window** and **view**.

Session – a set of users engaged in the use of GROVE on some common task. Users can enter or leave the session at any time.

Group window – a collection of windows whose instances appear on different display surfaces. Such instances are highly correlated: what is displayed in one instance will be close to, if not identical to, what is displayed in the others.

View – a representation of some portion of the shared environment. Such views will have controlled access, and may thus be of different types, typically: private, shared and public.

The group window shows all members of a view who are currently in a session. Part of the GROVE experiment was to give participants in a session the option of working in a more tightly coupled fashion than is possible in typical shared databases. The GROVE **concurrency control** algorithm allows fine-grained editing of the outline. The algorithm ensures that no matter what actions occur, or what their ordering, the replicated copies of the outline remain consistent. Additionally, users may explicitly lock out portions of the outline if necessary, or may rely upon **social protocols**; that is, agreement about who will do what and when.

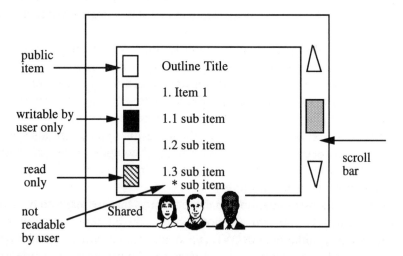

Figure 5.10 *Drawing a member's view.*

If 'shared view' is selected, a list of all project team names appears and the user has to select which team members are part of the subset. When a view is created, it is displayed as a public window on the screens of all members of the view who are also in the session (Fig. 5.10). Each item is on a new line.

A number of CSCW issues have been addressed in the process of developing GROVE, including WYSIWIS, group dynamics, screen space management, group protocols, and concurrency control. These are elaborated on below.

WYSIWIS, or 'What You See Is What I See' is an acronym used to describe an approach to multi-user interface design. Strict WYSIWIS implies that the shared context of a system will appear exactly the same to all users. GROVE relaxes this strict implementation in order to indicate an individual user's write permissions with colour (black text is read/write, whereas grey is read-only).

The interface of a CSCW system must reflect the dynamics of group work. For example, with a group editor such as GROVE, it is not suitable for characters to appear in a shared document as they would in a single-user application, one character at a time. To address this, they have developed a 'cloudburst' model of multi-user editing which displays text differently according to how 'old' it is, and who entered it (see below).

The screen of a single-user application can easily become congested with a large number of windows. For a CSCW system, where the activity of other group members can affect the windows on a user's screen, this problem is aggravated. The approach taken with GROVE was to adopt a rooms approach to grouping windows into sets related by their function. Users can move from room to room, with associated windows opening and closing as appropriate.

An issue touched upon elsewhere is that of group or social protocols. These are defined as 'mutually agreed upon ways of interacting'. They may be 'hard-wired' into the hardware and software of the system, in which case they are termed technological protocols, or left to the discretion of the users and referred to as social protocols. The most common protocol to be discussed and implemented in systems, is floor control. In GROVE, social protocols are used to govern the scrolling of shared windows. Any user can scroll such a window at any time, but this is disruptive to the other users viewing the window, and so the group members soon learn to add a verbal explanation before performing the action.

Concurrency control resolves conflicting operations performed simultaneously by the users. A number of approaches from distributed systems and CSCW have been developed to address this problem, including simple locking, transaction mechanisms, turn-taking protocols, centralized controllers, dependency detection, reversible execution, and operation transformations. All these approaches impinge on concurrency issues such as responsiveness, group interfaces, wide-area distribution, data replication, and robustness, which are exaggerated by real-time groupware. GROVE makes use of operation transformations, which the authors describe as dependency-detection with automatic conflict resolution. Each user has a local copy of the editor, on which their own operations are performed immediately. These operations are then broadcast to the rest of the group as a state vector, which includes information about operations processed recently from other users. Each editor compares the incoming state vectors with its own, and if they are the same, then the operation is performed as requested. If there is a difference, then the operation is transformed before execution, the transformation depending upon the type of operation, and a log of operations already performed.

Development has taken place on both personal computers, and UNIX workstations. The papers available are more concerned with the understanding of what is being supported, and reporting the results of evaluations, rather than any details of how the software has been implemented.

GROVE also provides features to support awareness of colleagues' work in a collaboratively-authored document outline. First, when a shared view of an outline is created, scanned-in images of the other group members in the subgroup (or their names if no images are available) are displayed at the bottom of the window. Further to this, they experimented with a 'cloudburst' model of multi-user text editing, which was made up of two techniques. The first technique 'ages' text, so that it gradually changes colour from light blue to black, the longer it is since it was entered. The second technique displays 'clouds' over regions of text that another group member is working on, with the cloud's position and size roughly indicating the location and extent of the editing. Once the modification is complete, as determined by the other user having stopped typing in that region, the change is broadcast to the other group members, and aged as above.

5.4.2 University of Calgary, Canada

The department of Computer Science at the University of Calgary has produced various researches into, and implementations of, synchronous CSCW. Greenberg examined synchronous, collaboration transparent use of single-user applications by multiple users, with the use of a group viewing system that allows choice of turn-taking protocol. Early research focussed on a drawing tool called GroupSketch, which later developed into GroupKit, a toolkit for developing synchronous CSCW, or groupware, applications. GroupSketch is a stand-alone real-time freehand drawing application that runs on Sun workstations.

The initial experiment with GroupSketch was implemented for Sun workstations using C. This has to be launched on the workstation with no windowing system running, and the application takes up the whole screen. Each user has a cursor which identifies them by name, and optionally with a caricature icon. The cursor can be used as a pencil, eraser, or large pointer, through the use of the three mouse buttons. A GroupSketch Registrar

Margin notes:

Groupware Toolkits (Gibbs, 1989)

Post-session Feedback (Rein, 1991)

Grouplab (Greenberg, 1992)

process must be running on one machine, and all users register with this process.

GroupKit provides support, in toolkit form, for the development of real-time 'work surfaces', with numerous activities supported. The developers have implemented paint programs, editors, brainstorming tools, and structuring tools, all for synchronous use by a distributed group.

Groupkit (Roseman and Greenberg, 1992)

GroupKit is a set of C++ classes and applications which provide 'common groupware components', and is based on the InterViews user interface toolkit, developed at Stanford University. GroupKit applications work on UNIX workstations, running X Windows. Each GroupKit application is based on a similar architecture to GroupSketch, that is, a single machine has a Registrar process running on it that all users register with centrally. One Registrar process exists for each installation, and each user can create one or more Registrar Client processes that implement particular registration policies and user interfaces. GroupKit applications are called Conferences, and they are controlled from a user's Registrar Client via a Coordinator process, which allows for multiple conferences with the same interface, membership, and so on. Users can therefore create a number of Registrar Clients for the various groups that they are a member of, and a number of shared applications for each group.

Personalizable Groupware, (Greenberg, 1991)

GroupKit also provides two types of overlays that can be used with any conference. These enable gestural communication through the use of multiple cursors, and annotative communication via freehand drawing. These overlays are transparent windows that are placed on top of a conference window, providing users with the capability to point or draw over the contents of a conference window without interfering with the application running in it.

It is assumed by the developers that an audio link is set up in parallel with a GroupKit-based application, such as using a conference call with speaker telephones.

5.4.3 NTT Human Interface Labs, Japan

Also looking at support for synchronous collaboration, Hiroshi Ishii at NTT Human Interface Labs has concentrated on providing rich communication channels to support 'seamless' CSCW, bridging the gap between CSCW shared workspaces, and what he terms 'interpersonal space'. He has built a number of prototype systems to support (predominantly) diads working on design tasks. TeamWorkStation is based on a personal computer, and ClearBoard is dedicated drawing board hardware and software.

Clearboard (Ishii *et al.*, 1992)

TeamWorkStation is intended to create an open shared workspace for a small group of users, typically two members, but possibly more. It does this by integrating the computers and the desktops of the collaborators. In doing so, it provides synchronous support for a distributed group, the members of which could be collaborating on any task. ClearBoard is more specifically targeted at a pair of collaborators, who are working together on a drawing board. Once again, the users are working synchronously whilst distributed geographically.

Characteristic of all of Ishii's prototypes is the highly interactive multimedia connection between users.

ClearBoard started as a simple vertical sheet of glass mock-up (ClearBoard-0), which the two users sat either side of and drew on the opposite sides. This was developed into the first distributed version (ClearBoard-1) which consisted of a configuration of video camera, half-mirror, polarising filters, and projection screen for each user. This simulated the physical presence of the users by projecting a video image of each user plus their part of the drawing to the other user, and vice versa. Users drew with colour markers directly onto the mirror surface. ClearBoard-2 went one step further, by making use of a multi-user paint program (TeamPaint, running on networked Macintosh computers) to overcome the difficulties with using marker pens. These included having to use thick pens because of low video resolution, which in turn caused problems with filling up the drawing area quickly, and also difficulties with recording and clearing the drawings. The image from TeamPaint is back-projected onto an angled projection sheet and glass drawing board, which also incorporates a digitizer sheet. The user 'draws' onto the board with a digitizer pen, which provides pen input to TeamPaint. A video camera situated above the angled board captures the image of the user and their gestures for transmission to the other user, and a video overlay board superimposes the images from the video cameras and TeamPaint. This combination provides each user with a projected image of a Macintosh Desktop running TeamPaint, superimposed with a (reversed) video image of their collaborator over the drawing in the TeamPaint window. What this, in turn, allows the users to do is to monitor where the other is directing his or her attention. Not only can the users make eye contact, they are also able to see where on the drawing the other user is looking, a phenomenon that Ishii calls gaze awareness. It is also possible to see other gestural information such as head movement and pointing with the hand or pen.

With TeamWorkStation, each user has an individual screen, and a shared screen, on two separate monitors, but contiguous in video memory. Therefore, a user can share a piece of their information by dragging it from individual to shared screen. Shared screen is strict WYSIWIS, with the individual screen relaxing the WYSIWIS space constraint. There are also two video cameras at each workstation, one for the user, and one for their desktop. Four networks connect each user, transmitting data from the computer, input devices, video, and audio (via speaker telephones). A number of different video overlay effects are possible, allowing, for example, one user's desktop image to be superimposed over another's computer windows on the shared screen. It is also possible to connect all the input devices to a single computer, whose screen is shown on the shared screen alone. This is useful for 'tightly coupled' tasks such as collaborative editing. The images

TeamWorkstation
(Ishii and Miyaki, 1992)

(Ishii and Arita, 1991)

of other users' faces can also be superimposed as small windows over the shared screen, allowing a view somewhat akin to that on ClearBoard. Their implementation of these video overlays depended upon the theory of selective attending, which accounts for our ability to choose which image to attend to when presented with more than one superimposed.

5.4.4 University of Arizona, USA

The systems produced at the University of Arizona's Department of Management Information Systems originated with the Arizona Planning Lab, or PLEXSYS. This is now known as GroupSystems, or under its guise as an IBM product, TeamFocus. They are real-time Electronic Meeting Systems (EMS), supporting brainstorming, description, and prioritization of ideas in 'anonymous' face-to-face sessions.

Meeting Systems (Nunamaker *et al.*, 1991)

The University of Arizona team coined the term Electronic Meeting Systems to describe the work that they were doing. In collaboration with IBM, they have implemented a number of meeting room facilities, complete with hardware and software at each seat, in order to support various sizes of meeting. The facilities are primarily used for 'same-time, same-place' meetings, with up to 48 team members supported, but other modes of work are possible.

(Dennis *et al.*, 1990)

GroupSystems is implemented as a number of facilities, each of which consists of a specially-designed meeting room, with networked PCs that are embedded into the work-tops, and large displays for the projection of public information.

(Valacich *et al.*, 1991)

GroupSystems tools are designed to 'deliver process-related structure to a meeting phase'. The authors define three distinct styles of meeting process, namely, chauffeured, supported, and interactive. These terms respectively denote the cases when only one person interacts with the system, as a scribe; when the whole group switches between talking together, and typing into the system; and when virtually all the group communication takes place via the system, with almost no verbal interaction. Furthermore, there are three areas supported by GroupSystems tools: session planning and management, group interaction, and organizational memory.

One tool, Session Manager (SM), is provided to support session planning and management, and is used primarily by the session facilitator. The tool has three components: pre-session planning, in-session management, and post-session organization. An electronic questionnaire is provided to ensure that no aspects of meeting planning are ignored, and an agenda tool assists with agenda development. In-session management is provided by the control menu, from which all GroupSystems tools are initialized, launched and closed. A task assignment tool records details about who is assigned to which task, and a read-only copy of this is made available to all participants.

Group interaction support is further divided into four areas: exploration and idea generation, idea organization, prioritizing, and policy development and evaluation. A number of tools are available under each heading, for example, four tools have been implemented to support idea generation. Electronic brainstorming (EBS) is an interactive process, in which users enter ideas on separate discussion topics, with each topic being held in a separate file. These files are shared randomly between the group members, such that each user has no control over which discussions they will receive. EBS provides two windows for a discussion; one is read-only, and contains previous comments in the discussion, while the other can be written to and allows the user (limited) space to enter their own comment. A user has only one discussion open at a time, and on entering a comment, the discussion file is written back to the file server in exchange for another. Electronic Discussion System (EDS) was developed for research use, and works in a similar manner to EBS. The major difference is that all comments can be stored in a single file, allowing all participants to join in to a single, unstructured, discussion.

Topic commenter (TC) also provides an interactive process, but in this case the discussions are displayed as a number of 'record cards' that each user may select in order to enter comments. In comparison to EBS, this allows the user to decide where they wish to comment, rather than being at the whim of the random allocation of discussions. Group outliner is similar to TC, but allows a set of cards to be developed by the group in a supported process, and then discuss them in an interactive process. The cards in this case may be organized into a hierarchical structure.

As for the rest of the group interaction support: idea organization is supported by the idea organizer, issue analyser and group writer; prioritizing by vote selection, alternative evaluator, group questionnaire and group matrix; and policy development and evaluation by Stakeholder Identification and Policy Formation. Each tool is designed to be used in a certain process, with participants expected to work as individuals in some situations, and as a group in others. The tools are selected with SM by the facilitator at the beginning of a session, depending on the task being performed.

Finally, support for organizational memory is provided by a number of tools that aim to provide task structure and task support. These tools are meant to move GroupSystems away from the common EMS situation where a meeting is viewed as an isolated entity, rather than a part of a larger whole. The tools do this by providing facilities to capture additions to organizational memory, and access to them in subsequent meetings. The tools are: Brief Case, Enterprise Analyser, Graphical Browser, and Group Dictionary.

5.4.5 Cooperative requirements capture, UMIST, Manchester

The CRC project has been a three-year collaborative project between ICL, Brameur, Human Technology, and UMIST's Department of Computation. It is essentially about providing support for distributed requirements capture teams and a prototype tool has been developed at UMIST.

The CRC prototype is intended to provide support for a requirements capture team that is at the earliest stage of identifying the requirements for a computer-based system. Macaulay puts the case for treating requirements capture as a cooperative activity, in contrast with more 'traditional' approaches. The prototype supports a fragment of a requirements capture method which gets the group to generate a list of objects for the proposed system and to describe them.

The CRC prototype has both centralized and distributed components. There is a central monitor process which runs on one machine and coordinates the activity of the users on their distributed workstations. Each workstation has the interface component of the prototype running, which provides the user with private and shared workspace, messaging capabilities, agenda information, and information about other group members. One user, the facilitator, has extra functionality provided in their interface in order to assist them in their role of supporting the group throughout the requirements process. This functionality included information about the group as a whole, and also about individual group members' activity on the system.

A distinction is made between group and personal messages. The former are analogous to notes in a computer conferencing system, being stored centrally and accessible at any time by any member of the group, while the latter are more like electronic mail. Standard X Windows editors are used for creating and editing text.

When generating ideas for objects, the group members make use of a brainstorming window which allows the entry of items to a shared list which is displayed in the public window. Once objects have been entered, descriptions can be supplied for them, once again using standard editors. These descriptions are displayed in separate windows, which can be dismissed or organized into a stack.

The prototype was developed on Sun SparcStations using X Windows and Franz Inc.'s Allegro Common Lisp and Common Windows, incorporating CLOS, the Common Lisp Object System. Most components in the prototype are stored and manipulated as CLOS objects, including users, messages and objects themselves.

In summary, the systems described above use different enabling technologies but all are considered to be CSCW systems. The design of the user interface to these systems is particularly difficult because of the many people who are potentially communicating with the system and with each other via the system at the same time. In order to gain a better understanding of the design issues, there follows a discussion of the role of the user interface. The author then attempts to draw out some of the general characteristics of CSCW user interfaces.

5.5 The role and characteristics of CSCW user interfaces

How is the CSCW
interface different
from a single-user
interface?

The role of the user interface in a single-user system is to support the interaction between the user and the system in order that the user can achieve his or her task. A CSCW user interface still needs to support users in this way but users will also need support in achieving their part in the group task.

5.5.1 The role of the CSCW user interface

The CSCW UI
supports the indi-
vidual task.

In a CSCW system, the role of user interface can be thought of as follows.

1. Supporting interaction between the user and the system in order that the user can achieve his or her individual task. (This is the same as for single-user systems.)

2. Supporting interaction between the user and the system in order that the user can achieve his or her part of the common task of the group. (This is different from single-user systems because the user is part of a group and the group itself has a task to achieve.)

The CSCW UI also
supports the shared
task.

3. Supporting social interaction between group members.
    (This is different from single-user systems because the user needs to communicate with other group members in order to achieve both the individual task and the common task.)

CSCW user interfaces generally combine the complexities of direct manipulation graphical user interfaces with multimedia and computer-mediated communication. From the user's point of view they also display the following five characteristics:

The CSCW UI also
supports interaction
between group
members.

1. *Order dependency*
    At the task level there may be some order dependency. For example, a meeting agenda prescribes which task should be performed and in what order.

The CSCW UI
combines GUIs,
multi-media and
computer-mediated
communication.

2. *Order-independence*
    At the dialogue level (within each task) the users can decide what to do and in what order. For example, users can send messages to any other user in any order and they can decide which objects to manipulate and in what order.

3. *Multithreading*
    Users may be involved in more than one 'thread of interaction' at once. For example, a user could be holding a discussion on more than one object at a time, moving freely between an editing window and a messaging window.

The dialogue does
not occur in any pre-
dictable sequence.

4. *Concurrency*
    Users may enter information in a private window at the same time as the

public window is being updated or at the same time as a message is being received. A multimedia user interface displaying animated images or outputting sound would result in additional concurrency.

There can be more than one thread of interaction at once.

5. *Sociability*

Users develop a sense of community or of being part of a group. They may have images, static or animated, of other group members or other ways of communicating with group members. The design of the user interface may add to or detract from the users' sense of sociability.

User interface design is particularly complex, and it is not at all clear that appropriate software tools are available to build such interfaces. For example, to what extent do current GUI toolkits enable us to build CSCW user interfaces? Do we need group widgets, for example, or WYSIWIS windows, group pointers or shared scroll bars? What dialogue specification techniques are appropriate? Will dialogue network diagrams suffice or are they only for sequential dialogues? Will object oriented be more appropriate? In the sections which follow, a method is described which will at least help the designer develop a specification of **what** needs to be designed, although the detailed design specification will depend on the tools available to build the user interface.

Many inputs to and outputs from the UI can occur at the same time.

5.6 A method of specifying and designing user interfaces to CSCW systems

The CSCW UI contributes to the sense of being part of a group.

Approaches to designing group user interfaces often make the assumption that a single-user interface will satisfy the needs of all the group members. While this may be sufficient for certain types of system, such as group editors, there are situations in which a number of distinct user interfaces will be required. Here, a method of specifying and designing multiple-user interfaces to a CSCW system is described. The objective of the method is to provide the designer with a way of thinking about the complexities of the situation and of identifying what needs to be designed.

First it is proposed that the designer undertakes an initial analysis of the group who are the intended users of the CSCW system and together with the group, identifies the overall role of the proposed system in supporting the group's work. Next an analysis of the users within the group is necessary in order to find out whether all the group members have the same role within the group. A user role is defined as a set of privileges and responsibilities attributed to a group member. Different user roles may well require different user interfaces to be designed or one user role may require different features from another. For example, a project manager may have different privileges and responsibilities than the other members of the team and may require views of group member progress and participation that other group members do not need.

CSCW UI design is complex and current GUI toolkits are inadequate.

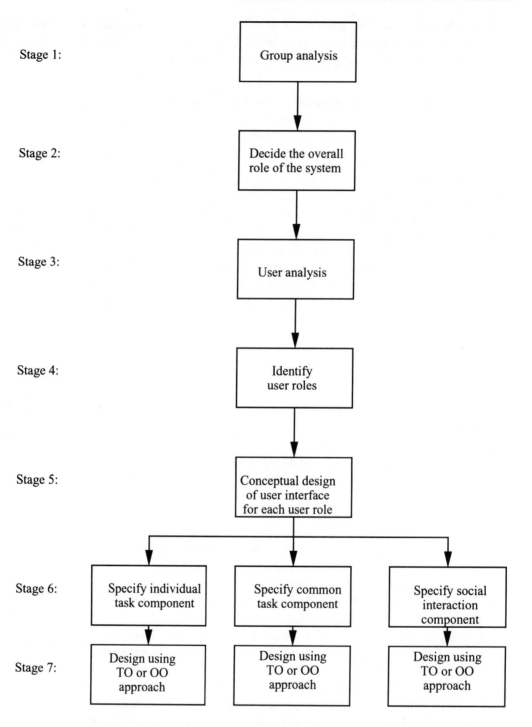

Figure 5.11 *Stages in specifying and designing user interfaces to a CSCW system.*

The next stage in the method is to develop the conceptual design of the user interface. If there is only one user role within the group, that is, all members have the same set of privileges and responsibilities, then there will only be one user interface to design. If there is more than one user role, then there will be one conceptual user interface design for each user role.

The conceptual design has three component parts. Firstly a description of the individual task component associated with the user role, secondly a description of the common task component and thirdly a description of the social interaction component. Once each component has been described the next stage is to develop a more detailed specification. These specifications will then form the basis for the more detailed design.

At this point, the designer must decide whether to proceed with a task-oriented approach to user interface design (section 3.6), or to proceed with an object-oriented approach (section 4.7) to user interface design. The design of each component will, of course, depend on the technologies available for building the proposed system. Thus at this point the designer needs to produce a design for each component using the specification of the user interface component together with a knowledge of the technology available for building that component. For example, for the social interaction component, in one situation, a basic e-mail system may be all that is available, whereas in another, a multimedia conferencing system may be available. It is at this point that the creative skills of the designer become paramount. Figure 5.11 provides a summary of the main stages.

Each stage is now described in more detail:

5.6.1 Stage 1: Group analysis

At this stage an analysis of the group is undertaken to a sufficient level of detail to enable the designer to describe the group, what the group members do and how they communicate with each other in the 'now' situation, that is, prior to use of the proposed computer support.

Group analysis falls into three parts: Firstly, a description of the group itself in terms of group mission, structure, location, size, dynamics (leadership style etc.) and cohesion. Secondly, the group task is described together with its characteristics such as task timing, fragmentation, task inputs and outputs, and other constraints such as costs or level of quality of work products. Finally, how communication and cooperation between group members is facilitated now is described, for example, through a project leader, memo passing, face-to-face meetings with a chair or facilitator, use of electronic mail or use of teleconferencing.

Having understood the 'now' situation, the next step is to identify what should change and what should remain the same in the 'proposed' situation i.e. when the group use the proposed computer support. In line with good HCI practice at this stage the acceptability of change to the group members

This method helps the designer to unravel some of the complexities.

and the costs and benefits of change to the organization would be considered. As a result of these analyses a description can be developed of the group and the group tasks that the system should support.

5.6.2 Stage 2: decide the overall role of the system

The next stage is to decide the overall role of the system in supporting social interaction. Here the designer needs to identify what level of facilitation of communication and cooperation will be needed. This will vary according to whether the group is working synchronously or asynchronously, distributed or face-to-face. The issue in question here is the protocol for interaction between group members. What are the current social protocols and to what extent should these be automated — that is, become technological protocols?

Identifying facilitation requirements leads to a debate concerning the role of the computer system in supporting cooperation. Such questions as: should decision making be automated through enforced voting or should group members reach decisions through discussion and be allowed to develop their own social protocols? Should turn taking be enforced when editing documents? Should the system be designed such that one member always leads the group or should leadership be distributed among all members?

5.6.3 Stage 3: user analysis

The next step is to consider each of the members within the group and to develop an understanding of each user and his or her task needs. The 'typical' group members must first be identified and each one described in terms of knowledge, skills, experience, motivation, what task(s) can be undertaken and his or her contribution to the group task.

5.6.4 Stage 4: identify user roles

The term role is used here in the sense described in CSCW literature, and refers to a set of privileges and responsibilities attributed to a person. This step requires identification of the number of distinct roles which can be attributed to group members. There may be five group members but only one distinct role; for example, in the GROVE editor described earlier in this chapter, there is only one role, since all group members have access to the same set of privileges and responsibilities. There may officially be a head of a group but within GROVE the head only has the same privileges as other members. If the head of the group was given a distinct set of privileges and responsibilities, this would constitute a distinct role.

Role identification is concerned with identifying the number of distinct sets of privileges and responsibilities associated with the users of the proposed system.

5.6.5 Stage 5: conceptual design of the user interface for each user role

Figure 5.12 shows the main components in the conceptual design of the user interface.

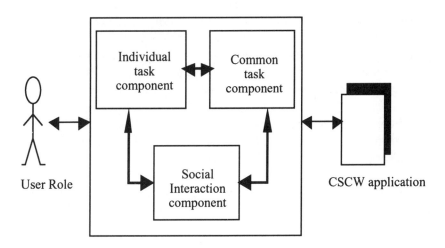

Figure 5.12 *Conceptual design of the user interface for each user role.*

The individual task component supports that part of the user interface which deals with the user's individual task. For example, the user may need to create a draft of a part of a document before presenting it to the group for consideration. In doing so, access to other personal applications may be required. The user interface may need to allow the user to switch from one work area to another, and to provide support for the user to 'tidy up' each work area before moving on to the next. The user interface may need to support the transfer of objects from the individual work area to the common work area.

The common task component supports that part of the user interface which deals with the common task of the group. This might include support for the workprocess, for example, through displaying an agenda or a project plan. It will include for the work content, for example, the use of shared editors or drawing tools and the provision and maintenance of a public window.

The social interaction component supports social interaction between team members. The user interface may include images of group members, conferencing facilities, decision support facilities, shared pointers, facilities for setting and agreeing on social protocols.

5.6.6 Stage 6: specify individual task component, specify common task component, specify social interaction component.

Specify individual task component. This could take the form of a written description, task hierarchies or an object model.

Specify common task component. Similarly, this could take the form of a written description, task hierarchies or an object model.

Specify social interaction component. In addition to the use of a public screen, what other mechanisms are needed to facilitate cooperation between group members? For example, restricted access to subgroups, cooperative editing, monitoring and feedback of participant activity. This component will include a detailed description of these components.

5.6.7 Stage 7: design each component using a TO or OO approach

At this point the designer must decide whether to proceed with a task-oriented approach to user interface design (section 3.6) or to proceed with an object-oriented approach (section 4.7) to user interface design. The design of each component will, of course, depend on the technologies available for building the proposed system. Thus at this point the designer needs to produce a design for each component using the specification of the user interface component, together with a knowledge of the technology available for building that component.

The next section uses a case study to illustrate the suggested approach to specifying and designing user interfaces to CSCW systems

5.7 A case study in user interface design for a CSCW system

5.7.1 Background to the case study

The cooperative requirements capture (CRC) project was concerned with the development of computer support for a multidisciplinary team whose members actively collaborate in the capture of requirements for a proposed computer system. Typically, this team will have an initial formulative face-to-face meeting and will then return to their respective places of work. Thus, they will be geographically distributed and will often need to work asynchronously.

5.7.2 Stage 1: group analysis

A general description of the CRC team was given earlier in this chapter. In summary, our 'proposed' system should support synchronous or asynchronous working for a distributed, multidisciplinary group. The size of the group will vary from five to 12; they are not a cohesive group but only meet to achieve the requirements capture task. They are constrained by cost, time and quality of the work-product. They must also reach a consensus on the content of the work-product, that is, the requirements document.

5.7.3 Stage 2: decide the overall role of the system

In the CRC project we modelled our approach to facilitation of cooperation on the scenario of face-to-face meetings which are managed by a professional human facilitator. In the CRC project it was thought important to emulate social protocols which occur in a face-to-face meeting. For example, decisions will be reached by discussion rather than by use of, say, computer-supported decision-making techniques.

It should support the following user tasks:

1. Producing a list of objects.

2. Analysing the list of objects (i.e. discussing, withdrawing/adding items on the object list).

3. Facilitating social interaction between team members.

Tasks 1 and 2 use social interaction techniques of brainstorming to produce the object list, and discussion for evaluating the list.

Brainstorming
Brainstorming was identified as a suitable technique for allowing CRC team members to contribute suggestions in order to build up a single list of system objects. The characteristics of brainstorming are the rapid generation of a single pool of ideas by individual group members, with evaluation and criticism being discouraged at this stage. Therefore the interface for brainstorming needs to provide the members of a distributed team with a means of inputting a suggested object at their terminal, and sending it to update a common area seen by all team members.

Discussion and analysis
To enable group members to agree on the list of objects produced by brainstorming, it was decided to provide computer support for discussion between members, allowing them to send messages to each other in a similar way to a mail tool. After the brainstorming session is over, members may propose amendments to the object list in the form of a message sent to the other team members. Comments on the proposal can then be contributed in the form of replies, linked to the proposal and to other related replies, so that the discussion can be followed and the evolution of objects and their descriptions can be traced. It is normally possible to reach a consensus by this method, but the facilitator may intervene if necessary.

Facilitating social interaction
In addition to brainstorming and analysis, the prototype also supports facilitation of social interaction between team members. This takes the form of specific support for a human facilitator. In particular, the facilitator will set the agenda for the group to follow, that is, what they should do, associated time constraints and with what outcomes or deliverables. The facilitator

monitors the group progress through the task, getting feedback from the system as to the activity of the group members. In addition to monitoring the group, the facilitator may choose to intervene in order to resolve any problem occurring between team members.

5.7.4 Stage 3: user analysis

Each team member or 'stakeholder' has a particular motivation for being involved in the requirements capture process and will have specific objectives they wish to maximize. They each also have certain knowledge and experience to contribute. Stakeholders will typically be senior designers, systems analysts, market or business analysts, user managers, user representatives or project managers. They will typically be senior members of staff experienced in requirements capture and in idea formulation. They will also be experienced in team working, often acting as project managers themselves. Figure 5.13 shows a summary of the user analysis.

Users	Motivation	Knowledge and skills	Contribution to the common task
Software designer(1)	To produce a technically excellent system	In latest techniques and creative design skills	Suggest objects, discuss them and agree upon a final list
Software designer(2)	To reuse existing software tools or designs	Knowledge of existing systems	Suggest objects, discuss them and agree upon a final list
Systems analyst	To produce requirements specification on time	Expertise in problem analysis	Suggest objects, discuss them and agree upon a final list
Technical author	To develop learning materials which meet user needs	Authoring skills, documentation design	Suggest objects, discuss them and agree upon a final list
User representative	To introduce change with minimum disruption and maximum benefit	Knowledge of organization, users and tasks	Suggest objects, discuss them and agree upon a final list
Training and User support staff	Support existing accounts generate future revenue	Knowledge of current user problems	Suggest objects, discuss them and agree upon a final list
Business/market analyst	To be 'better' than the competition	Knowledge of business/ market needs	Suggest objects, discuss them and agree upon a final list
Project manager	To complete the project successfully within given resources	Knowledge of project planning and of previous overrun projects	Suggest objects, discuss them and agree upon a final list
Professional facilitator	To help the group reach an agreed outcome	Social skills knowledge of the method	Manage the agenda, encourage participation and intervene if any problems occur

Figure 5.13 *Summary of user analysis.*

5.7.5 Stage 4: identify user roles

Within the CRC project there are two distinct roles: the stakeholder role and the facilitator role. Although the stakeholders are from a diversity of backgrounds and are quite different in terms of knowledge and expertise, as far as the particular task of requirement capture is concerned their roles are similar. Each stakeholder has a responsibility to contribute his or her knowledge and expertise, to participate actively and to cooperate with other team members. Each stakeholder has access to the same shared information, has the same rights to amend information and the same communication rights.

The facilitator role on the other hand has a different set of privileges and responsibilities. The facilitator has the responsibility of setting the agenda, identifying when a problem is arising between group members and to intervene and propose a strategy for solution. The facilitator is afforded certain privileges by other group members in that they look to this person for arbitration and leadership on what to do next.

5.7.6 Stage 5: conceptual design of the user interface for each user role

The user interface for the facilitation role
Individual task component. The facilitator must start the 'meeting', introduce group members, state the objectives, set the agenda, review progress of the group, intervene when necessary and close the 'meeting'.

Common task component. The facilitator does not have an active part in the common task because he or she is not a member of the requirements capture team,. The facilitator is external to the team and brought in specifically to help members arrive at an agreed set of requirements.

Social interaction component. The facilitator will need to follow the agenda and respond to requests from group members.

The user interface for the stakeholder role
Individual task component. Each stakeholder will be responsible for brainstorming a list of objects, which can be viewed by other group members and added to the overall list of objects.

Common task component. Each stakeholder will need to review the object list generated by the group members, request object descriptions, provide object descriptions, discuss amendments of objects and respond to proposals made by other group members.

Social interaction component. Each stakeholder will need to follow the agenda, to respond to any facilitator requests, to respond to requests from other group members, to inform the facilitator of any problems and to take part in group discussions.

5.7.7 Stage 6: specify individual task component, specify common task component, specify social interaction component.

Each component is described here using a task hierarchy.

Facilitator user interface
The individual task component for the facilitator is shown in Fig. 5.14.

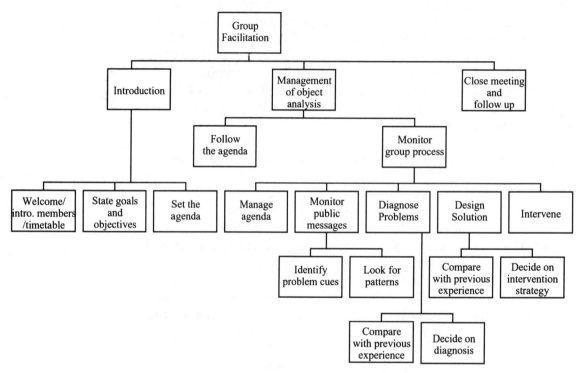

Figure 5.14 *Individual task model for the facilitator.*

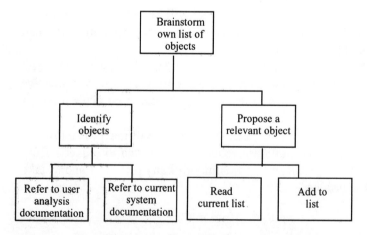

Figure 5.15 *Stakeholder's individual task component.*

Stakeholder user interface
The individual task component for the stakeholder is shown in Fig. 5.15.

The common task component for the stakeholder is shown in Fig. 5.16.

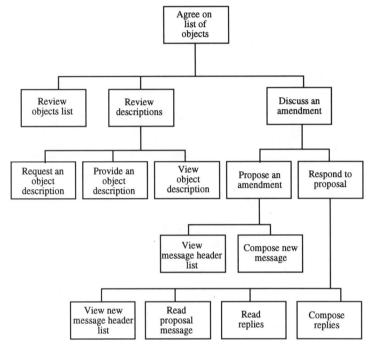

Figure 5.16 *Common task component for the stakeholder.*

5.7.8 Stage 7: design each component using a TO or OO approach
In the CRC project an object-oriented approach was adopted. Below is a description of the prototype and an example screen showing the facilitator's user interface and a stakeholder's user interface.

Overview of the prototype
The system consists of a central component — the monitor — which performs the routing of messages and the maintenance of the object and message bases. These are the repositories within which are stored the objects and messages that have been generated by the team using the prototype. There is also a distributed component of the prototype for each stakeholder that uses it. This runs locally on the stakeholders' machines, and provides them with functions for message exchange, and for interacting with the shared workspace. This distributed part of the system is the user interface and is identical for all the stakeholders.

Figure 5.17 provides a schematic overview of the main features of the prototype showing several team members and a facilitator logged onto the prototype. The prototype has been designed using a client-server model in which there is a central resource through which all communications are sent and data is redirected to its intended destination.

A further feature of the design is that the user interfaces are designed as separate modules and hence when running the CRC prototype on a team member's workstation only the user interface module needs to be mounted. This will enable the user to simply open the CRC window alongside other unrelated applications. In particular, the design of the software is such that the interface modules could be written in different languages or mounted on different host machines.

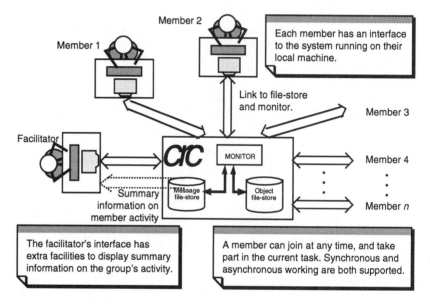

Figure 5.17 *Schematic of CRC prototype.*

In the CRC project the stakeholder role was provided with a public window for viewing the objects generated by the group; a brainstorming window for adding objects; group and personal communication windows for message passing and composition, with associated message viewing windows; an agenda window to display information on the current task and timing, and a group members' window for interactions with other stakeholders. A typical screen is shown in Fig. 5.18

The facilitator role also had a public window in order to view the outputs from the group; windows for message passing and viewing as for the stakeholder role; an agenda window to allow updating of task and timing information and a group members' window for interactions with the other group members, and to allow the facilitator to access further information about the group's activity. A typical screen is shown in Fig. 5.19.

A more detailed description of the user interface is provided below.

The CRC prototype is a single window, taking up almost the whole screen. It contains a number of 'child' windows.

The group communication window
This window is situated in the middle of the main window above the personal communication window. It functions in an identical way to the personal communication window, except that new messages are loaded automatically as they arrive. A separate message viewer window is provided for displaying the contents of messages.

CRC agenda window
This window is situated at the bottom-right of the main window, and is used to display messages about the current and future tasks to be performed.

The public window
This is the uppermost window on the right-hand side of the main window. Its purpose is to display items that are shared amongst the whole group; it therefore always displays the same information on each of the group members' screens. The items that it displays are objects that have been generated as part of the brainstorming session, and are represented as 'active regions' in the inner region of the window.

Description windows
A description window is created for an object in the public window by selecting the object with the mouse. The windows are created in a 'stack' on the left-hand side of the main window, and the system provides a number of functions to help with managing them.

The brainstorming window
This window is situated in the upper-middle of the main window, directly to the left of the public window. It is used during the brainstorming phase of a group session to allow group members to enter their ideas into the system, for display on the public window. It maintains a private copy of all the objects generated in a single session by that user.

The CRC group members' window
This window appears bottom-left in the main window, and contains a sub-region for each group-member, the facilitator, and the group as a whole (the 'table'). There is a menu associated with each user icon and with the table icon. Small icons which appear near a group member's head indicate what that member is doing at the time. A pair of glasses means that the group member is reading a message, a light bulb means that they are engaged in brainstorming and an exclamation mark means that the system cannot work out what the user is doing!

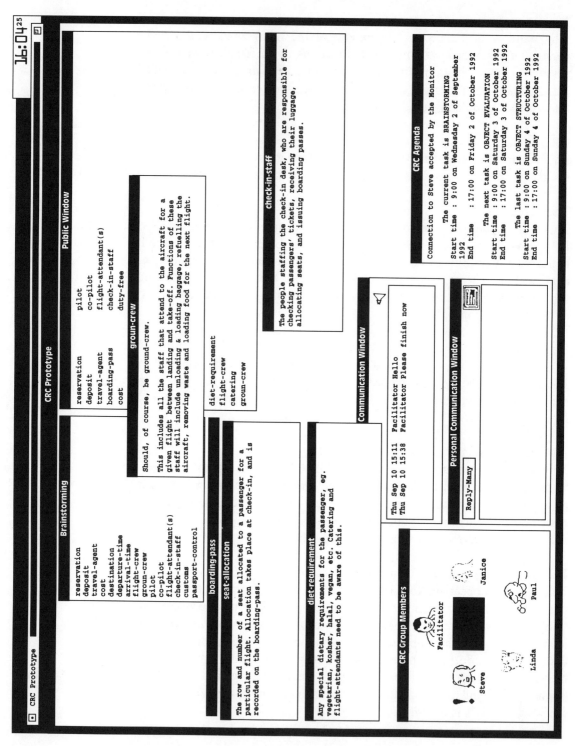

Figure 5.18 *A stakeholder screen providing object descriptions for an airline reservation system.*

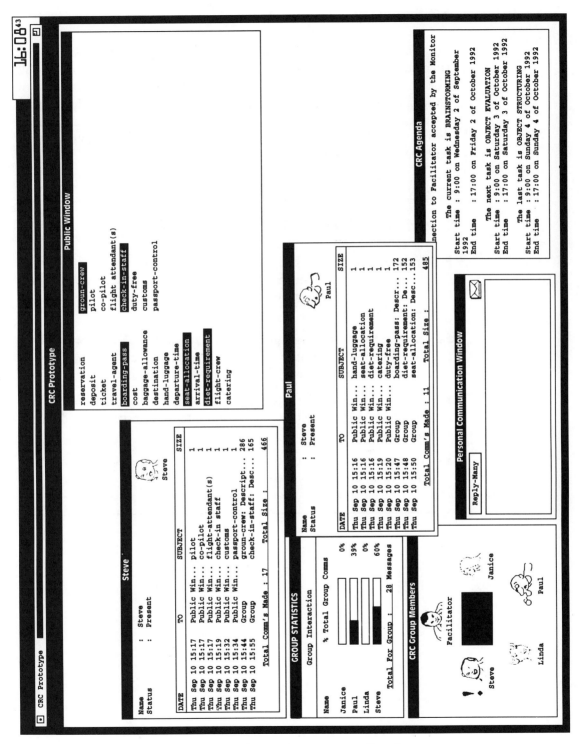

Figure 5.19 *The facilitator user interface a few minutes after the screen shown in Fig. 5.18.*

5.8 Summary

This chapter has provided a brief introduction CSCW systems and has attempted to provide some understanding of the characteristics of CSCW user interfaces. In order to assist the designer in the complex task of designing such user interfaces an approach to specifying and designing user interfaces to CSCW has been suggested. This approach provides a means of dealing with the complexities in smaller 'chunks' and was illustrated with reference to a particular case study.

Exercises for Chapter 5

5.1 Computer support for cooperative working can be broadly categorized into: support for face-to-face meetings; support for electronic meetings and support between meetings. Briefly describe one example of a system in each category.

5.2 Suppose you were designing a Group Editor. What are the major HCI issues you would consider? Include in your answer factors relating to the group window and views of the shared environment.

5.3 Give three major differences between designing user interfaces to support group working and designing user interfaces to support individual working.

5.4 Name and describe five principles of good user interface design which apply to all computer-based systems.

Chapter 6

Usability

The objectives of this chapter are:

- ☐ to distinguish between 'easy to use' and usability;
- ☐ to discuss the user, customer and designer view of usability;
- ☐ to introduce usability specification in terms of objectives and success criteria;
- ☐ to review briefly the techniques for usability evaluation;
- ☐ to illustrate how to plan a usability evaluation;
- ☐ to introduce ISO standards associated with usability.

6.1 Introduction

It is now generally understood that computer systems should be designed to be 'easy to use'; indeed ease of use is often a key factor in marketing systems. What is less well understood is the actual meaning of 'easy to use'. When a product is marketed as 'easy to use', does it mean that it is easy for anyone to use, in any situation, no matter what they are doing or what knowledge and skills they possess? Has the product been tested for ease of use and if so, with whom and under what circumstances?

What does 'easy to use' mean? Does it mean the system will be easy to learn for first-time users? Does it mean that experienced users will be able to use the system very quickly? Does it mean that the system is actually effective in supporting the user in their job? Does it mean that users enjoy using the system?

In the HCI community, the term **usability** is preferred to 'ease of use'.

The definition of usability includes ease of learning, ease of use, flexibility of use, effectiveness of use and user satisfaction with the system. Below is a definition of usability.

Usability includes ease of learning, ease of use, flexibility of use, user satisfaction and effectiveness of use.

Definition of usability
(ISO CD 9241-11.3, version 8.8, May 1993)

Usability is the effectiveness, efficiency and satisfaction with which specified users can achieve specified goals in particular environments.

Effectiveness is the accuracy and completeness with which users achieve specific goals.

Techniques for specifiying and measuring usability are described.

Efficiency is the accuracy and completeness of goals achieved in relation to resources expended.

Satisfaction is the comfort and acceptability of using the system.

Later sections in this chapter explain the definition in some detail and identify how to specify usability for a given system and what techniques can be used to measure whether usability has been achieved. The use of appropriate HCI standards can contribute significantly to the capability of designing a usable system and a section on standards is included in this chapter. The final section includes a case study of usability evaluation.

First, there is a discussion of the importance of usability to the user and to the customer, and an introduction to usability evaluation from the designer's point of view.

6.2 The user's, customer's and designer's viewpoint

The customer has different requirements at different stages of their usage cycle.

Figure 6.1 shows the customer usage cycle. At each stage in the cycle the customer will have different requirements with respect to the usability of a system.

At the 'needs assessment' stage, the customer will have identified the need for a new system to support some business requirement. Here the supplier will need to demonstrate the system to the customer and it is critical that the users can see an effective demonstration of key features. Given that the customer purchases the system, the next stage is 'installation'. The user must unpack and install the system, and it is critical that this can be done successfully and in the shortest possible time. Once the system is installed the users must learn to use the system features in order to perform their job. Thus at the 'introduction and training' stage the system must be easy to learn, and any supporting materials must be consistent with the software and training courses.

At the 'limited usage' stage, users will be left alone to use the system and will be expected to perform their jobs effectively. Thus ease of use and speed of completing most frequently-performed tasks become critical. At the next

stage, 'full usage', the users will be expected to make full use of all the
system features provided and to exploit the full potential of the system. Here
it is critical that users can explore system features which they are unfamiliar
with and that they can find out from the system itself how best to exploit its
capabilities.

Three main stages
are introduction and
training, limited
usage and full
usage.

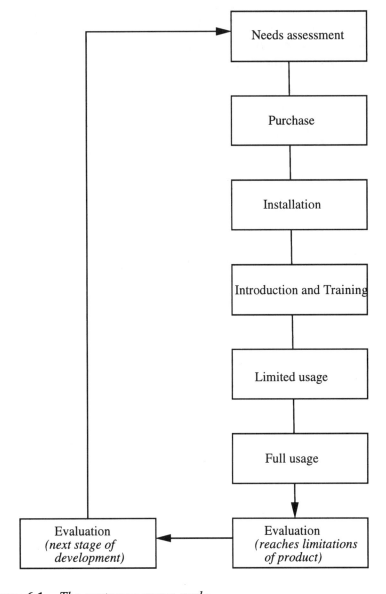

Figure 6.1 *The customer usage cycle.*

Once the users have fully exploited the features of the system and their job
needs change and develop, the customer goes through a period of 'evaluation'. The limits of the current system have been reached and the customer

is looking towards the next stage of computer support, and the next purchase.

Poor usability represents a cost to suppliers as well as customers.

At each stage in the customer usage cycle there are different usability requirements. For example, at the introduction stage, ease of learning is critical; at the limited usage stage, ease of use is critical; at the full usage stage, speed of performance is critical.

At each stage in the usage cycle the customer will be evaluating the system in terms of value for money. Depending on their experience with the system their perception of value may increase or decrease. Figure 6.2 attempts to show the costs of poor usability to the customer and the supplier.

Users may not be able to find out how to use features which are available.

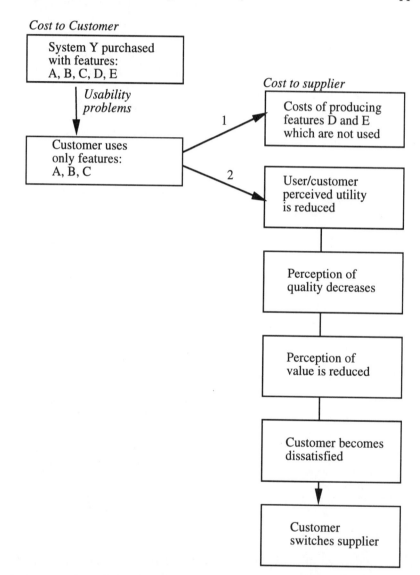

Customers and users may become dissatisfied.

Figure 6.2 *Costs of poor usability to the customer and the supplier.*

First of all, a cost to the customer is incurred when purchasing the system. Suppose a customer has purchased system Y because it has features A,B,C,D and E. The system is installed, the users are trained to use it and they go through the 'limited usage' stage using features A,B and C which they were taught on the training course. However, they are unable to reach the 'full usage' stage, either because they are unable to find out whether the system supports features D and E, or how to use these features if they do find them — or perhaps they are not even aware that if they were to use features D and E, they would significantly improve their performance. These are considered to be usability problems.

Thus the customer has purchased a system with features A,B,C,D and E but the users can only use A,B and C. This is not only a cost to the customer but also a cost to the supplier. The supplier has produced features D and E which are not used, and has therefore wasted development time and effort.

The customer on the other hand perceives that the system cannot perform features D and E and their perception of the usefulness of the system is reduced — it is not the system they thought they had purchased. The customer becomes dissatisfied with the product and when the 'evaluation' stage of the customer usage cycle is reached, the customer switches to a different supplier.

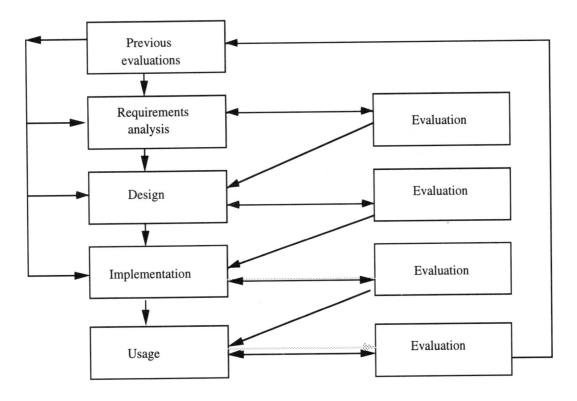

Figure 6.3 *The design life cycle and the role of evaluation.*

Thus usability problems not only incur costs to the users and customers but also to the suppliers of systems. A supplier should seek to ensure that the users have positive usability experiences at each stage in their usage cycle.

Suppliers must identify and create positive usability experiences.

Usability specification is concerned with identifying, for a given situation, what will constitute a positive usability experience. Usability evaluation is concerned with testing a prototype or a system to find out whether it is usable according to the specification.

Figure 6.3 shows when usability evaluations can be carried out. Different evaluation techniques will be used depending on the stage of the design lifecycle at which the system is tested.

Specifying and measuring usability can also do the following.

1. Help the customer to select products by comparing effectiveness, efficiency and satisfaction in two products when they are used in the same context.

Measures of usability can help the customer distinguish between two products.

2. Help the design teams to recognize the breadth of design issues associated with usability.

3. Help the supplier and customer when specifying requirements for the procurement of custom built-systems.

6.3 Usability specification

Testing for usability, or usability evaluation as it is more generally referred to, can only take place if there are some objectives or targets which are to be tested. The first stage, therefore, is to specify the usability objectives for the system. Usability specification must start with an understanding of the users and their tasks and identification of those tasks which are to be shared between user and computer. It is the shared tasks for which usability will be an issue, since it is in carrying out these tasks that the user is actually using the system.

The first stage is to specify usability objectives.

Usability specification should take place as part of system design. Usability objectives should be set as part of the requirements for the system so that the designer can design the system and the user interface with these objectives in mind. For example, contrast usability objective 1 with objective 2:

Usability objective 1: 'The CAL system to teach Stage 5, part 4 Mathematics must be capable of being used by schoolchildren aged eight, without reference to manuals and with no teacher intervention. It must enable the children to learn the key points of the part 4 lesson within 15 minutes, and 80% of the children should enjoy using it.'

Usability objectives are dependent upon the context of use.

Usability objective 2: 'The bank teller system should support tellers in answering customer enquiries by telephone. The teller will be given a one week training course, followed by one month on-the-job training and will have a supporting reference manual. After the training period, the teller should be able to deal with 85% of customer enquiries within three minutes.'

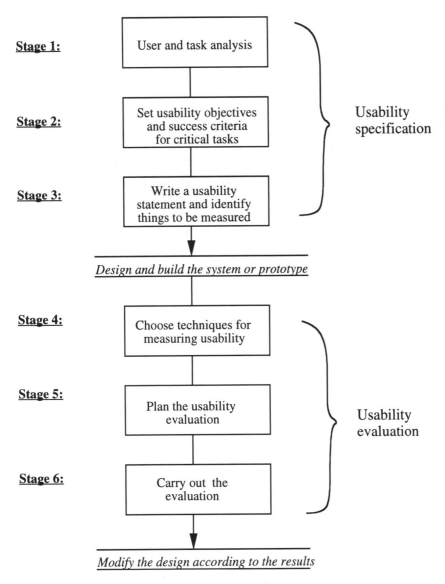

Figure 6.4 *The main stages in usability specification and evaluation.*

Objective 1 might lead to the designer to consider a multi-media user interface with graphics and sound supporting the key points of the lesson. The system may also need to be highly interactive, so that the child can be tested to see if the key points have been learnt. The key aspects of objective 1 are user enjoyment and effectiveness.

In contrast, user enjoyment is not an objective for the bank teller system; rather, speed and effectiveness are the main factors. In contrast to the CAL system, the user interface is not the only source of user support — the

Usability objectives
are also design
objectives.
designer can rely on additional support for the user from the training courses and manuals. The user will also need to speak to the bank customer at the same time as using the system, so speed of system response will be paramount. The designer might consider a user interface with minimal keyboard input, driven mainly by mouse control, with rapid routes through different sources of information.

The usability objectives provide key requirements for the design. The software designer needs to be clear what the objectives are before design begins.

The remainder of this chapter is concerned with the main stages associated with usability specification and usability evaluation. In essence, usability specification is about identifying critical success factors and usability evaluation is about measuring them.

The main stages in usability specification and evaluation are shown in Fig. 6.4 and are described in the sections which follow.

6.4 Stage 1: user and task analysis

A usability objective:
who are the users,
what are their
characteristics, what
tasks do they carry
out, under what
circumstances and
with what success
criteria?
A usability objective is a statement of who the users are; their characteristics; what tasks they are undertaking; under what circumstances they are undertaking the tasks and what the success criteria are.

The techniques for understanding users given in Chapter Two can be used to provide a statement of who the users are, their characteristics and tasks.

The circumstances under which the tasks are carried out can include the physical environment or the learning support. Some typical examples of systems, user characteristics and environments are given below:

Office systems

Systems	Database systems, spreadsheets, management information systems, decision support systems.

Some users are
discretionary users.

Users	Users can be expected to devote effort to learning the basics of the technology if it is central to their work. Some discretionary and intermittent users. Users can be expected to have basic keyboard skills and/or be familiar with other input devices.
Environment	Support available from colleagues. Likely to be a 'local expert'. Plenty of documentation and manuals. Telephone 'hot lines' often available.

Public information systems or walk-up-and-use systems

Systems	Automatic teller machines, public information databases, home teleshopping, automatic ticket machines.
Users	Members of the public who have a wide variety of skills,

knowledge and physical capabilities. Many intermittent, discretionary and casual users. Users may not possess keyboard skills, mouse skills or other specific interaction techniques.

Some users are casual users.

Environment
Little opportunity to provide user support. Users cannot be expected to read large amounts of documentation before using the system. Rarely a 'local expert' to help. Highly variable environment in terms of cost, ease of access and time constraints.

Knowledge-based systems

Systems
Planning, diagnostic and advice-giving systems.

Users
Users may be experts in their field, using an expert system to help in decision making and are therefore expected to devote energy to learning the system. Alternatively, users may be novices in the field seeking to obtain expertise, and may be casual users.

Some users are experts in their field.

Environment
Usually access is provided to on-line help and other user support. The documentation may be difficult to understand because of the size of these systems. In-depth training courses may be needed for first-time users.

Complex, real-time systems

Systems
Control systems used in civilian and military aircraft, large plant processing and monitoring systems (as used in nuclear and chemical power stations, oil-rigs), missile and rocket guidance systems. Known as safety-critical systems where safety is paramount.

Some users are highly trained.

Users
Users typically highly trained. Have to monitor many aspects of the systems simultaneously. Have to deal with the demands of real-time control. No discretionary or casual users.

Environment
General support unlikely to be available. Considerable training required to be used effectively. Many things may be happening extremely quickly.

Some users are novices.

Computer supported cooperative work (CSCW)

Systems
Electronic mail (e-mail), electronic conferencing, electronic meetings, joint authoring systems.

Users
Many casual and novice users. Likely to be many discretionary users, because other methods of working can offer alternatives.

Environment   After initial training, on-line support must be available. Cooperative setting may provide 'local expert' assistance.

The above examples illustrate how the user characteristics and environments will vary from system to system. However, it is not sufficient for the designer to think only in terms of the general characteristics that typical systems display but they must also understand users within a specific setting.

6.5 Stage 2: setting usability objectives and success criteria

A usability objective must have associated success criteria, which are capable of measurement.

Each usability objective must have associated success criteria, which is capable of measurement. Examples of success criteria include:

- 85% of users enjoy using the system.
- Users can recall 70% of system commands after two weeks of not using the system.
- Users can learn to use 75% of the systems features within 15 minutes.

Success criteria must be stated in such a way that they are capable of being measured; for example, through user opinion survey, through observation or through laboratory-based experiments.

Usability objectives may be different for different stages of the customer usage sycle.

Usability objectives may be set for different stages of the customer usage cycle (Fig. 6.1). For example, learning objectives may be set for the introduction and training stage, effectiveness objectives may be set for the limited usage stage or efficiency objectives may be set for when the system is fully in use.

Usability objectives relate to specific tasks.

Usability objectives will be related to specific tasks as well as specific users. It is normally not practical to set objectives for every shared task because of the costs associated with undertaking an evaluation. Some tasks will be more important than others, depending on the situation in which the system is being developed. Examples of reasons for selecting tasks are:

- *Competitive edge*
  Usability in some particular aspect of the system may differentiate your system from a competitor's system. For example, one theatre booking system may take two days for users to learn to book seats, whereas another might take only one hour.
- *Market requirements*
  For some types of system, usability is a prerequisite because all other systems of that type are usable. For example, automatic telling machines must be usable otherwise they simply would not get used.

Some tasks will be more 'important' than others.

- *Tasks performed first*
  Often the users' first impression of a system can be a key factor. If users have a good experience with the first task they attempt, they are more likely to be positive towards the rest of the system, or it may be that the

users' experience with the first task will be a deciding factor in purchasing the system.

- *Tasks performed most frequently*
  Once the system is in use, the task performed most frequently becomes critical. If a user is performing a routine operation 100 times a day, then it is important whether the operation takes three minutes or 30 seconds. Efficiency becomes a key usability objective.

A task may be 'important' because it is performed most frequently or because it is the first task to be performed.

Other usability objectives may be related to, for example, tasks where, if errors were made, the integrity of data would be affected, or tasks which are safety critical.

Figure 6.5 shows, for a given system only, how a small number of usability objectives should be set. Certain critical tasks should be chosen, here tasks 3, 8 and 9, and specific objectives set depending upon the stage of usage.

Usage cycle / Task	Introduction and training	Limited usage	Full usage
Task 3	Effectiveness Satisfaction		
Task 8			Efficiency
Task 9		Effectiveness	

Figure 6.5 *Usability objectives are set for critical tasks.*

Usability objectives should be set for 'critical' tasks.

Examples of usability objectives:

- *Objective: efficiency, usage cycle: full usage*
  Estate agent clerks with little or no computing experience, in a busy office environment, should be able to match a client to a suitable available house within five seconds.

- *Objective: effectiveness, usage cycle: introduction and training*
  Theatre booking clerks with low motivation, no computing experience
  and no previous training, working in a small and hectic box office are able
  to learn to reserve seats within a one hour period.

6.6 Stage 3: Writing usability statements and identifying measures

A usability statement provides requirements for the design.

Writing a statement specifying usability should be part of the requirements process. A typical usability statement should include:

1. Title, purpose and brief description of the system.

2. A description of the intended users and their characteristics (for example, knowledge, skills, motivation).

3. A brief description of the shared tasks and their characteristics (for example, frequency, timing).

4. A brief description of the equipment to be used, hardware, software and any other items.

5. A description of the environment (for example, physical, learning and support environment, workplace conditions).

6. A specification of the usability objectives for a particular context.

There are ISO standards for writing usability statements.

A specific ISO standard called 'Guidance on Specifying and Measuring Usability', Part 11 of the ISO 9241 standard *Ergonomics Requirements for Office Work with Visual Display Terminals*, addresses the problem of usability statements. The designer is advised to obtain the latest version of this standard from his/her local ISO Standards Office.

ISO CD 9241-11.3 ,v8.8, May 93 states that:

Products have no intrinsic usability.

The objective of designing and evaluating for usability is to meet the needs of users to achieve their goals.

The specification and evaluation of usability has to be placed in the context of an overall system consisting of the users, tasks, equipment (hardware, software and materials), and the physical and social environments which influence the interaction.

Part 11 of the ISO 9241 explains the way in which these components of the context of use should be described and how usability can be specified or evaluated. The standard deals with usability in terms of user needs. It emphasizes that products have no intrinsic usability because usability is determined by the characteristics of the users, tasks and environments in addition to the characteristics of the product itself.

Usability objectives provide a statement of the success criteria associated with the usability of the system in a given context. The statement should include a description of what has to be measured. It may be user satisfaction — for example, the fact that 85% of users enjoy using the system — or it may be effectiveness — for example, the fact that staff can learn to reserve seats within one hour. In the first example, users' enjoyment of the system must be measured; in the second example, the time taken to complete a task must be measured. Each usability objective must contain a statement of the thing to be measured.

A usability statement includes a description of what has to be measured.

Further examples of things which can be measured include:

- number of keystrokes;
- number of commands used;
- number of user actions required to complete a task;
- time taken to perform keystrokes, commands or tasks;
- time taken to learn a set of commands;
- number of commands remembered;
- knowledge of system use;
- attitudes and opinions;
- availability of support materials;
- errors: of understanding, typographical;
- time to recover from errors.

Success criteria and measures.

The usability statement which includes the usability objectives and the things to be measured provide the designer with clear design objectives. A prototype may then be developed to test some aspect of the system design or a version of the full system may be developed straight away. In either case, the next stage is to consider how the system or prototype should be tested to find out whether usability objectives have been met.

6.7 Stage 4: choosing techniques for measuring usability

Although it is possible to identify things which should be measured, it is not always so easy to carry out the measurement itself. There may be various problems.

Identifying measures may be easy but carrying out the measurement may be very difficult.

1. *Problems with users who take part*
   The performance of a user may be affected by the fact that they are being measured or the memory of the user may be affected by events which occur between the user undertaking the task and being questioned about their attitudes towards it.

2. *Problems with the person carrying out the measurement*
   Some measurement methods require very specific skills. For example, a laboratory-based experiment which measures number, frequency and type of errors may require the use of statistical techniques in the analysis

Some measurement techniques require specialist knowledge to carry out.

of the data. The designer may not have the knowledge and skills to design an experiment and to carry out the analysis. Another example might involve the designer being asked to lead the discussion in a focus group, and it may be that he or she will bias the discussion towards positive aspects of the system, possibly feeling defensive about any problems there may be within it.

3. *Problems with how the results of the measurement are interpreted*

Some measurement techniques require the designer to be given expert advice.

There may be bias in the conduct of an evaluation or in the interpretation of results. If a designer is asked to work through the transcript of an audio recording of a focus group and to summarize user problems, he or she may interpret negative user comments as if they were personal criticisms and limit the number or strength of such comments in the summary report.

Thus each measurement technique must be applied carefully if it is to have any value. In some cases, the designer will be able to apply the technique; in others, the advice of HCI experts or psychologists will be needed.

Some measurement techniques are easy for the designer to use.

There follows a brief description of some of the techniques which can be used to measure aspects of usability. Three groups of techniques are introduced:

1. The first group are those techniques which require specialist psychological knowledge, either to apply the techniques or to carry out the analysis. Or it could be those which require an expert in user interface design, someone, for example, to make an expert assessment of user interfaces developed. The designer should be involved in setting up the evaluation and acting upon the results.

See Sweeney *et al.* (1992) for a survey of current practice.

2. The second group are those techniques which the designer can use but only with expert advice. In the use of questionnaires, for example, the designer would possibly be involved in specifying the purpose and broad content of the questionnaire but expert advice would be needed to design the structure of the questionnaire, to choose the number and style of questions and to undertake any statistical analysis.

3. The third group are those which the designer can use without expert advice. Cooperative evaluation, for example, has been designed specifically so that it can be applied by designers without the assistance of HCI experts.

Group 1 techniques need specialist knowledge and experience.

6.7.1 Group 1 techniques

Technique	*Role of the designer*
Analytical evaluation	Needs psychological knowledge to apply. The designer should be involved in setting up the evaluation and acting on the results.

Expert evaluation   Needs an HCI expert by definition. The designer should act upon the results.

See Preece (1993) for more detail.

Experimental evaluation   Needs knowledge from experimental psychology. The designer should be involved in specifying what has to be measured and acting upon the results.

Analytical evaluation

Analytical evaluation techniques can be used early in the design lifecycle. They are based on descriptions which predict user performance. The user interface is represented using a formal or semi-formal specification language which enables designers to analyse and predict expert performance of error-free tasks. Tasks are described in terms of cognitive and physical operations, as illustrated in the single-layer model in Fig. 6.6.

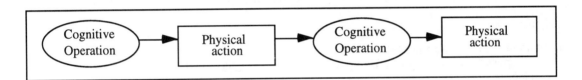

Figure 6.6 *Analytic evaluation, single layer model.*

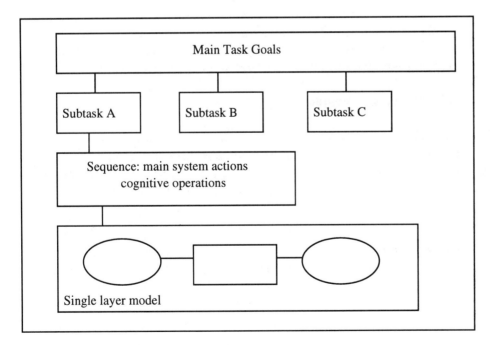

Figure 6.7 *Analytical evaluation, multi-layer model.*

The single-layer model is used to describe the user interaction at the level of keystrokes, while a multi-layer model can be used to describe interaction at the task level (Fig. 6.7).

The main advantage of analytical evaluation is that designs can be evaluated without developing prototypes and without user testing. The disadvantages are that the underlying models assume that users are expert and are capable of error-free interactions. Also they require expert psychological knowledge to apply and can therefore be costly and time consuming.

An HCI expert carries out the evaluation.

Expert evaluation

This usability evaluation method employs HCI experts — experienced human factors personnel — to review a user interface. The expert is given some realistic task to perform on the system and asked to give an impartial view of the interface. The expert may use the design principles of naturalness, flexibility, supportiveness, non-redundancy and consistency, or some other criteria, to evaluate the design, and would write up the results in a report.

Experiments require the help of applied psychologists or human factors experts.

Experimental evaluation

Experiments can be used when an evaluator wishes to manipulate a number of factors associated with the interface design and study their various effects on performance. Experiments must be planned with the help of an applied psychologist or human factors expert. An experiment will have a specific purpose: variables which can be changed or kept constant, and things to be measured such as time, keystrokes and completion rates. Experiments must be planned with specific hypotheses and measures and a statistical test selected. Experiments are normally preceded by a pilot study to enable any problems with the experimental design to be identified.

6.7.2 Group 2 techniques

Group 2 techniques require the designer to seek expert advice.

Technique	*Role of the designer*
Observation in a usability laboratory	Laboratory-based observations require an HCI expert to set up and record. The designer should view users or the video recordings of users using the system. The designer and the HCI expert should discuss the video recordings.
Observation in the workplace	Observations of the system in use in the workplace can be carried out by the designer, although expert help may be needed on how to record observations.
Questionnaires	The designer could design a questionnaire with the help of an expert or could use a generic usability questionnaire provided the instructions

See DTI Usability Guide (1991) for more detail.

for use were followed carefully.

Interviews   Interviews with users could be conducted by the designer if assistance was obtained on avoiding bias. A better scenario is for the designer and an HCI expert to conduct an interview together, to compare notes and to prepare a joint report.

Focus groups   Focus groups can be conducted by designers if they possess some facilitation skills and if they are willing to listen to what is being said. They should facilitate discussion between users rather than participate in or lead the discussion.

Observation

Observation can be carried out in a usability laboratory or in the user's normal place of work. In a usability laboratory, video cameras and data logging allow designers or evaluators to view users using the system and to analyse any problems after the user has completed their tasks. In the user's normal place of work, the evaluator would need to observe the user in an unobtrusive manner and make a log of user actions and user problems. Users can be asked to say out loud what they are doing and this can be recorded on audio tape for later analysis.

Surveys, interviews and questionnaires

The purpose of survey methods is to gather users' opinions through the use of either interviews or questionnaires. Interviews can be highly structured with the evaluator having a fixed list of questions which the user must answer, or can be flexible, whereby the evaluator will have a list of questions but will pursue certain threads of discussion depending on the response of the user.

Questionnaires can be used for survey evaluation. Questionnaires need to be carefully designed. The evaluator should either seek expert opinion in the design of a questionnaire or should use one which was already designed for this purpose, for example the SUMI questionnaire or the QUIS question-naire.

SUMI (Software Usability Measurement Inventory).

QUIS (Questionnaire for User Interaction Satisfaction).

Types of question vary between questionnaires. Questions can be open, for example, asking users to give a general statement about some system feature, or can be closed, requiring an answer of yes or no. A closed question is illustrated in Fig. 6.8.

Questions can be phrased in different ways — for example, the multi-point scale in Fig. 6.8 asks the user to tick how they feel. Figure 6.9 shows a Likert scale where the user is asked to agree or disagree with a given statement.

The semantic differential scale shown in Fig. 6.10 shows two adjectives which are at the opposite ends of a spectrum (for example, easy and difficult) and asks the user to rate a drawing package on that spectrum.

Closed Questions

Can you use the following text editing commands?			
DUPLICATE	yes	no	don't know
PASTE	yes	no	don't know

Multi-point scales

Rate this course on the following scale:

very useful | | | | | | | of no use

Figure 6.8 *Closed questions and multi-point scales.*

Likert Scale (strength of agreement with a clear statement)

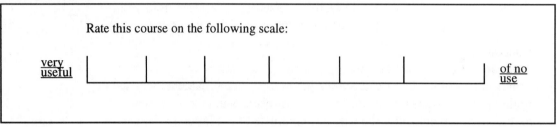

Figure 6.9 *Example of a Likert scale.*

Rate the Superpaint drawing package along the following dimensions:

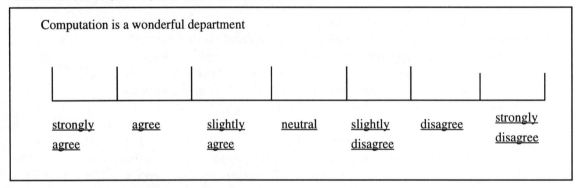

Figure 6.10 *Example of a semantic differential scale.*

Ranked order questions can also be used (Fig. 6.11). However, different types of questions should never be mixed together in the same section of a questionnaire.

Place the following commands in order of usefulness:
(use a scale of 1 to 4 where 1 is most useful)

PASTE ☐   DUPLICATE ☐   GROUP ☐   CLEAR ☐

Figure 6.11 *Example of ranked order questions.*

Focus groups

The purpose of a focus group is to allow a group of users to talk in a free-form discussion with each other, in the presence of an investigator. As an evaluation technique it can be used as a debriefing session after the users have had some exposure to the system being evaluated. The investigator, who could be the designer, should get together an audio recorder and ideally between four and six users, and should prepare a list of topics for discussion. The topics should be introduced one at a time, the main aim being to find out how people think naturally about the topics. The investigator should not take part in the discussion but should facilitate free discussion between the users. A focus group would typically last about 45 minutes.

> A focus group allows a free-form discussion between users.

If the users have been carrying out particular tasks on a system, the topics for discussion could relate to those tasks. For example, topic 1: how did they get started with the first task? Topic 2: were they able to complete the first task, and if not, what difficulties did they have? Such open questions should trigger the group to discuss problems and share experiences. The investigator can listen to the group at the time and to the audio recording after the focus group has finished. Often it is useful to have a transcript of the discussion, though this is very time consuming.

> A focus group will give the designer insights into how users think.

Focus groups will give the designer insights into how users think and what things are important to them. It is difficult to achieve this with other techniques.

6.7.3 Group 3 techniques

> Group 3 techniques can be carried out by the designer.

Technique	Role of the designer
Feature checklists	A feature checklist can easily be compiled by the designer.
Incident diaries	An incident diary can be readily prepared by the designer.

Cooperative evaluation   This approach was specifically developed for
                                     designers to use with users.

Feature checklists
The purpose of a feature checklist is to find out which features available on
the system are actually used by the users. They can also be used to find out
why certain features are not used. This checklist could simply be a list of
features with a column asking the user whether they use that feature or not.
For example, Fig. 6.12 shows a simple checklist of edit commands available
within Hypercard, where the user is asked to tick if they have heard of the
command or if they have used it.

Hypercard Edit Commands	Heard of?	Used?
Background	✓	✓
Copy	✓	✓
Cut	✓	x
New Card	✓	✓
Paste	✓	x
Text Style	x	x
Undo	✓	x

Figure 6.12 *A simple feature checklist.*

This can, of course, be elaborated upon further by adding more columns in
order to obtain more information. For example: how often does the user use
the command? Does the user know the short cut for the command? How did
the user learn about the command? If the answers required are not a simple
yes or no, then some instructions will be needed, as follows.

Q3: How did the user learn about the command? ('Learnt?' Figure 6.13)
Answer Q3 with a 0,1, 2, 3 or 4.

0 = do not remember
1 = found it in the menus
2 = read about it in the manuals
3 = heard about it on the training course
4 = heard about it from a colleague

Q4: How often do you use the command? ('Frequency?' Figure 6.13)
Answer Q4 with a 0,1, 2, 3 or 4.

0 = less than once a week
1 = once a day or less
2 = once an hour or less
3 = every ten minutes
4 = more often

Fig. 6.13 shows an expanded feature checklist.

Hypercard Edit Commands	Heard of?	Used?	Frequency?	Learnt?
Background	✓	✓	2	1
Copy	✓	✓	3	2
Cut	✓	x	0	
New Card	✓	✓	4	3
Paste	✓	x	0	
Text Style	x	x	0	
Undo	✓	x	0	

Figure 6.13 *Expanded feature checklist.*

The designer can evaluate the use of the system from the responses made on the checklist. This is a low-cost and effective evaluation technique.

Incident diaries

The purpose of the incident diary is to provide the user with a means of recording incidents which occur while using the system. The user is provided with structured forms on which he or she can record what happens. The forms contain a series of questions, such as if the designer wants the user to record whenever he or she has a problem. A problem can be defined as something which causes them to stop working. There will be one page for each problem and each page will contain the following questions:

An incident diary can help the designer find out where users are having problems.

1. At what time did the problem occur?

2. What started the problem?
    (i) did not know how to carry on;
    (ii) unhelpful error message;
    (iii) other, please state.

3. Which help facilities did you try?
    (i) on-screen help;

(ii) manual;

(iii) asked another user;

(iv) watched another user;

(v) other, please state.

4. Did the information obtained resolve your problem?
   (i) yes, completely;
   (ii) yes, partly;
   (iii) no.

5. How long did you spend trying to resolve the problem?
   (i) less than a minute;
   (ii) between one and five minutes;
   (iii) other, please state.

Incident diaries are useful when there are specific events that the designer wants to know more about, although they can be tedious for the user to complete, especially as they must be completed accurately to be of use. The users may require some training and practice in completing the diary prior to use.

Cooperative Evaluation involves users and designers working together (Monk *et al.*, 1993)

Cooperative evaluation

Cooperative evaluation is a practical technique developed at York University, UK. It is described in a small handbook specially prepared for designers to follow and use. Cooperative evaluation is a procedure for obtaining data about problems experienced by users when working with a prototype.

Users and designers evaluate the system together. Users are encouraged to ask the designer questions about interacting with the system and the designer asks the users about their understanding of the system. The handbook contains a step- by-step guide of how to recruit users, how to prepare tasks for them to do, how to interact with users and to record what they say and do, and how to summarize observations made. The author recommends the designer to consult the handbook for further details.

The techniques described above are representative of those available. In most situations, a usability evaluation will involve the application of more than one technique. In stage 5, the next stage in the process, a plan of a usability evaluation session is developed.

6.8 Stage 5: planning a usability evaluation

Any usability evaluation will probably require the use of more than one evaluation technique, and users and tasks must be carefully chosen. An evaluation requires careful preparation and planning. Two examples are given, one to illustrate the testing of a prototype and the other to illustrate testing a system which is already in use.

Example 1: testing a CSCW prototype

When evaluating the CRC prototype, users were selected to be representative of the target user population, that is, project managers, designers, people who were experienced in team working and in requirements capture. A series of tasks were designed to encourage users to use different aspects of the system. Users were provided with training in the use of the system prior to carrying out each task; they were given written and verbal instructions as to what to do and quick reference guides to help them remember basic system features. A full day was taken for one team to take part in an evaluation of the system.

See Macaulay *et al.* (1994) for more details.

Following is a summary of the plan for the day:

8.30am	Introduction/coffee.
9.00am	Training for task 1.
9.30am	Briefing for task 1.
	Task 1 (Competition — 20 mins).
	Completion of incident diary 1.
10.00am	Break/coffee and focus group 1.
10.45am	Briefing/training 2.
	Task 2 (Job advert — 45 mins).
	Completion of incident diary 2.
12.00noon	Lunch.
1.15pm	Briefing for task 3.
	Task 3 (Requirements task — 1hr).
	Completion of incident diary 3.
2.30pm	Break/coffee.
2.35pm	Focus group 2.
4.00pm	End.

A combination of a simplified incident diary and focus groups were used to obtain feedback from users. Several such one-day evaluations took place.

Feedback from users helped to develop a full specification of the requirements for a CRC tool.

Example 2: testing a system which is in use

The second example is from a usability evaluation to test a booking system which was in use in a number of theatres in England and Wales. The purpose of the evaluation was to provide feedback to the designers of the system on ways in which its usability could be improved. The Theatre Booking System was, at the time of the evaluation, being marketed to theatres throughout the UK, and a key selling point was its ease of learning. More specifically, it was claimed that box office staff could learn how to make a booking within half an hour of using the system. This was in contrast to other theatre booking systems on the market which required staff to attend a one-day training course to learn how to use the system. The suppliers of the system were anxious to ensure that their system would also be easy to use by frequent and experienced users.

This evaluation centred around two theatres, Theatre 1 and Theatre 2 who were already using the Theatre Booking System (TBS). The evaluation took place in a number of stages:

1. First, before visiting the theatres the evaluators had to decide what questions to ask on the visit. The checklists in CRC stage 1 formed a basis for identifying which users and tasks should be the subject of questioning.

2. In the initial investigation, a visit was made to Theatre 1 and Theatre 2. The initial visit was made to find out what usability evaluation techniques could feasibly be used. It was decided that observation was the only practicable technique to use. Video recording would be too obtrusive. Questionnaires were unacceptable to the box office staff.

3. On the second visit to both theatres, the evaluator observed the system in use and recorded details concerning patterns of use, timings, system performance times and user attitudes. From this, the evaluator was able to identify common usability problems with the system at both sites. These problems were confirmed by visiting a third theatre.

4. A third visit was made to the two original theatres, this time to undertake further observation of the specific aspects of system use which were causing problems. This time the evaluator looked specifically for problems using the criteria associated with the HCI design principles of naturalness, flexibilty, non-redundancy, supportiveness and consistency.

5. The evaluator prepared a report highlighting specific user problems.

This report was used as a basis for the designers to produce a better user interface design for the next release of the product.

6.9 Summary

In this chapter, distinction has been made between ease of learning and ease of use, and a fuller definition of usability presented. The author has shown how to specify usability for a given system and what techniques can be used to measure whether usability has been achieved. The software designer should use techniques with care and, where appropriate, seek the advice of an expert. No matter which techniques are used, the designer should be involved in some way in the evaluation. The main reason for undertaking a usability evaluation is to get feedback that can be used to improve the product.

HCI standards are reviewed in the next chapter.

Exercises for Chapter 6

6.1 FT Travelodge offers quality overnight accommodation for the travelling motorist. It employs over 800 staff operating in 80 Travelodges with approximately 40 bedrooms per lodge. FT Travelodge identified the need to enhance the effectiveness of its reservations system and developed a new centralised system known as Travelodge Roomline. Operators were inexperienced in computer systems and the management recognized that its new system had to be easy to use.

FT planned to undertake an evaluation of the system before going live. The evaluation had the following objectives: to identify and eliminate problems with the system before going live; to ensure that the system was easy to use by inexperienced operators; to test the effectiveness of training material and documentation. FT had access to the IBM Usability Evaluation Centre in London.

Briefly describe the range of usability evaluation techniques which FT could employ to test for ease-of-use and discuss the relative merits of using each technique.

6.2 Below is a selected quotation from the European Council Directive (90/270/EEC) on the minimum safety and health requirements for work with visual display screen equipment which became a legal requirement on 31st December 1992.

OPERATOR/COMPUTER INTERFACE
In designing, selecting, commissioning and modifying software, and in designing tasks using display screen equipment, the employer shall take into account the following principles:

(a) Software must be suitable for the task
(b) Software must be easy to use and, where appropriate, adaptable to the operator's level of knowledge or experience.
(c) Systems must display information in a format and at a pace which are adapted to operators.

Three of the minimum requirements for the operator computer interface are described in (a), (b) and (c) above. What techniques would you use when designing the interface to ensure that the above requirements were met?

6.3 Consider the following usability objective:

Theatre booking clerks with low motivation, no computing experience and no previous training, working in a small and hectic box office, are able to learn to reserve or book seats within a one hour period.

What measures could be taken and which techniques would you consider appropriate to test whether this objective was met?

Chapter 7

HCI standards

The objectives of this chapter are:

- ☐ to provide an overview of standards associated with HCI design;
- ☐ to introduce aspects of user documentation;
- ☐ to highlight some important developments;
- ☐ to conclude this tutorial text.

7.1 Introduction

Standards play an important role in improving the usability of systems. Various standards have already been referred to within this book: ISO standards for icon design in section 4.2; computer manufacturers' standards such as styleguides in section 4.4 and standards for writing usability statements in section 6.6. The purpose of this chapter is to provide an overview of current standards associated with HCI design, including standards for writing user documentation.

7.2 HCI standards

The level of HCI standards varies from in-house standards developed within a single organization to international standards spanning the world.

For many users, the most immediate HCI standards are those which are developed in-house and are applied to all systems used within the organization. Such standards are particularly important where large systems are being developed by different teams. Once the overall system is integrated, inconsistencies within the user interface can be difficult to resolve and can lead to errors, inefficiencies and frustration. Many user organizations are turning to consistent user interface standards to avoid such problems and to allow easy transfer of staff between departments and increased interworking across traditional organizational boundaries.

Similar market pressures apply to software suppliers and they too are developing their own proprietary standards. If the supplier is large enough or sufficiently influential, then its proprietary standard can become a *de facto* industry standard (for example IBM's Common User Access). In some cases consortia are formed to create standards, for example, for X Windows.

A number of national and international standards bodies are concerned with HCI standards, for example, the International Organization for Standardization (ISO), the European Computer Manufacturer's Association (ECMA), the British Standards Institution (BSI) in the United Kingdom or the German national standards body, the Deutsches Institut fur Normung (DIN). There are many other standards bodies and the reader is advised to consult the most recent copy of the *Directory of HCI Standards* for a fuller picture.

The use of standards does not guarantee good design but they can provide a means of specifying interface quality. They can help users to set appropriate procurement requirements and to evaluate competing supplier's offerings.

Standards can help suppliers to check their products during design and manufacture and provide a basis for making claims about the quality of their products. They can also help regulators to assess quality and provide a basis for testing products.

Below are descriptions of three types of HCI standard, firstly those associated with the European Computer Manufacturer's Association, secondly those associated with the International Organization for Standardization and their links with the European Directive (90/270/EEC) *Work with Display Screen Equipment* and finally user documentation standards associated with the British Standards Institution.

7.3 European Computer Manufacturer's Association (ECMA)

The ECMA is a trade association of the European computer manufacturers; its members include, among others, IBM, Digital Equipment Corporation, Bull, Hewlett Packard and International Computers (ICL) Ltd. The ECMA develops trade standards and technical guidance and also acts as a channel for communication between the standards makers and the European computer industry. It has published ergonomic requirements standards; ECMA 110 for monochromatic visual display devices, ECMA 126 for colour display devices and ECMA 136 for non-CRT visual display units. It also has a technical committee on User System Interface.

7.4 International Organization for Standardization (ISO)

ISO is the world-wide standardization organization responsible for developing international standards and identifies four distinct sets of aims for standards:

- mutual understanding;
- health, safety and the protection of the environment;
- interface and interchangeability;
- fitness for purpose.

The ISO technical subcommittee SC4 is responsible for the development of the multipart standard ISO 9241 which is the main standard which affects HCI design. ISO 9241 is the *Ergonomics requirements for office work with visual display terminals (VDT's)* and is in 17 parts. Each part is briefly explained below:

Part 1: *General introduction*
Provides an overview of the multipart standard.

Part 2: *Guidance on task requirements*
Deals with the design of tasks and jobs involving work with visual display terminals.

Part 3: *Visual display requirements*
Deals with the design of visual display terminals. In addition to design specifications, this part contains a proposed user performance test as an informative annex.

Part 4: *Keyboard requirements*
Deals with alphanumeric keyboard design and ergonomic aspects but not layout.

Part 5: *Workstation layout and postural requirements*
Deals with the ergonomics requirements for a visual display terminal workplace which will allow the user to adopt a comfortable and efficient posture. It covers the chair and ancillary items such as footrests and document holders as well as work surfaces and desks.

Part 6: *Environmental requirements*
Deals with the ergonomics requirements for the working environment in which a visual display is used in order to prevent environmental sources of stress and discomfort and to promote efficiency. It covers visual, acoustic and thermal environments.

Part 7: *Display requirements with reflections*
Details methods of measuring glare and reflections from the surface of display screens.

Part 8: *Requirements for displayed colours*
Deals with the requirements for multi-colour displays.

Part 9: *Requirements for non-keyboard input devices*
Deals with ergonomic requirements for devices such as the mouse and other pointing devices and includes a performance test.

Part 10: *Dialogue principles*
Presents high-level ergonomic principles which apply to the design of dialogues between humans and information systems.

Part 11: *Guidance on usability specification and measures*
Provides a framework for an ergonomics requirements specification which includes descriptions of the context for use, the evaluation procedures to be carried out and the criteria to be satisfied when the usability of the system is to be evaluated.

Part 12: *Presentation of information*
Deals with specific ergonomic issues involved in representing and presenting information in a visual form. It includes guidance on ways of representing complex information, screen layout and the design and use of windows

Part 13: *User guidance*
Deals with various forms of user guidance including documentation, help screens, within-system aids and error-handling systems.

Part 14: *Menu dialogues*
Contains a large number of guidelines developed from the published literature and from other relevant research.

Part 15: *Command dialogues*
Deals with text-based command dialogues.

Part 16: *Direct manipulation dialogues*
Deals with direct manipulation dialogues and WYSIWYG dialogue techniques.

Part 17: *Form-filling dialogues*

Each part of the standard is at a different stage of development. For example, part 2 has been published as an international standard, whereas part 17 has not yet reached the committee draft stage. The reader is advised to contact the ISO standards office for the most recent information on these standards.

There is also scope in HCI for standards which address the design process itself. In an analogous way to the ISO 9000 quality assurance standards, there are aspects of the design process which can be covered by HCI standards. For example, one part of ISO 9241 deals with statement of usability for users wishing to include it as part of a purchase specification and for suppliers wishing to attest to the merits of a product.

7.5 European Directive: Work with Display Screen Equipment

Much of the information available in these standards can be used to help employers conform to the European Directive (90/270/EEC) *Work with Display Screen Equipment*, which specifies minimum safety and health requirements for work with display screen equipment. In Great Britain, this directive is implemented through *Health and Safety, Display Screen Equipment, 1992, L26 Guidance on Regulations* (available from HMSO). Each European country will have its own implementation.

This directive places obligations on employers, as follows.

For each user, the employer must:

(a) Assess the risks arising from their use of display screen workstations and take steps to reduce any risks identified to the 'lowest extent reasonably practicable'.

(b) Ensure that the new workstations ('first put into service after 1st January 1993') meet the minimum ergonomics standards set out in a schedule to the Regulations. Existing workstations have a further four years to meet the minimum requirements, provided that they are not posing a risk to their users.

(c) Plan display screen work to provide regular breaks or changes of activity.

(d) Inform users about the results of assessments, the actions the employer is taking and the users' entitlements.

In addition, for his or her own employees who are users, the employer must:

e) Offer eye tests before display screen use, at regular intervals and if they are experiencing visual problems. If the tests show that they are necessary and normal glasses cannot be used, then special glasses must be provided.

f) Provide appropriate health and safety training for users before display screen use or whenever the workstation is 'substantially modified'.

The associated schedule for the directive contains a number of general minimum requirements which apply to the workstation and to the task of the users. The main points are listed below under the headings:

1. Equipment.

2. Environment.

3. Human computer interface.

1. Equipment:

   Display screen:
   - well defined clear characters;
   - stable flicker-free image;
   - adjustable brightness and/or contrast;
   - easy swivel/tilt;
   - free of glare and reflections.

   Keyboard:
   - tiltable and separate from display;
   - space in front to support arms and hands;
   - matt, non-reflective surfaces;
   - 'adequately contrasted symbols'.

   Workdesk:
   - large low-reflectance surface;
   - document holder;
   - adequate space for comfortable position.

   Workchair:
   - stable but should 'allow worker easy freedom of movement'
   - adjustable in backrest height and tilt, and seat height;
   - footrest available.

2. Environment:

   Space:
   - dimensioned and designed to allow change of posture.

   Lighting:
   - satisfactory lighting conditions;
   - secondary adjustable lighting as appropriate;
   - avoid glare by layout of workplace/ design of lighting;
   - control daylight by suitable window covering.

   Reflections and glare:
   - no direct glare and no distracting relections on the screen.

   Noise:
   - avoid distraction when equipping workstation.

   Heat:
   - equipment heat must not cause discomfort.

   Radiation:
   - all electromagnetic radiation (except visible light) to be reduced to negligible levels.

   Humidity:
   - adequate level maintained.

3. Human computer interface:

   - easy to use;
   - adapted to user's level of knowledge;

- no checking of user performance without their knowledge;
- system to provide feedback to user;
- information to be displayed in format and at a pace adapted to user;
- follow principles of software ergonomics.

This European Directive has immediate implications for the software designer. The part of the Schedule relating to the human computer interface is particularly important.

7.6 BSI Guide to the Design and Preparation of Documentation for Users of Application Software

The BSI (British Standards Institution) guide (BS 7649:1993) is introduced here because it provides an excellent guide to the design of documentation. Its approach to the design of user documentation is very much in line with that of this tutorial text. The first stage in the design of documentation is analysis. The aim of the analysis stage is to find out what information the users need and to decide what set of documents should be developed to meet those needs. The guide suggests that the analysis of user requirements should address the whole product together, so that the software, the documentation, the training and the support complement each other.

The analysis includes gathering information about users and tasks in a similar way to that described in Chapter Two of this text. The guide includes documentation development activites which should be carried out at each stage of the product development cycle, covering project requirements and constraints; analysis; planning; development and review; production and distribution and evaluation and updating. The software designer who is responsible for designing or producing user documentation should acquire a copy of this easy-to-follow guide from BSI.

7.7 Summary and conclusions

The emphasis throughout this book has been on introducing techniques and tools which may be useful to the software designer, and on illustrating the use of the techniques through examples and case studies. The focus has been on the main responsibilty of the software designer within the HCI design lifecycle, that of user interface design.

Chapter Two discussed the role of the software designer in the requirements stage of a project. Techniques for understanding user needs were introduced, covering analysis of users and their characteristics, the tasks they carry out and the objects they interact with. Techniques for identifying the role of the proposed system were introduced. Finally the costs and benefits of alternative allocation of function were considered from the user point of view.

Chapter Three briefly introduced the main classes of user interface and five principles of good HCI design (naturalness, flexibility, non-redundancy, consistency and supportiveness). A task-oriented approach to user interface design was presented. This involves identifying interface tasks; techniques for specifying dialogues and a procedure and guidelines for designing a consistent set of screens and windows. Use of colour at the user interface was considered, firstly through a brief discussion on the use of colour in general, then by looking at some poorly-designed colour screens to identify some typical mistakes that designers make. Finally, a number of guidelines on the use of colour were presented. The chapter concluded with a case study of a ferry reservation system showing the application of techniques from Chapters Two and Three.

Chapter Four introduced the main elements of graphical user interfaces (GUIs) and discussed the design of icons and the use of metaphors. An overview of GUI styleguides and toolkits was presented and issues of portability between GUI environments were raised. The characteristics of GUIs lead to the need for an object-oriented approach to user interface design. The object-oriented approach includes identifying and describing interface objects, identifying user actions on objects, deciding on the user interface metaphor and GUI toolkit to be used, identifying relationships between objects (according to the metaphor) and finally deciding how to view objects in terms of icons, menus or windows. The chapter concluded with a case study using the ferry reservation system, as in Chapter Three. This enabled the reader to compare and contrast a task-oriented approach to user interface design with an object-oriented approach.

Chapter Five provided an introduction to cooperative working systems by describing an number of systems and highlighting their general characteristics. A number of components of groupware were described together with systems being developed by leading edge research groups. This led to a discussion on the role and characteristics of user interfaces to CSCW systems and a method of specifying and designing user interfaces was introduced.

Chapter Six presented the case for designing systems which are usable from the user's, designer's and customer's point of view. It briefly introduced techniques for specifying and evaluating the usability of a system. Included in this were techniques for identifying success criteria, writing usability statements, identifying appropriate measures for testing for usability and considerations associated with planning a usability evaluation.

In Chapter Seven there was an overview of the BSI standards for user documentation and the current ISO standards for HCI design.

These methods should enable the reader to apply the methods suggested to design, build and test user interfaces which meet the needs of users and their organizations.

This text has concentrated on what can be done to design better user interfaces given the technology available today. There are many exciting developments taking place which will significantly affect the way in which humans communicate with computers in the future. There are arguments in favour of achieving better integration between the real world and the computer world, which takes us far beyond the use of graphics and mice. Mediaspaces, for example, which allow people to communicate through an audio, video and computer environment and 'augmented reality', which adds computational power to real-world objects. Other arguments are in favour of harnessing computer power to achieve better communication between people. Groupware products are a reality now, and tools are emerging which will help software designers design and build groupware, for example, Shared X, which is a window sharer available for UNIX workstations running X. However, it will be some time before 'group widgets' are available on GUI toolkits.

Finally, it should be remembered that HCI design is about designing systems for people, and people have many enduring qualities which will remain constant despite the ever-changing technology.

Appendix A:
Answers to exercises

Chapter 2

Exercise 2.1

Task sharing refers to who/what does what. Task control refers to who/what controls what and could include issues of speed, sequencing and interruptability. Passive support typically refers to the provision of general assistance with a task, whereas active support might typically include some element of decision making.

Exercise 2.2

A workgroup might find a new computer system unacceptable because of the following.

1. It results in a reduction in the size of the workgroup.

2. It results in unacceptable changes to the autonomy of the workgroup both in terms of what its members do and how they do it.

3. It results in a reduction in the status and prestige of this group relative to other workgroups.

(Changes to any of the social and organizational issues described in CRC stage 1 step 2 could be unacceptable)

Exercise 2.3

An invariant task is one which is fundamental to achieving the mission of an organization. It is a task which must be carried out even though the means of carrying it out may change.

Invariant tasks are important because identifying them enables the software designer to see which aspects of the user's job are fundamental (to the organization) and which aspects can be the subject of change. The designer can then apply his or her creative skills and knowledge of technological options to those aspects which can be the subject of change. This approach is more likely to result in an innovative design for the new system.

Exercise 2.4

The designer needs to acquire the following.

1. Knowledge of the user's present job. This will enable the designer to identify invariant tasks and the potential for acceptable change.

2. Knowledge of technological options. This will enable the designer to suggest possible alternative solutions.

3. Knowledge of the future system. This will enable the designer to develop a vision of what is needed and of what the user's future job will be.

Exercise 2.5
Arguments for the designer being part of a requirements capture team are as follows.

1. It helps the designer to develop a shared understanding of the organizational objectives for the proposed system.

2. It helps the designer to understand the constraints placed on the design.

3. It helps the designer to develop a realistic vision of the future system.

4. It enables the designer to contribute his or her knowledge and expertise to the requirements process.

Some arguments against the designer being part of a requirements capture team.

1. The designer may attempt to force his or her preferred solution before the alternatives have been adequately explored.

2. The designer may become impatient with the feeling of indecision during the discussions on requirements.

Chapter 3
Exercise 3.1
Five examples of how the screen design contravenes guidelines are as follows.

1. The use of capital letters when upper and lower case letters would be more readable.

2. No user assistance provided in completion of questions such as ' which performance?'. The user does not know the format of the data entry required.

3. There is unsufficient space for user responses.

4. The navigational instructions are confusing: Q for Exit to Main Menu; E for Quit.

5. The ordering of questions will result in unnecessary input by the user. For example, why ask about method of payment if this is only an enquiry? Why waste customer time asking for a name and address before the enquiry has been made?

Exercise 3.2
Dialogue design is used in SSADM to model the on-line screen handling and human-computer interaction of the required system. A flowchart, called a

logical dialogue outline or LDO, is used to represent the progression of screens for a particular event.

The objectives of the dialogue design step are to represent dialogue sequences, to communicate screen handling and interface concepts to the users and to provide a basis for the physical program design. Each LDO uses symbols similar to those used in flowcharts: a rectangle represents a single screen, a triangle represents a user decision point (one which requires a value judgment by the user) and start/stop and flow symbols are directly analogous to their flowchart equivalents.

Dialogue network diagrams are a specialization of state transition diagrams in which the progress of a dialogue between user and computer can be viewed as a series of transitions from one state to another.

The dialogue may be in a particular state awaiting input from the user, and it will progress to one of several possible states depending on the nature of the input received. Each state is represented by a node, denoted here by a circle. A node is defined as any point at which the dialogue outputs a message to the user or requests an input from the user. Transitions between nodes are indicated by directed arcs connecting two nodes; a label on the arc indicates the condition under which it is traversed. Note that there may be several arcs connecting two nodes, indicating that more than one condition can cause the transition to occur.

Exercise 3.3
Naturalness, supportiveness, non-redundancy, flexibility and consistency.

Exercise 3.4
The inconsistencies relate to the use of the Escape key. In Fig. 3.29, it is used to return to the main menu; in Fig. 3.30, it is used to return to the enquiry menu; in Fig. 3.32 it is used to return to the booking menu and in Fig. 3.33 it is used to cancel.

Chapter 4
Exercise 4.1
The organizational model of a graphical user interface as suggested by Peddie, 1992, should be used as a basis for comparison, level by level. Both Motif and OPEN LOOK are based on the X Window System and UNIX.

Exercise 4.2

- Visual appearance: this includes items such as the position and layout of menu and scroll bars, the design of icons used to represent applications and files and the shape and size of the mouse controller.
- Behaviour: the behaviour of an interface is the way in which it responds to actions taken by the user, e.g. a double click on a file icon will result in that file being activated.
- Metaphor: the term 'metaphor' is used to describe the analogy used in the design and implementation of the GUI. The use of a metaphor can help

users to foresee the consequences of their actions, e.g. the desktop metaphor.

Exercise 4.3

1. Main benefit: the ability to separate the application from the user interface, thus potentially being able to mount the interface on a different machine from that of the application.

2. The X client is structured into the Xlib, the X Intrinsics, the X toolkit widgets and the application itself.

Exercise 4.4
Form widget, box widget etc. Examples should be given from a GUI.

Exercise 4.5
Description of (Office) Workplace Environment showing the major classes of icons: application objects, system objects, folders, files, group items, buttons, plus description of typical attributes.

Chapter 5
Exercise 5.1
Face-to-face: facilitation services, group decision support, presentation support software, computer-supported meetings.

Electronic meetings: extensions of the telephone, personal computer software, computer conferencing, video teleconferencing.

Between meetings: project and calendar management software, group writing software, text filtering and conversational structuring.

Exercise 5.2
Group window, right of access, right of update, use of group mouse or pointing device, ability to have private views and shared views of the text, control mechanisms for updating or 'turn taking'.

Exercise 5.3

• the need to support informal communication between individuals;
• the need to facilitate group discussion and group decision making;
• the need to provide different views on the same data;
• the need to provide decision-making techniques such as voting, delphi;
• the need for public and private windows, etc.

Exercise 5.4
Naturalness, supportiveness, non-redundancy, flexibility and consistency.

Chapter 6
Exercise 6.1
Incident diaries: a low-cost effective way of getting users to record their problems when using the system.

Observation in a usability laboratory: an effective way of testing products prior to release; a video can be taken of the system in use and played back many times in order to identify the source of user problems. Experts would be on hand to help the designer to interpret findings. This is usually an expensive option.

Expert evaluation: needs an HCI expert. This technique would allow the training, documentation and user interface to be tested by an expert.

Exercise 6.2
All the techniques described in this book!

Exercise 6.3.
Observation in the workplace is probably the only realistic technique which could be used in these circumstances.

References

Chapter One

Alexander H. (1987) *Formally-based Tools and Techniques for Human-Computer Dialogues*, Ellis Horwood Ltd.

Barfield, L. (1993) *The User Interface Concepts and Design*, Addison Wesley.

Brown, C.M. (1988) *Human-Computer Interface Design Guidelines*, Ablex, Hove, UK.

Browne, D.P. (1994) *STUDIO, Structured User-Interface Design for Interaction Optimisation*, Prentice Hall International.

Creppy, M. (1990) Mind that user, *Eclipse*, Data General User Group, 4.

Dix, A.J., Finlay, J., Abowd, G. and Beale, R. (1993) *Human-Computer Interaction*, Prentice Hall International.

Johnson, P. (1992) *Human Computer Interaction: Psychology, Task Analysis and Software Engineering*, McGraw Hill International (UK).

Jones, S. and Downton, A. (1991) *Engineering the Human Computer Interface*, McGraw Hill Book Co. Europe.

Lowgren, J. (1993) *Human-Computer Interaction*, Chartwell Bratt.

Maddix, F. (1990) *Human-Computer Interaction theory and practice*, Ellis Horwood.

Laurel, B. (1990) *The Art of Human-Computer Interface Design*, Addison Wesley.

Preece, J. and Keller, L. (1990) *Human-Computer Interaction*, Prentice Hall with the Open University.

Preece, J., Rogers, Y., Sharp. H. *et al.* (1994) *Human-Computer Interaction*, Addison Wesley.

Sutcliffe, A. (1988) *Human-Computer Interface Design*, Macmillan Press.

Sutcliffe, A. and Macaulay, L.A. (eds) (1989) *People and Computers V*, Cambridge University Press.

Shneiderman, B. (1987 and 1992) *Designing the User Interface*, Addison Wesley.

Thimbleby, H. (1990) *User Interface Design*, Addison Wesley.

Chapter Two

Coad, P. and Yourdon, E. (1990) Object-Oriented Analysis, in *Systems and Software Requirements* (Eds R.H. Thayer and M. Dorfman), IEEE Computer Society Press, Los Alamitos, CA, USA.

Downs E., Clare, P., Coe, I. (1992*) Structured Systems Analysis and Design Method: Application and Context*, Prentice Hall.

Eason, K. (1987) *Information Technology and Organizational Change*, Taylor and Francis.

Jirotka, M. and Goguen, J. (1994) *Requirements Engineering, Social and Technical Issues*, Academic Press.

Macaulay, L.A. (1993) *Requirements as a Cooperative Activity* in the proceedings of RE '93, the first IEEE Symposium on Requirements Engineering, IEEE publication.

Marcus, A. (1992) *Graphic Design for Electronic Documents and User Interfaces*, Addison-Wesley.

Mumford, E. (1986) *Designing Systems for Business Success, the ETHICS method*, Manchester Business School Publication.

Singleton, W.T. (1974) *Man-Machine Systems Design*, Penguin.

Chapter Three

Coates, R.B. and Vlaeminke, I. (1987) *Man-Computer Interfaces: an Introduction to Software Design and Implementation*, Blackwell Scientific Publications.

Jackson, R., MacDonald, L. and Freeman, K. (1994) *Computer Generated Color: a Practical Guide to Presentation and Display*, Wiley.

Johnson, T. (1985) *Natural Language Processing: Commercial Applications*, OVUM Press.

Smith, S.L. and Mosier, J.N. (1984) *Design Guidelines for User-System Interface Software, Project No. 522A*, The Mitre Corporation, Bedford, Mass. USA.

Chapter Four

Berry, R.E. (1988) Common User Access – a consistent and usable human computer interface for the SAA environments, *IBM Systems Journal*, 27.

Diagnostic Research Inc (1988) *Macintosh or MS-DOS? A synopsis of what MIS managers and other professionals in Fortune 1000 companies have to say*, Apple Computer Inc, Cupertino.

Draper, S., Oatley, K., Weir, S. (1990) *Highly Interactive Visual Interfaces*, set of five videos, available from the Dept of Computer Science, Univ. of Glasgow.

Galitz, W.O. (1994) *It's Time to Clean your Windows: Designing GUIs that Work*, Wiley-QED.

Horton, W. (1994) *The Icon Book: Visual Symbols for Computer Systems and Documentation*, John Wiley & Sons Inc.

IBM, The Official Guide (1992) *Object-Oriented Interface Design*, IBM Common User Access Guidelines, QUE.

ISO standards, see contact details below.

OPEN LOOK (1989) *Graphical User Interface Style Guide*, Sun Microsystems Inc.

OSF/Motif User's and Style Guide, Vol. 1, OSF, 11 Cambridge Center, Cambridge, MA 02142, Mass. USA.

Peddie, J. (1992) *Graphical User Interfaces and Graphic Standards*, McGraw-Hill Inc.

Mansfield, N. (1993) *The Joy of X*, Addison-Wesley.

Myers, B.A., Guise, D., Dannenberg, R. *et al.* (1990) GARNET, Comprehensive Support for Graphical Highly Interactive User Interfaces, *IEEE Computer,* Nov.

Rogers, Y. (1989) Icon Design for the User Interface, *International Reviews of Ergonomics*, **2**, pp 129–54, Taylor and Francis Ltd.

Temple, Barker and Sloane Inc. (1990) *The Benefits of the Graphical User Interface*, Microsoft, Zenith Data Systems, Lexington, Mass. USA.

Webster, B. (1991) *The NeXt Book*, second edition, Addison-Wesley, Reading, Mass. USA.

XVT-Design manual, version 1.1 (1992), XVT Software Inc. Box 18750, Boulder, CO 80308, Colorado, USA.

Chapter Five

Bales, R.F. and Cohen, S.P. (1979) SYMLOG: *A System for the Multiple Level Observation of Groups*, The Free Press, New York.

Bly, S.A., Harrison, S.R. and Irwin, S. (1993) Media spaces: bringing people together in a video, audio and computing environment, *Communications of the ACM,* 36(1) pp 28–46.

Cook, P., Ellis, C., Graf, M. *et al.* (1987) Project Nick: meetings augmentation and analysis, *ACM Transactions on Office Information Systems*, 5(2) pp 132–46.

Dennis, A.R., George, J.F., Jessup, L.M. *et al.* (1988) Information technology to support electronic meetings, *Management Information Systems Quarterly*, 12(4) pp 591–624.

Dennis, A.R., Heminger, A.R., Nunamaker, J.F.J. *et al.* (1990) Bringing automated support to large groups: the Burr-Brown experience, *Information and Management* 18(3) pp 111–21.

Ellis, C.A., Gibbs, S.J. and Rein, G.L. (1991) Groupware: some issues and experiences, *Communications of the ACM* **34**(1) pp 38–58.

Galegher, J., Kraut, R.E. and Egido, C. (1990) *Intellectual Teamwork: Social and Technological Foundations of Cooperative Work*, Lawrence Erlbaum Associates.

Gibbs, S.J. (1989) *LIZA: an extensible groupware toolkit*, in CHI '89, ACM Press.

Greenberg, S. (1991) (Ed.) *Personalizable groupware: accommodating individual roles and group differences*, In ECSCW '91, The Second European Conference on Computer Supported Work, Kluwer, Amsterdam, Holland.

Greenberg, S. (1992) GROUPLAB, the Computer-Supported Cooperative Work and Groupware Research Laboratory, Demonstration at CSCW '92, Toronto, Canada.

Grohowski, R., McGoff, C., Vogel, D. *et al.* (1990) Implementing electronic meeting systems at IBM: lessons learned and success factors, *Management Information Systems Quarterly*, 14(4) pp 369–83.

Ishii, H. and Arita, K. (1991) *Clearface: translucent multiuser interface for*

Team *WorkStation*, (Eds L. Bannon, M. Robinson, and K. Schmidt), ECSCW'91, the Second European Conference on Computer-Supported Cooperative Work, Klewer, Amsterdam, Holland.

Ishii, H. Kobayashi, M. and Grudin, J. (1992) *Integration of inter-personal space and shared workspace: ClearBoard design and experiments*, (Eds J. Turner and R. Kraut) CSCW '92, Toronto, Canada.

Ishii, K. and Miyaki, N. (1991) Toward an open shared workspace: computer and video fusion approach of Team Workstation, *Communications of the ACM*, 34(12) pp 37–50.

Jennison, L. (1994) *Selected software for supporting cooperative working, in Computer Support for Cooperative Work*, (Eds E. Spurr, P. Layzell, L. Jennison *et al.*) John Wiley & Sons.

Macaulay, L.A., O'Hare, G., Viller, S. *et al.* (1994) *Cooperative requirements capture - prototype evaluation, in Computer Support for Cooperative Work* (Eds K. Spurr, P. Layzell, L. Jennison *et al.*) pp 169–95, John Wiley & Sons.

Nunamaker, J.F., Dennis, A.R., Valacich, J.S. *et al.* (1991) Electronic meeting systems to support group work, *Communications of the ACM*, 34(7) pp 40–61.

Olson, M.H. (1989) *Technological Support for Work Group Collaboration*, Lawrence Erlbaum Associates.

Rein, G.L. (1991) *A group mood meter*, Proceedings of HICSS-24, IEEE, Hawaii.

Roseman, M. and Greenberg, S. (1992*) GroupKit, a groupware toolkit for building real-time conferencing applications* (Eds J. Turner and R. Kraut), Proceedings of the CSCW '92, Toronto, Canada, ACM Press.

Sharples, M. (Ed) (1993) *Computer Supported Collborative Writing*, Springer-Verlag.

Stefik, M., Bobrow, D.G., Foster, G. *et al.* (1987) WYSIWIS revised: early experiences with multi-user interfaces, *ACM Transactions on Office Information Systems*, **5**(2) pp 147–67.

Valacich, J.S., Dennis, A.R. and Nunamaker, J.F. (1991) Electronic meeting support: the GroupSystems concept, *International Journal of Man-Machine Studies*, **34**(2) pp 261-82.

Wilson, P. (1991) *Computer Supported Cooperative Work: An Introduction*, Intellect Books and Klewer Academic Publishers.

Chapter Six

DTI (1990) *Usability Now! A Guide to Usability*, Open University Press.

Draper, S. and Oatley, K. (1991) *Practical Methods for Measuring the Performance of Human-computer Interfaces*, JCI Summer School notes.

Harrison, M.D. and Monk, A.F. (1986) People and computers: designing for usability, in *British Computer Society Workshop Series*, p 650, Cambridge University Press, York.

DTI Initiative, E. (1991) *Directory of HCI Consultants*, DTI.

DTI Initiative, E. (1991) *HCI Tools and Methods Handbook*, DTI.

Macaulay, L.A., O'Hare, G., Dongha, P. *et al.* (1994) Cooperative requirements capture: prototype evaluation, in *Computer Support for Cooperative Work* (Eds E. Spurr, P. Layzell, L. Jennison *et al.*) Wiley.

Monk, A. (1985) *Fundamentals of Human-Computer Interaction*, Academic Press Inc.

Monk, A., Wright, P., Haber, J. *et al.* (1993) *Improving your Human-Computer Interface*, Prentice Hall International with The British Computer Society.

Preece, J. (1993) A *Guide to Usability Human Factors in Computing*, Addison Wesley.

QUIS (Questionnaire for User Interaction Satisfaction), see address below.

Sweeney, M., Dillon, A. and Maguire, M. (1992) *A survey of current practices in usability evaluation and requirements for support within the European IT Industry*, HUSAT memo No. 585, HUSAT Research Institute.

SUMI (Software Usability Measurement Inventory), see address below.

Chapter Seven

BSI (1993) *Guide to the Design and Preparation of Documentation for Users of Application Software*, BSI Standards, see address below.

Beaudouin-Lafon, M. (1994) Beyond the workstation: mediaspaces and augmented reality in *People and Computer IX* (Eds G. Cockton, S.W. Draper and G.R.S. Weir), Cambridge University Press.

Shneiderman, B. and Plaisant, C. (1994) The future of graphical user interfaces in *People and Computer IX*, (Eds G. Cockton, S.W. Draper and G.R.S. Weir) CUP.

Stewart, T., *Directory of Human Computer Interaction (HCI) Standards*, DTI publication, see address below.

Useful addresses

Directory of HCI Standards
Tom Stewart
Systems Concepts Ltd.
Museum House
Museum Street
London
WC1A 1JT
UK

Questionnaire for User Interaction Satisfaction (QUIS)
University of Maryland Technology
Office of Technology Liaison
4312 Knox Road
University of Maryland
College Park
MD 20742
USA

ISO (International Organization for Standardization)
Central Secretariat
1, Rue de Varembe
Case Postale 56
CH-1211 Geneva 20
Switzerland

HUSAT Research Institute
The Elms
Elms Grove
Loughborough
Leics.
LE11 1RG
UK

SUMI (Software Usability Measurement Inventory)
Human Factors Research Group
University College
Cork
Ireland

XVT
XVT Software Inc.
Box 18750
Boulder
CO 80308
Colorado
USA

ECMA (European Computer Manufacturers' Association)
114 Rue de Rhone
CH-1204 Geneva
Switzerland

BSI (British Standards Institution)
2 Park Street
London
W1A 2BS
UK

DTI (Department of Trade and Industry)
IT Division
151 Buckingham Palace Road
London
SW1W 9SS
UK

Index

allocation of function   5, 6, 12, 20
analytical evaluation   186–188
arbitrary icons   98

brainstorming   153, 155
BSI Guide user documentation   205

case studies
    CAD   22–48
    CRC   154–171
    Fast Ferries   54–56, 75–92, 120–123, 127–135
ClearBoard   151
colour
    choice of   58–63
    examples of poor use of   60, 61
    factors   58–60
    guidelines   61–63
command language   51
communication beween people
    group members   143–145
    linear structures   12
    over the wall   12
    participation   14
    teams   14, 18
computer conferencing   142
computer supported meetings   138–140
concurrency control   148
concurrency in CSCW UI design   156
consistency   53, 56
control icons   99
cooperative evaluation   194
cooperative requirements capture
    case studies   22–48
    descriptions   17, 23
    prototype   154, 155
credibility ratings   39–41
CSCW
    characteristics of   143–147
    description of   9
    design of the user interface   157–171
    examples of   147–155
    the role of the user interface   156, 157

desktop metaphor   101

dialogue specification techniques
    dialogue network diagrams   65–67, 85–88
    SSADM Logical Dialogue Outlines   68–70
direct manipulation interfaces   52

Electronic Discussion System   154
examplar icons   97
experimental evaluation   187, 188
expert evaluation   187, 188

feasibility assessment   5, 6
feature checklists   191–193
flexibility   1, 8, 54, 56
focus groups   191
form filling dialogues   52
future vision   15, 16

Garnet   104, 105
graphical user interfaces (GUI)   2, 95–135
group decision support systems   140
group editor   147–150
group window   148
group writing   142
GroupKit   150
GroupSketch   150
groupware
    description of   3, 137
    examples of   138–143
GROVE Group outline editor   147–151
GUI design
    icons   97–100, 134
    look and feel   96
    metaphors   97, 100–104, 126
GUI Portability
    Architectures   109
    XVT   115–123
GUI styleguides and toolkits
    Garnet   104
    IBM's CUA   101–103, 126
    Macintosh   113
    Motif   110–112
    OPEN LOOK   112, 113
    Portability between GUIs   109–115
    Presentation Manager   114

X Window System   105–108

HCI design lifecycle   7, 10, 177
HCI design principles
　　consistency   8, 53, 56
　　flexibility   8, 54, 56
　　naturalness   8, 53, 55
　　non-redundancy   8, 53, 54
　　supportiveness   8, 53, 56

incident diaries   191, 193, 194
interactive icons   99
interpersonal space   151
interviews   189
ISO standards
　　ergonomic requirements   201, 202
　　icons   99, 100
　　usability   173, 174, 184

Macintosh GUI structure   113
menu systems   51
Motif   110, 111
multithreading in CSCW UI design
　　156

natural language   51
naturalness   53, 55
non-redundancy   53, 54

object icons   99, 100
object-oriented approach to GUI
　　design   123–135
objects
　　classification of   129, 130
　　descriptions   36, 37, 81, 82, 131–
　　　133
　　object-oriented user interface
　　　design   123–135
　　relationships between   126
　　visible objects   124–126
observation   189
OPEN LOOK   112, 113
order dependency in CSCW UI de-
　　sign   156
order independence in CSCW UI
　　design   156
organization of workprocess   146
organizational model of GUIs   109

physical object metaphor   101
pointer icons   99
Presentation Manager   114

questionnaires   190, 191

real-time groupware   147
real-time Meeting Systems   153
requirements
　　areas of knowledge   15
　　elicitation   13
　　document: list of contents   21
　　team formulation   18
　　user document   18
　　validation   19
requirements methods
　　CRC   15
　　OOA   13
　　SSADM   13
　　ETHICS   14
resemblance icons   97

Session Manager   153
shared objects   145
shared workspace   146
sharing of information   145
sociability in CSCW UI design   157
social protocols   148
software designer
　　role of   7, 8
stakeholders   14, 15
standards
　　BSI   9
　　ECMA   200
　　European Directive   203–205
　　ISO   9, 99, 100, 174, 184, 201, 202
status indicator icons   99
Step-by-step guides for
　　designing user interfaces to CSCW
　　　systems   158
　　object-oriented approach to UI
　　　design   124
　　task-oriented approach to UI
　　　design   64
　　understanding user needs   23
　　usability specification and evalua-
　　　tion   179
supportiveness   53, 56
surveys   189
symbolic icons   97

task-oriented approach to UI de-
　　sign   63–92
tasks
　　allocation of function   45–48
　　task analysis   42–45, 82–84, 180
　　task descriptions   32–35
　　task hierarchies   65
TeamFocus   153–154
TeamPaint   152
TeamWorkstation   151–153

tool icons   99
travel holiday metaphor   103

usability
    costs of poor usability   176
    customer usage cycle   175
    definition of   174
    directives   9, 203–205
    evaluation techniques   9, 185–194
    legal requirements   9, 203–205
    measures   9, 184, 185
    planning an evaluation   194–196
    specification and evaluation   20,
        178–180
    statements   9, 184, 185
    success criteria   9, 182–184
user interface
    classes of   51, 52
    importance   1–3
    role of   5
    time and cost   2
user interface design
    for CSCW systems   9, 156–171
    object oriented   9, 123–135
    planning the design   71–75, 89
    screen and window design   71–75,
        90–92
    task oriented   9, 63–92
user participation
    ETHICS   14
user support   5, 6, 205
users
    changing needs   4
    descriptions   29–31, 79–80
    primary   5
    productivity   1
    secondary   5
    tertiary   5

widgets   105, 108
workgroup
    computer support for   137
    descriptions   27, 28, 77–78, 127–
        128
WYSIWIS   141
WYSIWYG   96
X Window System   105–108
XVT – Design   116
XVT portability toolkit   115
XVT Tutorial   115–122